EDITORIAL REVIEW

Guard Your Heart: Hearing God to Master the Nine Issues of Life by Lloyd E. Wesley, Jr. is a valuable Bible-based self-help guide to help get your life out of the ditch. While you read this book, you'll feel like the author is talking to you one-on-one as he defines what he believes to be nine issues of life everyone has. Those in this simplified list are self-esteem, relationships, prayer life, health, education, vocation, prosperity, legacy, and eternal rewards. The book points out that perhaps of the nine, self-esteem is the most important as it often dictates how we handle the other eight issues on the list. Each issue has its own section in the book and is elaborated on in much more detail. These often overlap, which shows how interwoven they are with one another in our lives. Some of the book emphasizes listening to God, hearing God, and then acting on or doing what He is saying.

One thing that stands out about this book is how the author backs up what he is saying with Bible passages. This book may not be for everyone, and some would disagree with the content, but Wesley encourages readers to see themselves as God sees them--not so much as a child in need of punishment or wrath, but a child in need of guidance and love. I especially like how he explains the significance of the number nine in the Bible. Wesley's advice, along with his personal anecdotes and Scripture, can help unlock biblical secrets to success on a supernatural level, sometimes using spiritual gifts God gives us, therefore changing generations of defeating thoughts, behaviors, and choices. The author's style offers a practical approach that can be applied on a daily basis. The advice isn't philosophy or pep talk, it's a new way of Christian thinking that's been
along. It's a different way of listening to what Scripture h
people in general, about success, and about the future. *Gu
Hearing God to Master the Nine Issues of Life* by Lloyd
a book to help you get your life onto a brighter path.

GUARD
Your Heart

Hearing God to
Master the Nine Issues of Life

Lloyd E. Wesley Jr.

9/27/20

Felicia,

God has surprises &
the supernatural awaiting
you as you read & obey the
Lord's directions that you'll receive
as you venture through these pages.
Focusing on excellence,
only opportunities for solutions!

Of God, we are

Lloyd E. Wesley

"Keep thy heart more than anything that is guarded; for out of it are the issues of life."

~ Proverbs 4:23 (Darby) ~

Cover and interior formatting by Rooted Publishing
www.rootedpublishing.com
Heart cover and shield images from Pixabay.com
Published by Lloyd E. Wesley Jr.
Brownstown, Michigan

Library of Congress Control Number: 2020914130
Printed in the United States of America
ISBN: 978-0-578-73627-3

CONTENTS

ACKNOWLEDGMENTS

My gratitude goes firstly to my Heavenly Father who directed me by His Spirit about 10-12 years ago and *opened my eyes* to the revelation that there are actually *issues of life*, as I was studying Proverbs 4:20.

> "My son, attend to my words; incline thine ear unto my sayings. Let them not depart from thine eyes; keep them in the midst of thy heart. For they are life unto those that find them, and health to all their flesh. Keep thy heart more than anything that is guarded; for out of it are the issues of life. Put away from thee perverseness of mouth, and corrupt lips put far from thee."
>
> ~ Proverbs 4:20-24 Darby

The Lord originally showed me 5 issues of life, then 6, 7, and 8. At the point of the eighth being revealed, I really thought that was the finale; however, about five years ago the Lord said *now I'm going to show you another issue which is the most important one.* Issue number 9 is raising **your self-esteem to Christ-Esteem.** All the other issues of life are dependent upon it as it reveals how one views themselves and therefore, is of vital importance.

Next, my bride of 50 years, Pat... I thank her for her inspiration and example of walking in these issues of life successfully, as she trusts in the Lord with all of her heart, not leaning on her own understanding but acknowledging the Lord in all her ways (Proverbs 3:5-6). She has so many examples in her life of being a *guidepost* for myself, our family, congregation and neighbors. Honey, thank you for your patience and support, especially over the last 2 years as I have earnestly sought the Lord's direction in writing the manuscripts and the countless long hours that I've spent secluded in my office working on this project.

I'd like to thank a minister at the church and friend, Carolyn V. Robinson. The Lord told her approximately five years ago that this revelation "needs to be in a book." As the Lord spoke to her regarding this, He then showed her to gather my sermons, lessons from various teachings, Bible studies and conversations, and assemble them into book form. He told her to do this. She had no computer or laptop, so the Lord instructed her to go to the library and use the computers there… She obeyed. Then one day after a service, she presented me with the manuscript, gave me the Lord's message and let me know, "it's in your court now." It didn't stop there; she had to nudge me for years before I moved on the book. She has spent countless hours praying, patiently editing, and correcting the many directional flows of my writing and exhorting me to move forward. She also researched publishers and methods of getting this work into the hands of you, the reader.

Of course, my children Nicole and Jeremy and grandchildren Jayla, Shamiah, Deidre and Dante who have constantly used the line "daddy…granddad…when are you ever going to finish the book?"

Finally, I thank the congregation, the teachers and administrators of *How to go through Tribulation Victoriously*, of Grace Refuge Chapel, in Detroit, Michigan where Pat and I pastor, for their prayers, pushing me forward and patience… "Pastor Lloyd, when is the book going to be completed?" Well, it's finished… Thank you, Jesus!

Of GOD, I am

FOREWORD

As a young believer in Christ, I often wondered why so many Christians I knew, lived unsuccessful lives, including myself. It seemed to be such a mystery and the total opposite of what someone who wanted and tried to live right for God should be experiencing... But yet it seemed to be the norm. As I became a more mature Christian, it became an even greater mystery. And like so many others, I accepted unsuccessful living as *just the way it's supposed to be.* I adopted the philosophy that us *good people* would get our rewards when we got to heaven.

Then I met Pastor Lloyd E. Wesley, Jr. Pastor Lloyd had been teaching on nine issues of life for quite some time to us in his congregation. One day in 2015 while studying one of Pastor Lloyd's lessons on the nine issues of life, the Lord spoke to me, *This needs to be put in a book. There are more people that need this...* hence this book, *Guard Your Heart: Hearing God to Master the Nine Issues of Life,* began to become a reality.

In his book, *Guard Your Heart: Hearing God to Master the Nine Issues of Life,* Pastor Lloyd exposes the hidden issues that God has revealed to him that have kept God's people unsuccessful for generations, along with the keys that unlock the way to success in every area of life. Each issue of life overlaps another and requires that each is mastered God's way in order to acquire total success without the possibility of failure. Pastor Lloyd not only gives step-by-step details but provides the "how to" to get the desired results.

Often people reach for success, however, they don't know whether or not they are on the right track because success is a process that does not happen overnight. Pastor Lloyd outlines the way to measure the benchmarks to success God's way, a visible guide to gage whether the road you are on is right or not according to God's direct plan for your life. This comes by learning how to operate in the "hidden secrets" of God.

> "For I know the plans I have for you," declares the LORD, "plans to prosper you and not to harm you, plans to give you hope and a future." ~ Jeremiah 29:11 NIV

> "The thief only comes in order to steal and kill and destroy. I came that they may have and enjoy life, and have it in abundance [to the full, till it overflows]." ~ John 10:10 AMP

In this hour when men's hearts are failing, this book is truly a God send and should be a resource for every person, but especially every believer in the Lord Jesus Christ. Pastor Lloyd has outlined God's revealed strategies for lifelong success, both naturally and spiritually, in such a simple process that it would be hard for anyone to fail!

Minister Carolyn V. Robinson
Grace Refuge Chapel
Detroit, MI

INTRODUCTION

The number nine has special spiritual and scriptural importance. Nine represents completion, maturity, finality and judgement. During my time of pastoring, teaching and studying, I have noted that there are nine gifts of the Spirit, nine fruit of the Spirit, nine Christ-character traits, and nine weapons of spiritual armor. Nine marks the end, the conclusion of a matter. When nine has been achieved in a matter, results manifest. It is interesting to note that it takes nine months for a baby to come to full term and birth.

There is another set of nine that is just as important as the others. Through my study, prayer and walking in various experiences with the Lord, He has shown me nine specific issues which are a part of every person's life. The culminations of the results of these issues are determined by whether a person is eating of the *Tree of Life* or of the *Tree of the Knowledge of Good and Evil.*

> "And out of the ground made the Lord God to grow every tree that is pleasant to the sight, and good for food; the tree of life also in the midst of the garden, and the tree of the knowledge of good and evil…And the Lord God commanded the man, saying, Of every tree of the garden thou mayest freely eat: But of the tree of the knowledge of good and evil, thou shalt not eat of it: for in the day that thou eatest thereof thou shalt surely die." ~ Genesis 2:9, 16-17

DEFINITIONS OF MASTERY AND REVELATION

1. **Mastery**[1]: command or grasp, as of a subject: *a mastery of Italian. 2.* superiority or victory: ***mastery over one's enemies.*** *3.* the act of mastering. 4. expert skill or knowledge. 5. the state of being **master;** power of command or control.

2. Revelation[2]: 1a : an act of **revealing** or communicating divine truth b:something that is **revealed** by God to humans 2a:an act of revealing to view or making known b: something that is revealed *especially* : an enlightening or astonishing disclosure shocking *revelations* c: a pleasant often enlightening surprise; her talent was a *revelation*. Synonym: disclosure, divulgence or exposure.

OVERVIEW

This book is the result of years of teaching in church and in a business environment, during which God, by His grace, has given me revelations regarding the scriptures found in **Proverbs 4:20-24**. In verse 23 of this scripture, I found that as we hear the *sayings* of God, (His secrets) we discover that there are specific areas or issues in life. These *issues* have given me a wonderful relationship with God through Jesus, a joyful and healthy life, a marvelous marriage (50 years and counting) and a prosperous ministry and career. Therefore, it is not just to identify these 9 issues of life but to also show God's purpose and provision with His strategies on how to become the *head and not the tail* in each of these areas. The Lord has shown me 9 issues of Life that are a part of every person and how a person masters these issues will cause them to live the abundant life, not just exist, or live in squalor. As you get God's *Knowledge, Understanding* and *Wisdom* on these *issues*, which are God's **KUW**, you can determine whether you are eating of the tree of life or of the tree of the knowledge of good and evil.

The purpose of this book is to highlight God's plans for us to have a **supernatural**, healthy, abundant, flourishing, good life. The word **supernatural** must be underlined as it means to have thoughts or ideas that are apart from what is usual or normal and transcend the laws of nature. In chapter 1 of the book of Daniel we see that as Daniel, (Belteshazzar); Hananiah, (Shadrach); Mishael, (Meshach) and Azariah, (Abednego); decided not to follow the Babylonian ways of eating, but instead to dedicate their ways **to obey God's will**. God blessed them with superior knowledge, understanding and wisdom. After 3 years of all of the children of Judah that had been captured by the Babylonians and taken to the Babylonian country to serve king Nebuchadnezzar's government, as "…the king communed with them; and among them all was found none like Daniel, Hananiah, Mishael, and Azariah: therefore stood they before the king. And in all matters of wisdom and understanding, that the king enquired of them, he found them ten times better than all the magicians and astrologers that were in all his realm. And Daniel continued even unto the first year of king Cyrus" **(Daniel 1:19-21)**.

Take note, they were not found to be equally gifted as the magicians and astrologers who were the advisers to King Nebuchadnezzar that had years of preparation and schooling in the latest knowledge and technologies of the world, nor twice or even three times as gifted, <u>but instead ten times</u>! This transcended the normal laws of nature and was therefore <u>supernatural</u>!

One of the tools that will be introduced in this book is *meditation* as described in the scriptures. One of its purposes is to restructure our thinking to God's thoughts and ways. Once again, scripture states "as a man thinks in his heart, so is he" **(Proverbs 23:7A)**.

I have learned over the years that you cannot receive God's <u>supernatural</u> blueprint for your life without 3 elements: *knowledge, understanding* and *wisdom*. **KNOWLEDGE**, which is information for one to receive beneficial attributes not realized before. Next, the component of **UNDERSTANDING** must come on board. This gives one the WHAT and HOW to use the knowledge to be able to get results. In short, understanding turns on the light in a dark room. Lastly, the element of **WISDOM** must be attained which gives one the WAY, WHERE, WHY and WHEN to utilize the understanding of the knowledge gained. Summarized, wisdom gives one the strategy to accomplish a task.

KNOWLEDGE, UNDERSTANDING and WISDOM = KUW

"Wisdom is the principal thing; therefore get wisdom: and with all thy getting get understanding" **(Proverbs 4:7)**.

Here is an example of Knowledge, Understanding and Wisdom. An individual is standing on the sidewalk and is being barked and growled at by a dog that is across the street. The person has a can of dog repellant in their hand. The dog begins running towards them and is now halfway across the street, however, the individual feels comfortable because they realize that what's within the can they hold is against the dog (knowledge). The dog has crossed the street and is now on the lawn strip next to the sidewalk. The individual is confident because of what's in their hand...the dog is now biting the individual on the leg. The problem illustrated here is the person only had information. It was not enough.

The next example is another individual has the can of dog repellant in their hand, which gives them knowledge that what's in the can is against dogs along with that the repellant in the eyes or nose of the dog will repel it. The dog begins running towards them and is now halfway across the street, however, the individual feels comfortable because they realize that within the can they hold is repellant to the dog once in the dog's eyes or nose. The person begins spraying the repellant everywhere. The dog has crossed the street and is now on the lawn strip next to the sidewalk. The individual is confident because of the dog repellant in their hand, once applied, will repel the dog...the dog is now biting the individual in the leg. The failure here is the dog spray was used completely up by the time the dog was on the strip of lawn. **Understanding gives one the HOW and WHAT to use the knowledge to get the desired results but it needs one more element to manifest those results.**

The final example is another individual that has the can of dog repellant in their hand, which gives them knowledge that what's in the can will repel dogs along with understanding and wisdom. Once again wisdom gives one the WAY, WHERE, WHY and WHEN to utilize the understanding of the knowledge to get the desired results…to repel the attacking dog. Let's see what happens now… The dog begins running towards them and is now halfway across the street, however, the individual feels comfortable because they realize that within the can they hold is repellant to the dog once in the dog's eyes or nose. The person has wisdom enough to hold off spraying the repellant until the dog is in range of 4 to 6 feet from them. The dog has crossed the street and is now on the lawn strip next to the sidewalk. The individual doesn't begin to spray the repellant directly into the dog's eyes and nose until the dog is 4 to 6 feet away. The dog is instantly repelled and runs quickly away from the source of the repellant.

This simple illustration shows that as one attains knowledge, understanding and wisdom they will get the desired results of whatever activity they engage in. The hidden secrets in the passage of scripture Proverbs 4:20-24, comes forth as you utilize these 3 elements to attain the total blueprint available to you as stated in the verses.

In order to get the full benefit of these few lines of scripture we must understand them **in the context** in which they are stated. Reviewing them through **the context** means that it will greatly benefit your receiving a thorough knowledge, understanding and wisdom if you consider the verses by the information that came before and after them also. Take note of the following sentence as it relates to interpreting the meaning of a message that you are considering: *He does not like to see children hurt.* As you read this you discern that this person loves and has concern for children. Now, we take one word out of the sentence, *hurt*, and its entire communication changes. *He does not like to see children.* From this sentence we discern that the individual does not care for, love nor have concern for children. One word changed the entire communication, knowledge, and understanding and gave the wisdom of how this person should be engaged when it comes to children. So, it is as we consider verses of scripture, we need to read what came before and after along with the given scripture.

It is most important that we are cognizant of the reality that before the fall, Adam had the thoughts of God and had dominion and authority over everything above the earth, on the earth and in the sea. However, upon Adam's disobedience in the Garden of Eden he was separated from God and the thoughts and dominion he had. All of this was regained by Christ Jesus upon His resurrection and ascension to His Father, God. Jesus has opened the portal for the Kingdom of God to come into the earth through His thoughts to the church!

The authority and power that Adam had was because God's thoughts gave the availability of power due to the right relationship he had with God. This means according to **Isaiah 55:8-9,** he had the availability of thoughts and ways of God that were far above the earth as are the heavens. Think on that. Instead of trying to come back into a healthy status, he stayed in total health at all time. Instead of having thoughts of making a good living and being in a good neighborhood, he had lack of nothing, and nothing surpassed the Garden of Eden. Meditation and prayer are a major avenue back to the perfection in the Garden of Eden. He had a Utopian experience continually. All of this came from thoughts...God thoughts! This state of being, having God's thoughts in matters or issues, is available to every one of us. Effective meditation and obedient living will bring you back into the revelation-thoughts of God.

> "The secret things belong unto the Lord our God: but those things which are revealed belong unto us and to our children for ever, that we may do all the words of this law." ~ Deuteronomy 29:29

We have developed meditation exercises for your spirit just as if you were in an exercise club to get your body in top physical shape. They are on the website mentioned later in the book.

God wants us to have and has prepared us to experience more than a recall of Bible events spoken eloquently with revelations from the past. He wants us to have His knowledge, understanding and wisdom for our present situations and to know His ways for the Kingdom of God to come in the earth as it is in heaven.

There will be tools and a study course given throughout the pages of this book that will give examples, testimonies and encouragement to assist you in getting the secrets of God that He has provided for you in the issues of life.

As you journey through this book you will be introduced to even more processes that will further equip you to get actual results from God's word that can be demonstrated in your life. Those processes will be found in the resource section of the website, **www.guardyourheart.life**.

What I've been shown by the Lord in **Proverbs 4** is that Adam, before his sin and separation from the *spiritual life* of God, or the *God DNA*, had the Knowledge, Understanding and Wisdom for attaining God's intentions in every issue of life. The Knowledge, Understanding and Wisdom of God or the *KUW,* paves the path for one's self-esteem being returned to a far higher Christ-Esteem. The actual hearing from God shows our direction in life, gives words that impart effectual prayer and provides a peaceful resolution of every relationship issue: the healing and walking in health, achieving the necessary educational preparation for God's purposes, successfully achieving the vocational requirements of our position in the Body of Christ, and it reveals where and how we are to earn our living, while getting the financial resources for God's expected end for ourselves. Hearing God establishes our *legacy footprint* in the earth to give us the rewards God intended in eternity. In that light, the following scriptures open us up to God's promises hidden in our *perceived* problems.

"My son, attend to my words; incline thine ear unto my sayings. Let them not depart from thine eyes, keep them in the midst of thine heart. For they are life unto those that find them, and health to all their flesh. Keep thy heart with all diligence; for out of it are the issues of life. Put away from thee a forward mouth and perverse lips put far from thee."   ~ Proverbs 4:20-24

If a person moves to another city it is a major life change, a move to another state is a huge transformation, but to change country is revolutionary. Coming into the Kingdom of God multiplies all the others by an unknown number. It is not *joining a church* but is an altogether different life! Hearing the *sayings of God* will take you far beyond the actual words in the scripture to revelation that alters your thinking at its roots, which in turn will **supernaturally** transform every issue in your life!

God has all the solutions to all our life's issues. **Jeremiah 29:11, Matthew 7:7-11** show that there are simple keys to opening the lock of every door regarding them. We need to use His knowledge, understanding and wisdom **(KUW)** and not ours. In **Proverbs 3:5-6, Proverbs 23:7A** and **Psalm 32:8,** we find the way to resolve our every issue and to change our thinking into God's thinking. It has been my experience in life with people in every issue that is before them; that they need God's **KUW**. Those that don't get it find themselves in lack as compared to those who press on and find restoration.

In *Matthew 13:1-23, Mark 4:1-28* and *Luke 8:1-18,* Jesus gives the understanding of the parable regarding the sower sowing his seeds. Jesus goes on to explain to His disciples and those with them, that the sower plants the word of God and that the seeds fall on 4 types of soil which represent the type of hearts or minds that mankind possess. The first soil is *by the wayside,* or hard ground which represents a person who has numerous thoughts traveling in their minds and therefore, become hardened so that the seeds stay in the open on top of the hard ground and the fowls (demonic spirits) quickly take it away due to no penetration of understanding or light. No fruit is borne.

The next soil is rocky ground, and the seeds planted there, sense that the rocks or stones are preventing roots from penetrating. The seed sends a stalk of the plant directly upward with the moisture and nutrients within the seed. Although this person gladly receives the word sown, they only last for a short period of time because as soon as adversity arises, without water and nutrients supplied from the relationship provided through the roots, the plant dries up and dies bearing no fruit. Those stones are past hurts, disappointments, fears, abuses, unforgiveness, etc. that cause a hardening within the heart.

The next soil is that which is covered with thorns. Although the plant grows from the seed sown and begins the initial fruit development, said fruit never reaches maturity and cannot be used. This is caused by the thorns, which are *cares of the world, deceitfulness of riches and the lusts of other things,* that choke the plant that came forth from the seed sown.

The last soil in which the seeds are sown is the *good ground;* this ground, without the detriments of the other soil types, brings forth a harvest of 30-fold, 60-fold and 100-fold production in fruit. We find the reason for this abundance is **the seed is received**, "But that on the good ground are they, which in an **honest** and **good heart**, having heard the word, **keep it**, and bring forth fruit **with patience**" (**Luke 8:15**, emphasis added).

This parable references Jesus taking the disciples and a few others aside from the crowd and giving them a more in-depth understanding of the secrets within the parable which concern the Kingdom of God. He told them that it had been given to them, the chosen ones (**John 15:16, 1 Peter 2:9**) to understand the things of the Kingdom of God, but for those who were *outside* or *without the door*, the secrets are spoken in a parable or dark, mysterious, hidden method. The Lord goes on further to state that those who are on the *outside* see but don't perceive or realize *something* is there. They therefore have a painful or pleasant sensation but continue in the direction they're going in. The *outsider* also hears the answer but doesn't *understand* where to place it in the equation of life. They therefore remain in the dark in life, and keep stumbling, going nowhere. They therefore stay sick, broke, unpromoted, without peace or victory. Jesus went on to say regarding this parable that "If you don't understand this story, you won't understand any others." **The understanding of this parable and its application in your life is a major purpose of this book!**

At the end of each chapter for each issue of life there will be a spiritual inventory that will request what specific scriptures you have meditated and received a *revelation saying* from the Lord. The bottom line to this is: God's word is true just as gravity works: should I pick up a quarter and hold it between my thumb and forefinger, if I open up my thumb and forefinger the quarter, due to the natural laws of gravity, will fall. It does not matter what I know, the quarter will fall. It doesn't matter what I believe, the quarter will fall, and it doesn't matter what I understand, the quarter will fall. So, it is in the spiritual realm, if I get a *saying from God* and *obey* and *do the word,* **supernatural** results will follow. Here is a dynamic secret! Hidden within these words are the keys to unlock every problem, limitation, fear and lack in your life...

"My son attend unto my words, incline your ear unto my sayings. Let them not depart from your eyes, keep them in the midst of your heart. For they are life to those that find them and health to all their flesh. Keep and guard your heart with all diligence, for out of it are the issues of life. Put away from you a forward mouth and perverse lips put far from you." ~ Proverbs 4:20-24

Those discovered issues mean a source of life that escapes death and defeat!

A NOTE OF CAUTION

"Go to the ant, you sluggard! Consider her ways and be wise, Which, having no captain, Overseer or ruler, Provides her supplies in the summer, And gathers her food in the harvest. How long will you slumber, O sluggard? When will you rise from your sleep? A little sleep, a little slumber, A little folding of the hands to sleep— So shall your poverty come on you like a prowler, And your need like an armed man." ~ Proverbs 6:6-11 NKJV

Sluggard: The KJV translates Strong's Sluggard: H6102 in the following manner: <u>slothful</u> (8x), <u>sluggard</u> (6x). sluggish, lazy A. sluggard, 'âtsêl, aw-tsale'; from <u>H6101</u>; **indolent:**—slothful, sluggard. Indolent: (Niphal) to be sluggish, **'âtsal,** aw-tsal'; a primitive root; to lean idly, i.e. to be indolent or slack:—be slothful. (negligent, careless, remiss)[3]

"For I know the thoughts that I think toward you, saith the LORD, thoughts of peace, and not of evil, to give you an expected end. 12 Then shall ye call upon me, and ye shall go and pray unto me, and I will hearken unto you. 13 And ye shall seek me, and find me, when ye shall search for me with all your heart." ~ Jeremiah 29:11

Seek: The KJV translates Strong's Seek: H1245 in the following manner: <u>seek</u> (189x), <u>require</u> (14x), <u>request</u> (4x), <u>seek out</u> (4x), <u>enquired</u> (3x), <u>besought</u> (2x), <u>ask</u> (2x), <u>sought for</u> (2x), <u>begging</u> (1x), <u>desire</u> (1x), <u>get</u> (1x), <u>inquisition</u> (1x), <u>procureth</u> (1x). **bâqash,** baw-kash'; a primitive root; to search out (by any method, specifically in worship or prayer); by implication, to strive after:—ask, beg, beseech, desire, enquire, get, make inquisition, procure, (make) request, require, seek (for).[4]

Search: The KJV translates Strong's Search: H1875 in the following manner: <u>seek</u> (84x), <u>enquire</u> (43x), <u>require</u> (12x), <u>search</u> (7x), *miscellaneous* (18x). to seek (with a demand), demand, require to investigate, enquire, to ask for, require, demand, to practice, study, follow, seek with application, to seek with care, care for.[5]

Heart: The KJV translates Strong's Heart: H3824 in the following manner: <u>heart</u> (231x), <u>consider (with H7760)</u> (5x), <u>mind</u> (4x), <u>understanding</u> (3x), *miscellaneous* (9x). (mind, knowledge, thinking, reflection, memory, inclination, resolution, determination (of will), conscience.)[6]

"The company of the prophets said to Elisha, 'Look, the place where we meet with you is too small for us. Let us go to the Jordan, where each of us can get a pole; and let us build a place there for us to meet.' And he said, 'Go.' Then one of them said, 'Won't you please come with your servants?' 'I will,' Elisha replied. And he went with them. They went to the Jordan and began to cut down trees. As one of them was cutting down a tree, the iron axhead fell into the water. 'Oh no, my lord!' he cried out. 'It was borrowed!' The man of God asked, 'Where did it fall?' When he showed him the place, **Elisha cut a stick and threw it there, and made the iron float.** 'Lift it out,' he said. Then the man reached out his hand and took it."

~ 2 Kings 6:1-7 NIV, emphasis added

After Elisha was presented with the problem of one of his students having lost the needed piece of borrowed equipment to the bottom of the waterway, one must consider Elisha's response of cutting a branch from a tree and throwing it into the water where the iron axe head had sunk to the bottom. What was he thinking and why would he take such an odd action during an obvious emergency? It was due to his character of being an ardent disciple of Elijah… in following him with all fervency and diligence while being a daily and continuing meditator of God's word as instructed by the Lord. He trusted in the Lord with all his heart and did not lean unto the natural thinking of man but constantly acknowledged and was aware of God's presence. Being in that state of mind, he consulted God and received His higher thoughts that are available to everyone that has disciplined their minds to His omnipresence.

"For my thoughts are not your thoughts, neither are your ways my ways, saith the LORD. For as the heavens are higher than the earth, so are my ways higher than your ways, and my thoughts than your thoughts."   ~ Isaiah 55:8-9

I mention this at the beginning of this book to give a word of **caution** and **warning** as I have noted in life's experiences that there are many people who have fallen into the iniquitous state of *lazy-Christianity* and have become slack and even slothful and worldly when it comes to seeking and trusting the Lord with all their hearts. Those in that state will miss God, not repent due to being <u>**comfortable in the "traditions of men"**</u> and therefore miss the flow of God's Spirit in this end time season.

The good news is that the Lord has provided witty inventions along with His higher thoughts for direction to His secrets and revelations to bring the Kingdom of God in each issue of our lives.

So, I welcome you to *GUARD YOUR HEART, HEARING GOD TO MASTER THE 9 ISSUES OF LIFE*. One word of expectation… God's Kingdom is <u>**supernatural**</u>, and it is His plan and expectation for you to have and experience the <u>**supernatural**</u> in your everyday life… it is the norm in the Kingdom of God!

OF GOD, I AM

1. ***I am loved of God***, *love Him & by Grace, am restored to righteousness and Dominion through belief & faith in Christ Jesus being wounded, shedding His blood, dying & being raised from the dead for my sins & transgressions.*

2. ***He is my light*** *which gives understanding, & salvation; I therefore fear nothing, for He is the strength of my life & is greater in me than Satan in the world.*

3. ***I am predestinated*** *through His being bruised for my iniquities to being transformed by His thoughts to His image.*

4. ***I am built up*** *in Him through His nature inherent in my inner man by His Spirit; my Shepherd He is & has supplied all my need through His riches in glory.*

5. ***I walk in His peace*** *through His being chastised & have healing & divine health because of the stripes He received.*

6. ***He has Prepared a Prosperous Path*** *for me to Process His Promises out of Perceived Problems through the Predestined Power of His Purposes revealed in the Spirit through Prayer, Praise and Worship.*

7. ***I am led of His Spirit*** *which guides me into all truth for His name's sake; who shows & prepares me for things to come.*

8. ***I bear much fruit*** *to the glory of God that remains in the world; by diligent, steadfast connection to Christ Jesus's vine; empowered & ordained of God, in & through the abundance of His Word.*

9. ***I have goodness and mercy***, *through the grace of Christ Jesus, in & around me all the days of my life; & I shall dwell in the House of the Lord forever.*

I'm an heir of God; joint heir of Christ Jesus By,
Lloyd E. Wesley, Jr.

SECTION I

←————————→

SELF ESTEEM

Gain the knowledge and relationship with God and come
into how He views you.

TRANSFORMING CHARACTERISTIC
~ DILIGENCE ~

Make with haste to do something, to use speed, to
make effort, be prompt, or have an earnest, endeavor, labor,
study in God's word, thoughts and purpose in your life.

KINGDOM BENCHMARK
~ KNOWLEDGE ~

The secret information regarding the things pertaining to
God's Kingdom in the earth experienced by you.

1

THE ISSUES OF LIFE

Issues means, in the context of this book, the results manifesting from whatever has been done in one's life that yields victory or success. As an example: someone who is skilled in math has a love of reading, is very attracted towards things regarding math and all types of computations and is very good at them. They also associate themselves with people with the same interests, research subjects via the internet and social media regarding people or events surrounding mathematical interests. Therefore, that person has math related things, creative ideas coming forth from them continuously because their mind is full of thoughts regarding it.

A further definition of Issues is: The act of sending out or putting forth, promulgation,* distribution. An Issue is something proceeding from any source, as a product or effect, the result or consequence. Issue(s) would be the offspring or progeny of something, it is the going, coming or passing or flowing out, something that comes out. It would be the profit that comes from a venture. A simple description of issue(s) is that which comes out of a source that causes either a continued prosperity or destruction to that which will come from it in the future.[1]

1

As I said in the introduction, the Lord has shown me 9 major issues of life. The results of these issues come forth in a person's life from the abundance of thoughts that they have regarding each issue as shown in the following:

1. The **SELF-ESTEEM** of one being raised to **CHRIST-ESTEEM** (Coming into how God views us through hearing from Him and the intimate relationship that's produced by obedience to His revelations).

2. The **RELATIONSHIPS** between God and man and then between man and others (Obedience to God gives a good alliance with Him and mankind).

3. **RECEIVING DIRECTION FROM GOD AND EFFECTIVE PRAYER** (Hearing and being led of God while believing and speaking what He reveals into our circumstances).

4. **HEALING AND HEALTH** (Getting the results of the inheritance of healing and walking in health we have through what Jesus purchased for us by the stripes He took).

5. Being **EDUCATIONALLY PREPARED** (The purposed learning we acquire in order to contribute beneficially to the social-economic environment).

6. **VOCATIONS** (The work we do in life. The first relates to an individual being attached to God's purposes (occupation) in their church life and the second is the job by which one earns their living).

7. **FINANCE$** (Relates to obtaining God's resources to sponsor one's spiritual and natural activities in life).

8. **LEGACY** (Refers to an individual's influence that they have on those around them both now and after their transition).

9. **ETERNAL REWARD** (Refers to the return on investment of a person in the here-after based on what they've contributed in their life in God's purposes).

Each of these nine issues came from what the Lord has revealed to me in **Proverbs 4:20-23**. In each area God has purposed for us to have His secret knowledge. As you spend time focusing and obeying the words in scripture for each issue, God will speak to you on it. As you meditate what has been spoken and continue following the leading of the Holy Spirit, you will see God's Kingdom Blueprint for that issue and begin declaring His purposes for the "abundant life" in that issue of your life. Please note, you must go after it according to God's instructions…

"Only fear the LORD, and serve him in truth with all your heart: for consider how great things he hath done for you."

~ 1 Samuel 12:24

"And ye shall seek me, and find me, when ye shall search for me with all your heart." ~ Jeremiah 29:13

"Jesus said unto him, Thou shalt love the Lord thy God with all thy heart, and with all thy soul, and with all thy mind."

~ Matthew 22:37

As stated in the introduction, we must learn to effectively meditate the word of God which reconnects us to His **KUW**. We read in **Romans 8:26** that we don't know what to pray for as we should and that as we pray in the spirit or in tongues, the Holy Spirit prays the mind of God for us. This is explained in depth in the course, *First Foundational Steps in God,* which can be found at **www.guardyourheart.life**.

2

DEFINING SELF ESTEEM

The first issue of Life is self-esteem being raised to Christ-Esteem. Once this issue is mastered, it will lay the foundation for you to begin to master the other eight issues of life. But before we discuss how we can master the issue of self-esteem being raised to Christ-Esteem, let us define its meaning.

As we look at this compound word, self and esteem; of course, self refers to not only ourselves, but our inner most self. It places a microscope on the very core of our being. The word *self* is defined as "the union of element (as body, emotions, thoughts, and sensations) that constitute the individuality and identity of a person."[1] The word *esteem* is defined as "the regard in which one is held; the perceived worth that someone or something is afforded."[2] As we put these two words together, they multiply their meaning and purpose.

Self-esteem is a person's inward perception of themselves as compared and related to their feelings, beliefs and perceptions of how they and others feel, value and think towards them. It encompasses a person's overall sense of self-worth or personal value. Self-esteem determines how well or poorly a person will progress in caring for themselves in body, mind and spirit. It will control how a person's educational endeavors, relationships, finances, living conditions, attire and positioning will manifest in their lives. Once again, it must be reiterated that self-esteem is the center core of a person determining the present and future contributions or subtractions of their legacy in life.

We can see how important a person's self-esteem is to their overall quality of life.

POSITIVE AND NEGATIVE SELF-ESTEEM

Each of us comes to a point in life when we search for a sense of identity – who we are. How we identify ourselves directly affects our self-esteem. When we are young, we identify with our parents. The teenage years bring on peer identity comparisons. But as we get older, we begin to look for other ways to find our identities. How we identify ourselves directly affects our self-esteem. As we learned in the Introduction, self-esteem boils down to how we think about ourselves. Our thinking can cause us to have positive self-esteem or negative (low) self-esteem. But how do we know what to think of ourselves? Let's review positive versus negative self-esteem.

Positive Self-Esteem

Positive self-esteem is a healthy esteem. It's when a person knows who they are as it relates to their value. They have established morals and standards and are not intimidated or influenced by the majority or pressure from others. Individuals with a positive self-esteem realize that their happiness is not solely dependent on someone or something else. They understand that God is the true source of our happiness.

A person with a positive self-esteem strives to advance in whatever environment they find themselves in.

Negative Self-Esteem

A person with low or negative self-esteem will not strive to improve their lot beyond a particular point of reference (it differs with each individual); they simply try to blend in to not be seen. Negative self-esteem develops when a person does not have healthy thoughts about themselves. They do not put proper value on who they are. Usually our early life experiences develop our self-esteem. Therefore, having negative experiences in our life such as a lack of attention or encouragement while growing up will impact esteem negatively.

Low Self-Esteem Attributes

1. Dwelling on negative thoughts about ourselves.

2. Not placing proper value on who you are.

3. Lack of values, standards, and/or boundaries.

4. Dependent upon others for happiness.

5. Unrealistic expectations of one's self.

6. Not recognizing or acknowledging your gifts and talents.

The way we come into proper self-esteem is to come into proper thinking.

SCIENTIFIC STUDY AND DNA/CHROMOSOME ADVANCEMENTS

Scientists have studied for generations the complex structure of mankind's cellular structure and composition. In the last 70 years breakthroughs have been accomplished whereby they have been able to manipulate the chromosomes of various animals and have discovered ways to find out techniques from years of prolonged studies to determine and cure a few diseases that are inherited. Look at the 3 paragraphs below describing this.

Determining the order of DNA building blocks (nucleotides) in an individual's genetic code, called DNA sequencing, has advanced the study of genetics and is one technique used to test for genetic disorders. Two methods, whole exome sequencing and whole genome sequencing, are increasingly used in healthcare and research to identify genetic variations; both methods rely on new technologies that allow rapid sequencing of large amounts of DNA. These approaches are known as next-generation sequencing which was done in 1980.

The original sequencing technology, called Sanger sequencing (named after the scientist who developed it, Frederick Sanger),[3] was a breakthrough that helped scientists determine the human genetic code, but it is time-consuming and expensive. The Sanger method has been automated to make it faster and is still used in laboratories today to sequence short pieces of DNA, but it would take years to sequence all a person's DNA (known as the person's genome). Next-generation sequencing has sped up the process (taking only days to weeks to sequence a human genome) while reducing the cost.

With next-generation sequencing, it is now feasible to sequence enormous amounts of DNA. For instance, all the pieces of an individual's DNA that provide instructions for making proteins. These pieces, called exons, are thought to make up 1 percent of a person's genome. Together, all the exons in a genome are known as the exome, and the method of sequencing them is known as whole exome sequencing. This method allows variations in the protein-coding region of any gene to be identified, rather than in only a select few genes. **Because most known mutations that cause disease occur in exons, whole exome sequencing is thought to be an efficient method to identify possible disease-causing mutations.**[4]

Recently, in 2018, it was reported on the news that the assailant of a schoolteacher that had been raped and murdered around 1993, had been found, tried, and imprisoned. Detectives used forensic science, after exhuming the body, to check the DNA coding of the dead sperm that was still existent and then tracked down and identified the murderer. This was due to the fact that every individual's DNA is different. The rapist and murderer was located, tried in the courts with the evidence and put in jail.

OK, so what on earth does DNA have to do with an individual's self-esteem? The last 4 paragraphs relate the cumulative scientific research known by mankind that over the last 70 years has led to the ability to cure a few inherited diseases in humans and aid in criminal investigations, through working with just a few of the thousands of chromosomes found in the cellular make-up of our bodies. But let's look at Adam's abilities.

Adam's DNA/Chromosome Mastery

"Now Jesus Himself began His ministry at about thirty years of age, being (as was supposed) the son of Joseph, the son of Heli,… the son of Enosh, the son of Seth, the son of Adam, the son of God."

~ Luke 3:23, 38 NKJV

Adam gave the actual DNA of all the animals on the earth and birds of the sky, by hearing God and speaking their DNA structure into their beings!

"Now the LORD God said, "It is not good (beneficial) for the man to be alone; I will make him a helper [one who balances him—a counterpart who is] suitable and complementary for him." So the LORD God formed out of the ground every animal of the field and every bird of the air, and brought them to Adam to see what he would call them; and whatever the man called a living creature, that was its name. And the man gave names to all the livestock, and to the birds of the air, and to every animal of the field; but for Adam there was not found a helper [that was] suitable (a companion) for him."

~ Genesis 2:18-20 AMP

The scripture above tells us God brought every animal to Adam to see what Adam would name them. Let's investigate further <u>what it means to name something</u>. After being made in the image of God, man was given the authority and ability to do God's will.

> "And God blessed them, and God said unto them, Be fruitful, and multiply, and replenish the earth, and subdue it: and have dominion over the fish of the sea, and over the fowl of the air, and over every living thing that moveth upon the earth." ~ Genesis 1:28

With this authority and ability through the empowerment of God's Spirit in Adam, he named all the animals in the earth as God brought them to him. *"Naming"* **is this, as Adam heard the voice of God within himself regarding God's will for each one, Adam spoke the "nature" of the animal in them.** Adam gave them their DNA nature by calling (speaking into them) their name. To call, in this sense, means to *prophesy or to summon to a position or status.* Therefore, whatever Adam *"called"* the animals, that is what they became. This is POWER!

Scientists and biologists in the 21st century, through teams of the most brilliant people on the planet and years of research and study, are working with the chromosomes of living beings, adjusting their DNA by removing or adding particular chromosomes, to affect behaviors which results in changes in their nature. Adam did all of this by speaking whatever he heard God say for the complete DNA structure of thousands of creatures in a relatively brief period! Now STOP and THINK ABOUT IT...this is **POWER**, and **ABILITY** that far exceeds our abilities today! This is the **Self-Esteem** Adam walked in!!

It's All in the Name

The issue of naming in the Bible is extremely important! God named people (which caused them to take on the ability to perform and produce) according to their nature or purpose in the earth and universe. Abram, meaning *high father,* or *father of height,* had his name changed to Abraham which means *father of a multitude.* This came after the Lord told him he would have descendants as the number of stars in the heavens. Once the name is changed, so is the nature and results!

Sarai, the wife of Abram, who had been barren, whose name meant *head person of any rank,* was changed to Sarah, meaning, *female, noble, princess, queen,* once she was prophesied over about giving birth to a son who would have a multitude come from him. When Sarah heard the angels say she would bear a son being 89 years of age and barren; she laughed saying, "shall I have pleasure of Abram?" The angels challenged her unbelief and told her because of her laughter the child would be called Isaac, meaning *son of mocking laughter.* Methuselah, the longest recorded living person in the scriptures, lived to be 969 years of age. His name did not denote his many years but instead meant *the great deluge or flood,* because when he died the great flood came upon the earth. Adam stated, once awakening from the sleep that God put him in, to remove one of his ribs, and then make woman.

> "And Adam said, This is now bone of my bones, and flesh of my flesh: she shall be called Woman, because she was taken out of Man." ~ Genesis 2:19

So, as did the Lord, so did Adam in the naming or *naturing* all the animals in the earth and birds in the sky. He did so by the **POWER** resident in him via the Spirit of God. The number of animals in the earth and birds in the sky amounted to thousands as it relates to sheer numbers. This was an awesome task and ability all of which derived from Adam's **Self-Esteem**. Again, this is the **Self-Esteem** of Adam before his fall into sin.

You could be thinking… Would Adam have been made this smart; this gifted?! Let's look at the clues, the evidence.

"Then God said, 'Let us make mankind in our image, in our likeness, so that they may rule over the fish in the sea and the birds in the sky, over the livestock and all the wild animals, and over all the creatures that move along the ground.' So God created mankind in his own image, in the image of God he created them; male and female he created them. God blessed them and said to them, 'Be fruitful and increase in number; fill the earth and subdue it. Rule over the fish in the sea and the birds in the sky and over every living creature that moves on the ground.'"   ~ Genesis 1:26-28 NIV

Man was made in God's image and given dominion over all things in the earth. All things include Satan who God had expelled from heaven, which caused him to fall to the earth with a third of the angels that had joined in with him **(Revelation 12:3-4)**. Let me describe this in another way... Adam was over Satan.

The Impact of Iniquity on Adam's Self Esteem

The Lord showed that the iniquity that Adam and Eve received upon their disobedience was really an automatic mind programming. That programming set the minds of Adam and Eve against the thoughts of God. On the other hand, righteousness, which is established through man hearing and believing the spoken word of God, as shown in **Genesis 15:6** when "Abram believed in the Lord, and it was counted to him as righteousness." This righteousness is what Jesus talked about in **Matthew 6:33** when he said, "but seek ye first the kingdom of God, and his righteousness; and all these things shall be added unto you."

Righteousness brings one back into believing God and in proper alignment with God through His thoughts. Those thoughts come from the mind and mouth of God and are the *Rhema Word* of God. The *Rhema Word* of God is the communication of God to us that is coming directly from His heart and mouth to ours. While Adam was "naming all the animals and birds," he was receiving those thoughts from God Himself and the power and the light that was displayed from that communication. Satan could not try to come close to Adam and Eve because of the **LIGHT** power display that was going on!

It states in **Psalm 119:130**, "the entrance of Thy word gives light; it gives understanding to the simple." That *Light* is the same *Light* that God spoke in **Genesis 1:3**:

> "And God said, Let there be light: and there was light. And God saw the light, that it was good: and God divided the light from the darkness. And God called the light Day, and the darkness he called Night. And the evening and the morning were the first day."
>
> ~ Genesis 1:3-5

This Light was not coming from the sun, moon or stars but was the *glory-presence* of God Himself which disperses anything that is not of God or His nature! Therefore, Satan would not be able to approach Adam during this *naming of the thousands of animals and fowls*. During this "Naming-DNA-event," Adam was worshipping God as God's presence was there in the receiving of what to speak for each creature. It was a powerful and creative demonstration and it further amplified Adam's dominion over all things on the earth, sea and sky. This light chased away all darkness. However, once that *light and power display* was finished, and it could have been days, weeks, months or even years, Adam stopped worshiping God…which caused the atmosphere to be changed because of the *light of God's presence*. Once God was not in the presence from Adam's worship, Satan slipped in and brought his cunning lies to Eve who was with Adam. Did pride enter Adam because of the great accomplishments of the *naming/naturing* of the thousands of creatures? Let's look deeper into the plausibility of this.

The serpent was not always in the form that he found himself to be in in Genesis 3:1:

> "Now the serpent was more cunning than any beast of the field which the LORD God had made. And he said to the woman, "Has God indeed said, 'You shall not eat of every tree of the garden'?
>
> ~ Genesis 3:1 NKJV

The serpent's first estate was in heaven and he was a high-ranking angel that had the assignment of transporting all the praise and worship from the entire universe up to the throne of Almighty God. God created him to have pipes throughout his body so that the worship sounds and music could be channeled through his body and then to the throne of God. Look at the description of his body with its beauty along with his wisdom.

> "Moreover the word of the LORD came to me, saying, "Son of man, take up a lamentation for the king of Tyre, and say to him, 'Thus says the Lord GOD: "You were the seal of perfection, Full of wisdom and perfect in beauty. You were in Eden, the garden of God; Every precious stone was your covering: The sardius, topaz, and diamond, Beryl, onyx, and jasper, Sapphire, turquoise, and emerald with gold. The workmanship of your timbrels and pipes Was prepared for you on the day you were created. "You were the anointed cherub who covers; I established you; You were on the holy mountain of God; You walked back and forth in the midst of fiery stones. You were perfect in your ways from the day you were created, Till iniquity was found in you." ~ Ezekiel 28:11-15 NKJV

> "How you are fallen from heaven, O Lucifer, son of the morning! How you are cut down to the ground, You who weakened the nations! For you have said in your heart: 'I will ascend into heaven, I will exalt my throne above the stars of God; I will also sit on the mount of the congregation On the farthest sides of the north; I will

14

ascend above the heights of the clouds, I will be like the Most High.' Yet you shall be brought down to Sheol, To the lowest depths of the Pit." ~ Isaiah 14:12-15 NKJV

"By the abundance of your trading You became filled with violence within, And you sinned; Therefore I cast you as a profane thing Out of the mountain of God; And I destroyed you, O covering cherub, From the midst of the fiery stones. Your heart was lifted up because of your beauty; You corrupted your wisdom for the sake of your splendor; I cast you to the ground, I laid you before kings, That they might gaze at you. You defiled your sanctuaries By the multitude of your iniquities, By the iniquity of your trading; Therefore I brought fire from your midst; It devoured you, And I turned you to ashes upon the earth In the sight of all who saw you. All who knew you among the peoples are astonished at you; You have become a horror, And shall be no more forever." ~ Ezekiel 28:16-19 NKJV

We see that Lucifer's beauty, wisdom, power, success and high position caused him to be lifted up in pride and arrogance to a point of thinking he could be like the Highest God, *I will be like the Most High*. This iniquity, the thinking patterns that were against the knowledge of God, caused the sin against God. However, as the scriptures above showed, it caused him to be cast out of heaven and one-third of the angels were with him. Jesus spoke in **Luke 10:18**, "And He said to them, 'I saw Satan fall like lightning from heaven.'" John revealed in **Revelation 12:3-4**. Could Adam have been lifted with pride from the remarkable success he had in naming the creatures of the air and earth along with his status and power and dominion? I believe so. After Eve had listened to and thought on (meditated) what the serpent had said and then eaten of the forbidden fruit she gave it to her husband that was with her. By the way he had dominion over all things…he therefore had the power to easily subdue the serpent. However, it has been revealed to me that Adam, at this point had fallen into the same error as Lucifer. **That error was to be lifted with pride.**

Another revelation is given in scripture regarding all of this after Adam and Eve had eaten the fruit and found themselves to be naked. In Genesis 3:7,

> "Then the eyes of both of them were opened, and they knew that they were naked; and they sewed fig leaves together and made themselves coverings. And they heard the sound of the LORD God walking in the garden in the cool of the day, and Adam and his wife hid themselves from the presence of the LORD God among the trees of the garden. Then the LORD God called to Adam and said to him, "Where are you?"   ~ Genesis 3:7-9 NKJV

God is all knowing and all seeing, and was fully aware of the actual location of Adam and Eve; however, the question of **"where are you?"** was referring to, "where is the praise and worship that draws and welcomes me into the midst of you?" Once Adam's pride had exalted him, the worship ceased... the darkness came... and the serpent sneaked in and sprung the trap on Eve. Adam's pride blinded him even as Eve's ignorance and lack of experience, blinded her. She was not around during the power and glory of the *Light explosion* during the naming/DNA creativity, as she had not yet been made from Adam's side. Iniquity always precedes sin. The iniquity and then disobedience caused the fall of Adam and Eve; it then was passed to all that came after them in their generations and programmed us all with the same mind-set. The power that Adam had through his self-esteem being originated from God's Self-Esteem is further high-lighted from the fact that the ground became cursed. In **Genesis 3:17 and 18**, it talks about the earth becoming cursed because of Adam's sin and iniquity, bringing forth thorns and thistles and how Adam had to work out of the darkness he was in to earn a living.

The Lord states in **2 Chronicles 7:14**:

> "…if My people who are called by My name will humble themselves, and pray and seek My face, and turn from their wicked ways, then I will hear from heaven, and will forgive their sin and heal their land."   ~ 2 Chronicles 7:14 NKJV

There is a very informative 13:26 minute, YouTube video named Transformations-Revival Almolonga, Guatemala[5] that shows a city totally transformed from witchcraft, alcoholism, violence, wife-beating, sickness and impoverishment to fervent Christianity, peace, little to no violence, no jails, tremendous prosperity…and along with this, the actual land began producing crops that were 7-10 times the prior size with 3 harvests instead of 2 each year. The people went from sending out 4 truckloads of harvested crops each month to 160! **The land was healed!!!**

Please go on YouTube and watch the video. Adam's self-esteem was so powerful that it impacted the very earth once it was lost!

There are many books on Iniquity, however there are two that I've experienced that have had a great positive impact on myself; and I recommend to you, they are *Breaking Generational Curses,* by Marilyn Hickey and *Purging Your House Pruning Your Family Tree,* by Perry Stone.

3

A RENEWED MIND

In order to have a healthy, positive self-esteem we must have the right thinking. If you don't have a positive self-esteem, you simply must change the way you think. The wrong thoughts created by definition from people, experiences, environment, etc. have to be replaced with the thoughts God, our Creator, has for us.

Our thinking is the blueprint of our expression in our lives. If you think you are successful, you will be successful. If you think you are a failure, you are a failure. The blueprint of the Empire State Building does not resemble the blueprint for a country shanty. We could go on and on, but I believe you get the point.

Scripture records in **Proverbs 23:7a,** "For as he thinketh in his heart so is he." With this in mind, we can say that we are exactly what we think. Therefore, the outward environment of a person with a positive self-esteem (positive thinking) will change a positive outward environment to even a better one. They will also change a negative outward environment to a positive one. Likewise, the opposite will manifest through a person with a negative self-esteem (negative thinking). They change the negative to more negative or maintain it, while corrupting the positive to a downward trend or negative results. In short, the inward thinking and especially a progressive, God-right relationship alignment directly affects our self-esteem. The way a person thinks in their heart mirrors the same images in their environment and will manifest what they are thinking around them whether positive or negative. The way we think has a great impact on our lives.

The first two chapters of the Bible can help us with this. Firstly, it tells us we were created by God Himself. Secondly, it says we are created in His image and His likeness **(Genesis 1:26-27)**. Nothing else in the entire universe can make this claim. God chose us to be like Him!

In 1995 I became the acting postmaster for the City of Detroit. When I arrived, I found the mindset of a majority of the managers to be less than positive. This resulted in subpar performance in the various activities the unit was judged on, as compared to other like units in the country. At that time there were 85 districts in the country and the Detroit District with the Detroit Post Office rated as number 83, two from the bottom. By influencing the management staff and developing a can-do attitude within them through God's directing, within one year's time they advanced to the number one position in the country! Therefore, we stress in the interactive study course that we teach, *How to Go Through Tribulation Victoriously*, the absolute need to effectively meditate the word and thoughts of God. What better inward thoughts can there be but to hear the corrective up-building progressive life thoughts of the Almighty!? See, the managers began to think of themselves as being significant. They realized that they mattered and had purpose. In his book, *The Pursuit of Purpose*, Dr. Myles Munroe states:

"A lack of purpose and the impending tragedy that results from its absence is found not only in people but in all things. When elements of nature lose their purpose, chaos and destruction are the results.

20

When nations, societies, communities, organizations, friendships, marriages, clubs, churches, countries, or tribes lose their sense of purpose and significance, then confusion frustration, discouragement, disillusionment, and corporate suicide – whether gradual or instant – reign. Purpose is the master of motivation and the mother of commitment. It is the source of enthusiasm and the womb of perseverance. Purpose gives birth to hope and instills passion to act. It is the common denominator that gives every creature an element of distinction."[1]

One of the purposes of this book is for you to desire to hear God; and as you hear and obey, allow Him to change your self-esteem to Christ-esteem.

"But we all, with open face beholding as in a glass the glory of the Lord, are changed into the same image from glory to glory, even as by the Spirit of the Lord."   ~ 2 Corinthians 3:18

"For whom he did foreknow, he also did predestinate to be conformed to the image of his Son, that he might be the firstborn among many brethren."   ~ Romans 8:29

Factors That Influence Self-Esteem

1. Personal thoughts
2. Experiences (childhood, work, social)
3. Environment
4. Health issues
5. Culture
6. Denominations (doctrine)
7. Titles and roles
8. Other people's thoughts/opinions

These are just some of the factors that can influence self-esteem. However, our own thoughts about ourselves have the greatest influence on our esteem. Your thinking is very important to your overall self-esteem. The thoughts that manifest when you view situations and circumstances are an indication of your self-esteem. When you have healthy self-esteem, you feel good about yourself and see yourself deserving the respect of others. However, when you have negative or low self-esteem, you put little value on your opinions and ideas. We maintain low self-esteem with too much criticism and not enough positive, spiritual feedback.[3]

Healthy Self-Esteem Attributes

1. Assertiveness – having the ability to take a stand in situations that do not line up with your values

2. Confidence – the ability to make good decisions

3. Secure – the ability to make your own decisions and not feel guilty when not agreeing with everything someone else says

4. Realistic – knowing that no one can love us like God; no one else can make us happy, but ourselves

5. Flexible – the ability to handle taking a hit – everything is not always going to be perfect

6. Healthy feelings – do not have a "victim's" mentality

7. Mentally healthy

A Revelation of God's Love

One thing that is important to remember is the revelation of God's love frees us from needing to live *out of order*, to please others.

"May Christ through your faith [actually] dwell (settle down, abide, make His permanent home) in your hearts! May you be rooted deep in love and founded securely on love, That you may have the power and be strong to apprehend and grasp with all the saints [God's devoted people, the experience of that love] hat is the breadth and length and height and depth [of it]; [That you may really come] to know [practically, through experience for yourselves] the love of Christ, which far surpasses mere knowledge [without experience]; that you may be filled [through all your being] unto all the fullness of God [may have the richest measure of the divine Presence, and]become a body wholly filled and flooded with God Himself]!"

~ Ephesians 3:17-19 AMPC

Steps to Combating Negative Thoughts

1. **Convert negatives into Godly thoughts**
   - Find scriptures in God's word that talks about how God thinks about you
   - Meditate these scriptures by memorizing them, posting them around your house, office, car, etc., and repeating them until they become your truth.
   - Visualize in your mind what God's word says about you. Get a picture!

2. **Treat yourself with kindness and encouragement**
   - Love yourself. God makes it clear we are to love ourselves.

3. **Forgive yourself**
   - If God forgives you, shouldn't you forgive yourself? 1 John 1:9 says

4. **Don't put unrealistic demands on yourself**
   - Whenever you try to do anything without Jesus and His direction it puts an unrealistic expectation on you.
   - Don't try to live up to others' expectations of what they think you should do or be.

5. **Reflect on the abilities and talents that God has given you and be thankful**

6. **Reflect on something you have done well (not necessarily perfectly!)**

<u>WE THINK IN IMAGES</u>

While I was employed in the post office, I was used to do motivational speaking, whereby I was sent throughout the country to speak to various groups of people to assist them in changing their thinking to success. What I would do at times is bring someone up from the audience and ask them this question. "I am going to ask you to do something that is very easy and will take you one or two seconds to do. Will you agree to do it when I ask?" Of course, the person would say "Yes, I will." I then would say the following in my mind without speaking it aloud, "Will you pick up the cup or the piece of paper," that would be right in front of them, only remember, I said this to myself, they could not hear me. I would wait a second or two and of course they would not do what I had said inside myself because they could not hear me.

I would then repeat this, three times, while each time I would say, "Okay you said you would do it, but you didn't." They would become very confused. Of course, I wouldn't give them time to ask questions. I would say to them very quickly, "Okay I'm going to ask you again... that was strike one, then strike two and finally, strike three."

I would ask the audience how many strikes do you get before you strike out at bat? Of course, all laughing, would say three. I would then say, "Okay you just struck out; however, I'm going to give you another chance, but I want you to pay attention closely to what I say." Often the person would say, "But you didn't say anything!" I would say "Pay attention this last time." The 4th time, I would speak aloud. "Would you please hand me the cup or the piece of paper that's in front of you?" They very quickly would pick up the item and hand it to me. At this point I say, "Why thank you. Why didn't you do that the first three times?" Of course, they would say, you didn't say it out loud so I could hear you.... I would then say, correct! I would then state, let's go further into this that just happened.

"What happened in your mind when you heard me say pick up the cup or pen or piece of paper?" I would then direct them to what happened in their mind when they heard me say, "Would you hand me the cup or the paper or the pen?" They immediately had an image of the item in their minds.

<u>**Once you have the image in your mind you can then do it!**</u> Everything that we do in life comes from an image. Whether we put on our coat or sweater or put on a watch or shoes, we must first have an image of that thing in our minds. Everything that we do in our lives comes from the images that are in our minds. Except for breathing or our heart beating and things such as are automatic. We don't have to think... *I'm going to breathe now* and we don't have to think, *I'm going to let my heartbeat so that my blood pumps through my body.* We do those things automatically. However, everything else that we do, we must first have an image in our thoughts... a picture of the thing and that's how we're able to do it. Without the image, we can't do it. On the other hand, when we receive an image from a successful attempt or a pleasant personal experience, it builds the image within us of, *I can.* Now there are images within our minds of hurts from our past or things that we did not have success with repeatedly and those images in our mind cause us to have success or failure. Look at these two scriptural passages.

> "I beseech you therefore, brethren, by the mercies of God, that ye present your bodies a living sacrifice, holy, acceptable unto God, which is your reasonable service. And be not conformed to this world: but be ye transformed by the renewing of your mind, that ye may prove what is that good, and acceptable, and perfect, will of God."   ~ Romans 12:1-2

This scripture is referring to our yielding our lives to the Lord, learning of and obeying Him so that we discern His ascending thoughts that in turn, *transform (to change in form, appearance, or structure; metamorphose, to change in condition, nature, or character; convert, to change into another substance; transmute) our thinking! The Lord has been speaking, speaking, speaking for our minds to be *transformed*. It is a literal expectation and predestined provision that is to be, to bring forth His 30, 60 and 100-fold Kingdom results.

> "(as it is written, "I have made you a father of many nations") in the presence of Him whom he believed—God, who gives life to the dead and calls those things which do not exist as though they did; who, contrary to hope, in hope believed, so that he became the father of many nations, according to what was spoken, "So shall your descendants be." And not being weak in faith, he did not consider his own body, already dead (since he was about a hundred years old), and the deadness of Sarah's womb. He did not waver at the promise of God through unbelief, but was strengthened in faith, giving glory to God."
>
> ~ Romans 4:17-20 NKJV

This scripture is speaking to Abraham receiving faith from his "hearing God say," believing that which was heard and receiving an inner image of it whereby he could then do what he had an image of. It is called faith… hearing, then believing and doing what can't be seen with the natural eyes. Let me repeat this for clarity. Righteousness is hearing God and believing what was heard. Faith is hearing what God has spoken, believing and acting on that which was heard and believed without seeing or having sensory evidence of it.

"So then faith cometh by hearing, and hearing by the word of God" **(Romans 10:17)**. This scripture refers to how one gets faith. They must hear… it comes… from God's mouth… and believe. They hear and get a picture, an image, then they act on it… again, it's called faith!

Motivational Speaking Skit: Please Hand Me the Pen

Hearing gives an image.

Images' Impact on Belief

Here is a true story of an experiment with a pike, minnows, a glass wall and an aquarium. The pike is in a large aquarium and the minnows are released into the aquarium. The minnows are one of the favorite foods of the pike, and the pike would quickly swim to the minnows and eat them.

After some time, a glass wall was placed in the aquarium to separate the pike and the minnows. After this, the pike would swim rapidly as usual, over towards the minnows to eat them. As the pike did this, it would ram into the glass wall hurting itself, not reaching the minnows. This was done repeatedly and each time the minnows would be released into the aquarium, the pike would swim quickly towards them and run into the glass wall, causing pain.

After a period, every time the minnows would be released into the aquarium, it became the equivalent of pain and failure for the pike. Eventually, it came to the point where it would not even swim over towards the minnows at all. Well, after a while because of repeated failure and pain, the mind told the body of the pike that the minnows that used to mean food now meant pain and failure. Therefore, the pike would not only not swim towards the minnows when they would be released into the aquarium but would not even look in their direction. The repeated pain and failure gave the image that the pike could not eat the minnows... it screamed, *I can't eat the minnows!*

The glass wall was eventually removed but the pike would not attempt to eat the minnows when they would be released into the aquarium. The minnows would swim over right past the pike and he would never even open his mouth to eat them. Why? The minnows no longer meant a food source to the pike, but pain and failure. The pike ended up dying of starvation although he was surrounded by food.

The Pike, Fish, Glass Wall and the Aquarium

Where did this come from? Repeated failure and pain. This is the same thing that happens in our minds when we attempt something, or our parents or grandparents attempted something, and it did not work... it meant pain and failure. This is what causes the esteem to be changed negatively... when something has been attempted without success repeatedly. This plays havoc on the self-esteem and will transfer failure images to the next generations (See index for iniquity's definition).

Once Adam sinned and was cut-off from the thoughts, power, peace, and right relationship with God which gave favor, it worked towards degrading mankind's self-esteem from God's-esteem.

Jesus, through His sacrifice, death burial and resurrection, procured the success of "I can do all things through Christ which strengtheneth me," **(Philippians 4:13)** for all believers. However, only those who press into learning, believing and obeying what He is saying to them now will receive this inheritance. Take note of the following scriptures:

> "For **God so loved the world, that he gave his only begotten Son,** that whosoever believeth in him should not perish, **but have everlasting life.**"   ~ John 3:16, emphasis added

This scripture refers to God's great love towards us to the point that He sacrificed His only Son so that as we believe, we get the transference of everlasting life. Everlasting life does not only mean to live forever... people in hell live forever... but it means to have the things of the Kingdom of God now and forever. Things such as love of self just as God loves you, health, total provision and great relationships with the peace and power of God.

> "But as it is written, Eye hath not seen, nor ear heard, neither have entered into the heart of man, the things which God hath prepared for them that love him. But God hath revealed them unto us by his Spirit: for the Spirit searcheth all things, yea, the deep things of God.   ~ 1 Corinthians 2:9-10

This scripture means that God has already prepared tremendous, unimaginable Kingdom of God things for us now, right now, because of our love and obedience to God. However, these things are secret and not revealed to non-believers, surface Christians, (those that have accepted Jesus as their Savior, but don't obey His word) but instead are revealed to those Christians who obey and follow Him... are known as disciples.

> "Wherefore I also, after I heard of your faith in the Lord Jesus, and love unto all the saints, Cease not to give thanks for you, making mention of you in my prayers; That the God of our Lord Jesus Christ, the Father of glory, may give unto you the spirit of wisdom and revelation in the knowledge of him: The eyes of your understanding being enlightened; that ye may know what is the

hope of his calling, and what the riches of the glory of his inheritance in the saints, And what is the exceeding greatness of his power to us-ward who believe, according to the working of his mighty power."   ~ Ephesians 1:15-19

Breaking Down Your Walls

Now, let's go deeper regarding the pike, minnows, aquarium and the glass wall. The glass wall, which was invisible to the pike, represents the blockages in our thinking, preventing our receiving the provisions that are in the Kingdom of God. Scripture states that the kingdom of God comes without observation, but invisible images in our mind can be the wall that blocks our attaining them (Luke 17:20-21). On the other hand, Satan's kingdom is also invisible, we don't see it either and there can be strongholds in our minds that make-up walls to block attaining the provisions in God's Kingdom. The pike could not see the glass wall that it was hitting. But let's understand thoroughly that we represent the pike, and Satan's kingdom is the invisible wall blocking us from the provisions of God. If we react according to our intellectual and emotional senses towards health, financial provision, and relationship issues while Satan moves against us in the 9 issues of life, we're hitting the wall! What this means is this: if our only source of healing is from the medical doctors, our financial dependence being tied to the economy, the union or management association and our relational wellbeing is based on pleasing Mr. Ms. or Mrs. Doe…you're going to continue to hit that invisible wall and the pain and failure will increase!

The wall for mankind is sin, iniquity, and Satan's strategies. Here are the things that compose the wall; ignorance and disobedience to God's word, witchcraft, the occult, sexual sin, idolatry, fear, unforgiveness, pride, being a non-tither, negative emotions, past sins, *cares of the world, *deceitfulness of riches, (love of money) *and the lusts of other things (*See

Mark 4:19). Jesus already removed the walls… Hallelujah! Jesus removed the invisible wall that has been preventing us from coming into what is ours in the spirit, when He took our sins, washed them away by His blood, died and then rose from the dead. If the pike had the Spirit of God to show him the way to his provisions was through grace, righteousness, prayer, praise and worship while making faith declarations… it could have overcome that which he could not see. So, what's our problem?

Here it is:

> "For our light affliction, which is but for a moment, worketh for us a far more exceeding and eternal weight of glory; While we look not at the things which are seen, but at the things which are not seen: for the things which are seen are temporal; but the things which are not seen are eternal." ~ 2 Corinthians 4:17-18

Also:

> "Wherefore seeing we also are compassed about with so great a cloud of witnesses, let us lay aside every weight, and the sin which doth so easily beset us, and let us run with patience the race that is set before us, Looking unto Jesus the author and finisher of our faith; who for the joy that was set before him endured the cross, despising the shame, and is set down at the right hand of the throne of God. For consider him that endured such contradiction of sinners against himself, lest ye be wearied and faint in your minds." ~ Hebrews 12:1-3

So, the real issue is what's harbored in the core of our thinking; our minds must be changed.

> "I beseech you therefore, brethren, by the mercies of God, that ye present your bodies a living sacrifice, holy, acceptable unto God, which is your reasonable service. And be not conformed to this world: but be ye transformed by the renewing of your mind, that ye

may prove what is that good, and acceptable, and perfect, will of God."   ~ Romans 12:1-2

The pike could not renew his mind, but you can.

In each one of the issues of life, as you prepare yourself to meditate God's word until you hear the Spirit of God from His word on that issue and believe what you've heard from God, then begin to speak to the issue. At that point you'll remove that wall by the power of God that is in you.

"Wherefore I put thee in remembrance that thou stir up the gift of God, which is in thee by the putting on of my hands. For God hath not given us the spirit of fear; but of power, and of love, and of a sound mind."   ~ 2 Timothy 1:6-7

Hallelujah! So, although, in the natural, you can't get over to the other side of the invisible wall, you, by the Spirit of God, have in your renewed mind and mouth the tools and power to break it.

So, let's say that hypothetically you have an illness that you've been seeing the doctor for years on, or a relationship issue that is painful along with being a failure, or financial issues that will soon be in bankruptcy court; you've hit the wall unsuccessfully for so long and have gotten nowhere except for bruised emotions and depressed feelings; here is your way through that wall. I know, I've been there. Please go to the website, **www.guardyourheart.life,** go to the "Tools" tab and the Meditation Download Tool entitled "9 Issues of Life With 9 Scriptures" located in the list on the right-hand side. Ask the Lord to lead you to 1-3 scriptures regarding your specific issue and **meditate** them day and night until God speaks a *saying* to you. Continue with what God has spoken to you. He will speak further *sayings* while giving you direction and understanding with His empowerment in your issue. As you do this faithfully while getting rid of distractions and repenting from any sin that you may be led to come away from. Watch the results you'll obtain. There is a video on the website giving more explanations, training, and illustrations.

Love's Impact on the Change from Self-Esteem to Christ-Esteem

"Beloved, let us love one another: for love is of God; and every one that loveth is born of God, and knoweth God. He that loveth not knoweth not God; for God is love." ~ 1 John 4:7-8

When Adam was made in the image of God, love was a major component of man because God is love. Therefore, a major purpose of God is to express this love through that which He creates or makes. Whatever comes forth from God will manifest love in its functioning also. When I was a letter carrier, I delivered to an office of the Social Security department and in the mid 70's there were no computers and there must have been about 40-50 individual cubicles with agents working at each of them. As I would pass their desks daily in route to pick-up the outgoing mail, I would give a cheerful greeting to each at their desk. One day one of the agents snarled at me stating, "What makes you so happy?!" I turned and told her, "Jesus!" She quickly snapped, "I don't want to hear about no church!" I answered back, "I'm not going to tell you about any church but the person of Jesus." As I shared with her about the wonderful relationship that I experienced daily, she not only listened intently, but when asked if she'd like to get to know Him, she said yes and received His love that day. The next day as I made my delivery to that office, she received the baptism in the Holy Ghost. Why was I so happy as I delivered the mail? I had a special delivery package for everyone... the love of Jesus that was being shared from my heart **(Romans 5:5)**.

Jesus said that as we love back on Him through our doing what He says, we become His friend and He reveals the secrets of His Father to us because of the right relationship we have with Him.

> "Ye are my friends, if ye do whatsoever I command you. Henceforth I call you not servants; for the servant knoweth not what his lord doeth: but I have called you friends; for all things that I have heard of my Father I have made known unto you."   ~ John 15:14-15

In order for this to happen we must yield ourselves and learn of and obey God. As we obey, what He reveals to us changes our natures from those of the people in society who don't know of God, or have received Jesus as their Savior, but have not moved to the next stage of having Him become their Lord **(Romans 12:1-2)**. What this means is this... if someone disrespects you, or lies on you, or even treats you in an evil manner, your natural or normal *worldly* reaction to their treatment of you would be to give them the same treatment or worse that had been given to you. Let's see what Jesus says about that...

> "But I say unto you, Love your enemies, bless them that curse you, do good to them that hate you, and pray for them which despitefully use you, and persecute you."   ~ Matthew 5:44

Also, the Lord admonishes us:

> "If it be possible, as much as lieth in you, live peaceably with all men. Dearly beloved, avenge not yourselves, but rather give place unto wrath: for it is written, Vengeance is mine; I will repay, saith the Lord. Therefore if thine enemy hunger, feed him; if he thirst, give him drink: for in so doing thou shalt heap coals of fire on his head. Be not overcome of evil, but overcome evil with good."
>   ~ Romans 12:18-21

In this day of darkness of behavior, evil, disrespect, jealousy, envy and hatred, God has called His people to do far more than read scripture and show up in a building called *church*, on Sundays between 11am-12:30pm; but instead become an example of the same behavior that Jesus displayed as He walked in the earth. This in turn, the learning of God, hearing Him and doing His will at home, in the neighborhood, at school and at work will cause people to follow you to church on Sunday and other days.

This is a process of victory after the character of Christ has manifested in us moving past offense in love and releasing the character of Christ through us. Now as that happens then as stated in **John 15:14-15**, we become the friends of God, through love and obedience and Jesus shares the revelation secrets of God to us because He can now trust us with His authority and power! This causes the transference of our **self-esteem** to **Christ-esteem** as we continually walk in the **knowledge, understanding** and **wisdom** that comes from the "revelation secrets" of God in the issue now and all issues of life.

As you really hear from God, believe what He has said, obey it and meditate it until it becomes your predominant thoughts… it will be what comes forth out of your mouth.

> "A good man out of the good treasure of his heart bringeth forth that which is good; and an evil man out of the evil treasure of his heart bringeth forth that which is evil: for of the abundance of the heart his mouth speaketh."   ~ Luke 6:45

You will become what you believe and speak!

SPIRITUAL INVENTORY

Give at least 3 scriptures the Lord has given you from which you have received revelation secrets. . . "God's sayings." List your revelation also.

_____

_____

_____

_____

_____

_____

_____

_____

_____

_____

_____

_____

_____

_____

SECTION II

RELATIONSHIPS

God's plan is for you to have very good relationships.

TRANSFORMING CHARACTERISTIC
~ FAITH ~

Having a pressed focus, meditation, getting the water
of the Word spoken from the mouth of God and then
acting on it. Just do it!

KINGDOM BENCHMARK
~ UNDERSTANDING ~

Knowing how to utilize the "knowledge" of God in
the appropriate circumstances

4

RELATIONSHIP
WITH GOD

A good alliance with God gives good associations with mankind. Proverbs 16:7 says, "When a man's ways please the LORD, he makes even his enemies to be at peace with him."

Here's a magnificent revelation! No one, starting with you, is perfect!!! With this being an undisputed statement of fact... or should we say TRUTH in life, you will have associations that will be unpleasant. When that occurs, and it will daily, weekly, monthly and throughout the year, there are behaviors that need to be displayed from you that will cause things to go better, even pleasant.

The relationship that we have with God greatly influences for the good, our relationship with others. God is omnipotent (having all power), omniscient (knows all things), and omnipresent (being everywhere at the same time). God has a personality that is not flawed like ours, but He has a personality. He expects reverence, respect, consideration, and obedience. As we give Him the reverence, respect, obedience, and consideration, He gives us His favor and blessings in our lives. We must go by His blueprint for He is the master architect of success, power, and peace.

39

"The earth is the LORD's, and all its fullness, The world and those who dwell therein."   ~ Psalm 24:1

In 2016 my wife and I selected a home to be built. We chose the model type, the plot of land along with the doors, walls, woodwork, floors, kitchen countertops, carpet color and type, cabinets, bathroom showers, etc. We also approved the blueprint of how things would be constructed and as the home was being built, we came in and checked it out at various stages; a couple times during the building process, we found things that were not according to our instructions nor the blueprint and had it changed to match the instructions and the blueprint. In a few cases we changed what was in the blueprint according to our desire. God also has a blueprint of what He wants in our lives, **it's the knowledge of Him**. It shows His expectations and direction which, when followed, give a right and good relationship with Him and causes us to be blessed and not cursed as we **obey** and **continue to follow** that blueprint. Let's look at a few scriptures that will assist in supporting this:

"This book of the law shall not depart out of thy mouth; **but thou shalt meditate therein day and night, that thou mayest observe to do according to all that is written therein:** for then thou shalt make thy way prosperous, and then thou shalt have good success."
~ Joshua 1:8, emphasis added

"For I know the thoughts that I think toward you, saith the LORD, thoughts of peace, and not of evil, to give you an expected end."
~ Jeremiah 29:11

"Blessed is the man that walketh not in the counsel of the ungodly, nor standeth in the way of sinners, nor sitteth in the seat of the scornful. But his delight is in the law of the LORD; and in his law doth he meditate day and night. And he shall be like a tree planted by the rivers of water, that bringeth forth his fruit in his season; his leaf also shall not wither; and whatsoever he doeth shall prosper."   ~ Psalm 1:1-3, emphasis added

"But you have not so learned Christ, if indeed you have heard Him and have been taught by Him, as the truth is in Jesus: **that you put off, concerning your former conduct, the old man which grows corrupt according to the deceitful lusts, and be renewed in the spirit of your mind, and that you put on the new man which was created according to God, in true righteousness and holiness.**"

~ Ephesians 4:20-24, emphasis added

"**Therefore, leaving the discussion of the elementary principles of Christ, let us go on to perfection, not laying again the foundation of repentance from dead works and of faith toward God, of the doctrine of baptisms, of laying on of hands, of resurrection of the dead, and of eternal judgment.** And this we will do if God permits. For it is impossible for those who were once enlightened, and have tasted the heavenly gift, and have become partakers of the Holy Spirit, and have tasted the good word of God and the powers of the age to come, if they fall away, to renew them again to repentance, since they crucify again for themselves the Son of God, and put Him to an open shame."

~ Hebrews 6:1-6, emphasis added

God created human life so that He can have a personal relationship with us. This makes our relationship with God the most important relationship we have. God Himself chose us to be His creation. Therefore, our lives are to be centered around our relationship with Him since He created us for Himself. Jesus Himself tells us in **Matthew 6:33**, "But seek ye first the kingdom of God, and his righteousness; and all these things shall be added unto you."

"And you shall love the Lord your God with all your [mind and] heart, and with your entire being, and with all your might."

~ Deuteronomy 6:5, AMP

While many people believe that God is real, many also believe that He is only *watching them from a distance* and has no real desire to know them personally… but the opposite is true; God is actually very interested in you and desires for you to have a personal relationship with Him; so much so that God thinks about you all the time. Imagine that – God thinking about you.

> "How precious are your thoughts about me, O God! They are innumerable! I can't even count them; they outnumber the grains of sand!"   ~ Psalm 139:1–18b NIV

Not only does He think about you, He has made lasting plans for your relationship. Just think of relationship in terms of having a long life together.

> "For I know the plans I have for you', says the LORD. They are plans for good and not for disaster, to give you a future and a hope."
>   ~ Jeremiah 29:11 NIV

God is first to know that words can be cheap in any relationship if not backed with action, so He goes on to prove it…

> "God showed how much he loved us by sending his one and only Son into the world so that we might have eternal life (relationship) through him."   ~ 1 John 4:9 NLT, brackets added

In the beginning, Adam and Eve lived in a perfect relationship with God and as the Bible put it, God viewed it as "very good". However, Adam and Eve disobeyed God. Because of their disobedience, sin entered into the world (into the perfect relationship, if you will) and because of sin, humankind was separated from God. You see, God is pure and holy and can only be joined in a perfect union and cannot be jointed together with sin. It makes no difference how much or how little you've sinned; you still fall short of God's perfection. "For all have sinned; all fall short of God's glorious standard" **(Romans 3:23 NIV).**

Now this puts us in a bind because God tells us in His word that the punishment for sin is death. Not just physical death, but a spiritual death which will cause separation from relationship with God and His Kingdom for eternity; that is what sin does; it is the great divider. It caused a breach in the relationship.

The Good News is that God wants us to spend eternity in heaven with Him. About 2,000 years ago God sent His Son, Jesus Christ, to come to this earth and die on the cross to pay the penalty for our sin. Christ is the "repairer of the breach, the restorer of path to dwell in" **(Isaiah 58:12).**

> "For God so loved the world that He gave His one and only Son, that whoever believes in Him should not perish but have everlasting life."   ~ John 3:16 NIV

Remember, God is thinking about you. Do you remember how he has been making plans for your future? In other words, even though you are separated from God because of your sin, God's plan made a way for you to come back to Him by offering salvation to you as a free gift. All you have to do is believe it to receive it. Remember, although the gift is free, at no cost to you; it cost God His only begotten son, Jesus. And it cost Jesus His blood and His life. That's how much God loves you. "But God commends his love toward us, in that, while we were yet sinners, Christ died for us" **(Romans 5:8).**

Now that you believe in Jesus Christ, you can say with confidence that your relationship has been restored and you are completely accepted by God. You can now begin to live a life that truly pleases Him. He did all of this for us because He loves us, He loves us, He loves you!

Essentials to Our Relationship with God

God wants us to know Him more intimately. He makes it clear, but the real question is what do you want? Do you want a closer walk with God? Do you want to walk and talk with Him "in the cool of the evening" like Adam once did? How bad do you want it? Listen, you are as close to God as you want to be. In other words, we, not God, determine our level of intimacy with Him.

Here are ways to make your relationship with God stronger. By putting these tools into action, you will not only please God, but also build up your faith in God at the same time:

➢ **Read the Bible.** The Bible is God's word. It is His mind – thoughts, desires, His will. By reading, searching and meditating on the word, we can get to know God. In this age of information, it is easy to be confused by the amount of data that bombards us every day. However, the Bible is unique in that it is God's message to mankind; a message that never changes.

➢ **Be transformed into holiness.** God is a Holy God; therefore, He is holy, pure, righteous, clean and without sin. God's expectation for us, by His grace through faith He gives us, is to be just as Jesus' walk in this earth as a man, holy.

For us to fulfill this commandment of God, we must apply effort, focus and diligence. God has already given us this "holiness" in His salvation package of grace. He has therefore given us the ability to become holy as we diligently pursue Him and have our minds transformed into His thoughts (see **Romans 12:1-2 and John 1:12-13**). In his book "The Pursuit of Holiness", author Jerry Bridges writes, "In the Declaration of Independence, Thomas Jefferson declared that one of the inherent and unalienable rights of men is 'the pursuit of happiness'. Professional Christians must be brought to realize that the preeminent desire and

44

demand of God for us is that of the continual pursuit of holiness of life, and the reflection of His own holiness."[1]

"Be ye holy; for I am holy."   ~ 1 Peter 1:16b

Throughout the New Testament we see scriptures that tell us to not be "conformed to the world: but be ye transformed by the renewing" of our minds **(Romans 12:2)**. We also see that we are to put off that which is of the worldly flesh nature, be renewed in the spirit of our minds and put on the new nature **(Ephesians 4:22-24)**. We see in **Romans 6**:

"Knowing this, that our old man is crucified with him, that the body of sin might be destroyed, that henceforth we should not serve sin. For he that is dead is freed from sin."   ~ Romans 6:6-7

As we walk in agreement with holiness, we are changed from glory to glory **(II Corinthians 3:18)** and therefore reflect the total attributes of Jesus in this earth to the glory of God the Father! This gives us His peace, His power and His righteousness whereby we reign in the earth as His ambassadors of the Kingdom of Heaven… "thy will be done on earth as it is in Heaven."

➤ **Talk to God in Prayer.** Prayer is simply talking to God from the heart. Our prayers don't have to sound *religious* and you don't have to use Christian-sounding words. God wants to hear from the real you and He wants to hear your deepest concerns and needs. Prayer is mainly a time for us to thank the Lord and to praise Him for the great things He has done in our lives.

Relationship Developed Through Obedience of What's Been Revealed in Meditation

There are instructions and behavioral traits expected and prepared for us by our Heavenly Father. It takes more than a casual reading of these scriptures to get revelation on them. But as we focus, meditate, get revelation and obey God, He leads us into a transforming process whereby our behaviors become molded into His likeness. Jesus states in **Matthew 16**:

> "He said to them, "But who do you say that I am?" Simon Peter answered and said, "You are the Christ, the Son of the living God." Jesus answered and said to him, "Blessed are you, Simon Bar-Jonah, for flesh and blood has not revealed this to you, but My Father who is in heaven. And I also say to you that you are Peter, and on this rock I will build My church, and the gates of Hades shall not prevail against it."   ~ Matthew 16:15-18 NKJV

As we seek to hear God and then believe what He says and obey what He is showing us, we find ourselves literally "walking with Him," causing us to receive **supernatural** impartations from His blueprint. The chapter on Meditation and the website give further information regarding the meditation of God's word with examples to assist you in *hearing what God is speaking to you* in His word regarding the various issues of life. Take note of the example below:

As we speak on the topic of relationship, I must consider my coming into obedience with the Lord in 1999. I was diagnosed with stroke level blood pressure. At that time the Lord instructed me to do two specific things. (I heard Him speak them to me) First, I was told to forgive and pray for a person who had lied on me and prevented advancement in my career. I obeyed the Lord (finally, after 3-4 months) and forgave and began praying for the person. OK, let me make a confession at this time; I obeyed after I had almost died.

One Sunday as I was serving communion, I had taken the congregation to 1 Corinthians 11:27:

> "Therefore whoever eats this bread or drinks this cup of the Lord in an unworthy manner will be guilty of the body and blood of the

Lord. But let a man examine himself, and so let him eat of the bread and drink of the cup. For he who eats and drinks in an unworthy manner eats and drinks judgment to himself, not discerning the Lord's body. For this reason many are weak and sick among you, and many sleep."   ~ 1 Corinthians 11:27-30

I really preached "up a sweat" in exhorting the congregation to obey the Lord in this matter. While doing so the Lord told me that I should heed the instructions I was giving them... I didn't. The next morning at work, my secretary advised me that I should go and see the doctor, because I really looked bad. This is when I received the stroke level diagnosis. On the way to my own doctor's office, the Lord reminded me of what He had told me the day before, and that's when I repented and prayed for the person who had done wrong to me.

Next, the Lord told me to meditate **Isaiah 53**, beginning in verse 4:

"Surely He has borne our griefs and carried our sorrows; yet we esteemed Him stricken, smitten by God, and afflicted. But He was wounded for our transgressions, He was bruised for our iniquities; the chastisement for our peace was upon Him, and by His stripes we are healed."   ~ Isaiah 53:4-5 NKJV

As I committed this to memory, began praying over each word for understanding and application in my life, repeating the verses over and over aloud with focus and concentration while praying in the spirit regarding the scripture; the Lord spoke the following to me regarding the blood pressure: *you are not on the defensive!* Now, please note that these words are not found in the two verses of **Isaiah 53:4-5** meditated.

Effective meditation causes one to hear and understand God's thoughts on a matter as God x-rays the limitations of our thoughts, corrects them and aligns them to His. In short, the Lord showed me with what He had spoken to me regarding the stroke-level blood pressure that I was on the offensive, not the defensive. I really didn't understand how I was on the *offense* regarding the stroke-level blood pressure. The Lord then took me to **Matthew 16:18** where Jesus had just asked His disciples who men were saying regarding who He, Jesus, was. His disciples responded with, *they're saying that you are Jeremiah, Elijah, John the Baptist or one of the prophets.* Jesus then asked His disciples, who do you say that I am? Peter responded with, "you are the Christ, the Son of the Living God" (Matt. 16:16b). At this point Jesus told Peter that flesh and blood (mankind) had not revealed this unto him, but His Father which is in heaven. Jesus told Peter, **"And I say also unto you, that you are Peter, and upon this rock I will build my church; and the gates of hell shall not prevail against it"** (Matthew 16:18, emphasis added). As the Lord spoke this, He was referring to the fact that those things revealed to man are the things that He was building His church upon.

> "The secret things belong to the LORD our God, but those things which are revealed belong to us and to our children forever, that we may do all the words of this law." ~ Deuteronomy 29:29

Next the Lord changed my thinking on the line that followed... **"and the gates of hell shall not prevail against it"** (Matthew 16:18b, emphasis added). The Lord told me that myself and a great number in the church has interpreted that line to mean that the church was struggling in its attempt to hold the gates shut to keep Satan from forcing his way in. **This is totally in error the Lord showed me!** The gates of hell represented all things that were not in and from heaven such as sickness, lack, fear, poor relationships, confusion, no direction, etc. He went on further to show me that Satan was the gate, not the church! Let me repeat that... Satan is the gate, not the church! What that means is Satan, who is the author of sickness, lack, confusion, fear, hatred, etc. is the one that is the gate and **we the church are the ones who are the battering ram knocking the gates of hell down!**

Now let me turn your attention to how all of this came about; when I finally obeyed the Lord, I was led into a path that brought about the healing. Had I not obeyed and come into a *right relationship* with the Lord, I very well might not be here today typing about this. I could have remained disobedient and died or had a stroke with the results being a tremendously limited lifestyle. I also would have not come into the benefits of a *right relationship* with the Lord whereby He gives the secret revelations that come with it.

How do we knock the gates of hell down? We accomplish this in the same manner that all the prophets of the Old Testament did and as Jesus did in the four books of the gospel (Matthew, Mark, Luke and John). How did they move in the **supernatural** causing great miracles (the plagues falling on Egypt, the Red Sea opening for the Israelites escape on dry land, Daniel interpreting Nebuchadnezzar's dream and staying untouched by the lions overnight, Elijah calling down fire from heaven to consume the offering unto God, Jesus healing the sick, casting out devils from the possessed, giving sight to the blind, turning sinners to God, walking on water, raising the dead, giving His life for the world, shedding His blood and removing the sins of the world, dying and being raised from the dead to give eternal life to all who believe on Him.) They did it through being in *right relationship* with God, learning of Him, seeking, hearing, believing with diligence and obeying that which they received from God. This is faith.

At this point the Lord showed me that I was on the offensive because what He would speak to me would place me in charge over Satan concerning the stroke level blood pressure. He then told me to begin speaking to my body that my blood pressure was better than normal blood pressure which is 120/80. He told me to begin speaking that my pressure was 116/76. A subsequent doctor's visit within two-three weeks from this event showed my pressure was better than the normal of 120/80 but was then 116/66! (I had to bring the 66 up a little) All of these things came from having a right relationship with God! It means to know Him and His ways… this is what God wants… for us to really know the ONE that has made us and loves us.

RELATIONSHIP ONE

I was sent to Chicago in 2001 to assist the Chicago postmaster in bringing his operation into success. I was given an office that had no windows along with an entrance and exiting door. One afternoon two different attractive women came into my office separately, while I was alone and tried tempting me sexually. They both came into my office over a 3-hour period. The first one came in with a truly short skirt and set in front of my desk in a very inappropriate, non-modest manner, fully exposing herself suggestively to myself as she crossed her legs. She remained in that manner, smiling while conversing, making it very apparent that she was available sexually. At that point I took my wallet out of my back pocket where I have a picture of my wife. I opened it and showed her my centerfold, advising her, this is the only person I sleep with and you can exit either door now! Her feelings were greatly damaged, and she left my office in a huff!

About an hour later, another young woman came in and she had a very low-cut blouse and before sitting down in front of my desk, she bent down purposely exposing her figure. Again, I took out my wallet and showed her my centerfold, a picture of my wife, advising her that this is the only one I sleep with. She also left in a great huff, with severely damaged emotions. My point in raising these two occasions, is due to my relationship with the Lord, I could not, nor did I desire to engage these young women, because it would be an affront to the one I love the most, Jesus.

I noticed shortly after that incident a number of people, especially the ladies in acting managerial positions, in the Chicago post office that were reluctant at my approaches to get them to move up the ladder in management, became more trusting and available in accepting my invitation for them to move up from their temporary positions. Could it be, that trust, the spirit of trust, began to move through the communication of the Holy Spirit from those two incidents? I believe so.

I also noticed a major turnaround that equaled success in the Chicago post office began developing. The question for you and all of us, is what kind of steadfast relationship with the Lord, will cause a major outreach by the Holy Spirit which is shed abroad from our hearts (Romans 5:5) to those on the fence and to the unbelieving that will draw them over to the side of life and light, in Christ Jesus through our behaviors?

SPIRITUAL INVENTORY

Give at least 3 scriptures the Lord has given you from which you have received revelation secrets. . . "God's sayings." List your revelation also.

_____

_____

_____

_____

_____

_____

_____

_____

_____

51

5

RELATIONSHIPS WITH OTHERS IN THE BODY OF CHRIST

There is a great need within the body of Christ for us to **truly** understand that we are *family*. The scriptures below clearly teach that our faith in the blood of Christ Jesus has given us the privilege to be forgiven for every transgression, offence, and sin we have committed against God and His word.

> "God presented Christ as a sacrifice of atonement, through the shedding of his blood—to be received by faith. He did this to demonstrate his righteousness, because in his forbearance he had left the sins committed beforehand unpunished—"
>
> ~ Romans 3:25 NIV

> "The Spirit you received does not make you slaves, so that you live in fear again; rather, the Spirit you received brought about your adoption to sonship. And by him we cry, "Abba, Father." The Spirit himself testifies with our spirit that we are God's children."
>
> ~ Romans 8:15-16 NIV

> "Of whom the whole family in heaven and earth is named,"
>
> ~ Ephesians 3:15

Not only have we been forgiven; we are now children of God and part of the whole family in heaven and earth. In the natural, children have their biological father's blood type. The same is true in the spirit – we all have the same blood type and that is faith in the blood of Christ Jesus – therefore God is our heavenly Father and we are in the family of God.

HOW WE ARE TO RELATE

The Apostles Paul and Peter wrote some wonderful letters, being inspired by the Holy Spirit, on Christians' relationship with one another. It is not enough to have a relationship with God and Jesus. The heart of God is that we have a godly relationship with our brothers and sisters in Christ. We are family so let us read of these powerful letters written by two great men of God to the Church.

"...And have put on the new man, which is renewed in knowledge after the image of him that created him:"   ~ Colossians 3:10

"Wherefore putting away lying, speak every man truth with his neighbour: for we are members one of another. Be ye angry, and sin not: let not the sun go down upon your wrath: Neither give place to the devil. Let him that stole steal no more: but rather let him labour, working with his hands the thing which is good, that he may have to give to him that needeth. Let no corrupt communication proceed out of your mouth, but that which is good to the use of edifying, that it may minister grace unto the hearers. And grieve not the holy Spirit of God, whereby ye are sealed unto the day of redemption. Let all bitterness, and wrath, and anger, and clamour, and evil speaking, be put away from you, with all malice: And be ye kind one to another, tenderhearted, forgiving one another, even as God for Christ's sake hath forgiven you."   ~ Ephesians 4:25-32

"Finally, be ye all of one mind, having compassion one of another, love as brethren, be pitiful, be courteous: Not rendering evil for evil, or railing for railing: but contrariwise blessing; knowing that ye are thereunto called, that ye should inherit a blessing. For he that will love life, and see good days, let him refrain his tongue from evil, and his lips that they speak no guile: Let him eschew evil, and do good; let him seek peace, and ensue it. For the eyes of the Lord are over the righteous, and his ears are open unto their prayers: but the face of the Lord is against them that do evil. And who is he that will harm you, if ye be followers of that which is good?"

~ 1 Peter 3:8-13

Jesus' Teaching on "Love One Another"

The love Jesus teaches is called *agape*. *Agape* love is the attitude of God toward His Son, humanity, and to believers on the Lord Jesus Christ. It is His will for His children concerning their attitude toward each other, and toward all men. He desires for us to express His essential nature. These attributes (characteristics) of God will manifest by faith and obeying the word of God, and as we remain in constant fellowship by coming into the presence of God through praise and worship. God is love. His love will pour out to us, which we shall pour out to each other. "...the love of God is shed abroad in our hearts by the Holy Ghost" **(Romans 5:5)**. "...praying in the Holy Ghost, Keep yourselves in the love of God" **(Jude 1:20b-21a)**.

"This is my commandment, that ye love one another, as I have loved you. Greater love hath no man than this, that a man lay down his life for his friends. Ye are my friends, if ye do whatsoever I command you. . . These things I command you, that ye love one another."

~ John 15:12

"He that saith he abideth in him ought himself also so to walk, even as he walked. Brethren, I write no new commandment unto you, but an old commandment which ye had from the beginning. The old commandment is the word which ye have heard from the beginning. Again, a new commandment I write unto you, which thing is true in him and in you: because the darkness is past, and the true light now shineth. He that saith he is in the light, and hateth his brother, is in darkness even until now. He that loveth his brother abideth in the light, and there is none occasion of stumbling in him. But he that hateth his brother is in darkness, and walketh in darkness, and knoweth not whither he goeth, because that darkness hath blinded his eyes."   ~ 1 John 2:6-11

The emphasis on love is important because it does define who God is. God is love; therefore, we are children of love. We are the image and likeness of our heavenly Father.

Loving in Action: Being a Doer of the Word

We as Christians are given the rarest of opportunities of any people on the earth. We are commanded to love our enemies, to bless (speak well of and to) those that curse us, do good to those that hate us and pray for them which despitefully use us and persecute us. When Jesus gave us command to do these things, He led the way by example, by doing them first Himself. In the Garden of Gethsemane, He told His disciples that He could cause the persecution to halt by requesting His Father to send twelve legions of angels. On the cross He told His Father to forgive them because they didn't know what they were doing. As we act lovingly in patience toward the unlovely, we are fulfilling His will in the earth and are releasing the power of His kingdom. Loving, patient and kind action toward the unlovely is exactly how God acts toward them.

"But I say unto you, Love your enemies, bless them that curse you, do good to them that hate you, and pray for them which despitefully use you, and persecute you; That ye may be the children of your Father which is in heaven: for he maketh his sun to rise on the evil and on the good, and sendeth rain on the just and the unjust."

~ Matthew 5:44-45

God's love, through His Spirit, is transferred from our hearts to the unlovely as we yield ourselves or crucify our flesh by letting it die on the cross prepared for us by the evil actions of the unlovely as Christ did dying on His cross. Through our love first to God in obedience, the Holy Spirit is transferred from God's Word engrafted into our hearts and unto them.

"And I will sanctify my great name, which was profaned among the heathen, which ye have profaned in the midst of them; and the heathen shall know that I am the LORD, said the Lord GOD, when I shall be sanctified in you before their eyes."   ~ Ezekiel 36:23

"And not only so, but we glory in tribulation also: knowing that tribulation worketh patience... And hope maketh not ashamed; because the love of God is shed abroad in our hearts by the Holy Ghost which is given unto us."   ~ Romans 5:3, 5

"Not rendering evil for evil, or railing for railing: but contrariwise blessing; knowing that ye are thereunto called, that ye should inherit a blessing."   ~ 1 Peter 3:9

"Herein is love, not that we loved God, but that he loved us, and sent his Son to be a propitiation for our sins. Beloved, if God so loved us, we ought also to love one another."   ~ 1 John 4:10-11

6

RELATIONSHIPS WITH THOSE WHO DO WRONG TO YOU

A good alliance with God gives good associations with mankind; Proverbs 16:7, "When a man's ways please the Lord, he maketh even his enemies to be at peace with him." Here's a magnificent revelation - no one, starting with you, is perfect! With this being an undisputed statement of truth in life you will have associations that will be unpleasant. When this occurs, and it will daily, weekly, monthly and throughout the year, there are behaviors that need to be displayed from you that will cause things to go better... even pleasant.

Let's look at a few scriptures that will assist in supporting this claim. The scriptures in the **NOTES** section in the back of the book are to be read and given careful attention. These are the instructions and behavioral traits expected and prepared for us of our Heavenly Father. It takes more than a casual reading of these scriptures, but a meditated, disciplined transforming of our character to Christ's.

Christians are given the rarest of opportunities of any people on the earth. We are commanded to love our enemies, to bless (speak well of) those that curse us, do good to those that hate us and pray for them which despitefully use us and persecute us. When Jesus gave us command to do these things, He led the way by example, by doing them first Himself. In the Garden of Gethsemane, He told His disciples that He could cause the persecution to halt by requesting His Father to send 12 legions of angels. On the cross He told His Father to forgive them because they did not know what they were doing. As we act lovingly in patience toward the unlovely, we are fulfilling His will in the earth and are releasing the power of His kingdom. Loving, patient and kind action toward the unlovely is exactly how God acts toward them.

> "But I tell you, love your enemies and pray for those who persecute you, that you may be children of your Father in heaven. He causes his sun to rise on the evil and the good, and sends rain on the righteous and the unrighteous." ~ Matthew 5:44-45

Years ago, while a letter carrier, another carrier received a portion of my route to carry due to additional volume I had. The carrier brought back the packages for the portion that she delivered. I brought the matter to her attention to no avail. I informed the superintendent of her failure to complete the assignment, again to no avail. I was enraged and showed that behavior to the young lady, to no avail. The resulting relationship between us became hostile. After about a week of these hostilities the Lord told me that although she had not carried out her responsibilities in delivering the packages on that portion of the route, my belligerent actions and negative attitude toward her had not aligned itself with **Matthew 5:44-45**.

God then told me that I was to forgive, begin praying for her, purchase two Christian paper backs (she was a Christian), wrap them nicely in gift paper, and present them to her with an APOLOGY. It took me three days to obey. I walked slowly to her assignment with the gift. Once I apologized, to her amazement and shock, the Lord told me, *Now ask her to forgive you.* Within myself I said, *If I had known you were going to tell me to ask her to forgive me, I wouldn't have come over here* The Lord responded with, *That's why I waited until you said you were sorry.* The results of my obedience caused the young lady to begin to come over to my case and ask questions concerning the scriptures. This eventually led to her and her sisters and families to begin coming to a Bible study that my wife and I conducted bi-weekly on Thursdays after work on my route. We saw several people come to salvation, healing and transformed lives! All of this came from my obeying God, shaming the devil and my flesh nature and praying for someone I did not get along with. God's Word works when we work it!

God's love, through His Spirit, is transferred from our hearts unto the unlovely as we yield ourselves, or crucify our flesh by letting it die on the cross prepared for us by the evil actions of the unlovely as Christ did dying on His cross. Through our love first to God in obedience, the Holy Spirit is transferred from God's word engrafted into our hearts to the unlovely. Note the following scriptures:

"And I will sanctify my great name, which was profaned among the heathen, which ye have profaned in the midst of them; and the heathen shall know that I am the LORD, saith the Lord GOD, when I shall be sanctified in you before their eyes." ~ Ezekiel 36:23

"And not only so, but we glory in tribulations also: knowing that tribulation worketh patience; And patience, experience; and experience, hope: And hope maketh not ashamed; because the love of God is shed abroad in our hearts by the Holy Ghost which is given unto us." ~ Romans 5:3-5

"Not rendering evil for evil, or railing for railing: but contrariwise blessing; knowing that ye are thereunto called, that ye should inherit a blessing." ~ 1 Peter 3:9

"Herein is love, not that we loved God, but that he loved us, and sent his Son to be the propitiation for our sins. Beloved, if God so loved us, we ought also to love one another."   ~ 1 John 4:10-11

Having a right relationship with God causes you to prosper in relationships with others.

"When a man's ways please the LORD, He makes even his enemies to be at peace with him."   ~ Proverbs 16:7

As we review what has been shared regarding having a right relationship with the Lord it includes being in the family of God, having an established knowledge of Jesus, and hearing, believing and obeying the word or thoughts of Him. It is to walk in faith and love. The Lord states clearly in *Galatians 5:6* that faith works by love and in *Hebrews 11:6*, He states that without faith it is impossible to please Him.

In the natural world, common sense pleases one's boss, but in the Spirit world, the Lord is the King of kings and the Lord of lords; He's the Boss of all things. "When a man's ways please the Lord, He makes even his enemies to be at peace with him" **(Proverb 16:7 NKJV)**. A man's ways pleasing the Lord means you have the Lord's thoughts. Having His thoughts gives His behaviors, His character, and being connected to Him once again. Therefore, saying that you have the Lord's ways, thoughts, and character reconnects you to Him yielding the Lord's purposes, plans and ideas into your character and then into the earth. Jesus said in the Lord's prayer for His Father's Kingdom to come and His will to be done on Earth as it is in heaven. Having his ways will produce His kingdom for **"as a man thinks in his heart so is he"** (Proverbs 23:7a, emphasis added). Having His ways means having his thoughts, His nature and therefore His image. **Psalm 1:1-3** states:

"Blessed is the man that walks not in the counsel of the ungodly nor sits in the seat of the scornful nor stands in the way of sinners. But his delight is in the law of the Lord; and in his law doth he meditate day and night. And he shall be like a tree planted by the rivers of water, that bringeth forth his fruit in his season; his leaf also shall not wither; and whatsoever he doeth shall prosper." ~ Psalm 1:1-3

Therefore, a man's ways pleasing the Lord equates to that person being **blessed**. Therefore, a man's ways pleasing the Lord, equates to that person meditating God's word and thoughts and doing them. Why? Because that person is in love with the Lord; and what he sows, he shall reap. As you stay in the same atmosphere with an individual, in this case the individual being the Lord, then you will hear His thoughts, understand and therefore **know His ways**. You will see what the Lord is doing at the particular time frame, and therefore seeing that you hear and see, you know what the Lord is doing at a specific time. You will bring what the Lord says into the present moment. A perfect example of this is the woman caught in the act of adultery being brought to Jesus by the Pharisees and Sadducees with stones in their hand prepared to throw them and kill her **(John 8:1-12)**. They demanded of Jesus according to what Moses had written in the Bible, that anyone caught in adultery is to be stoned to death. Jesus ignored them, stooped down and wrote in the ground with his finger while waiting for what the Lord was speaking and doing in the moment; having received God's direction, He arose and spoke what the Lord was showing and speaking; *"you who are without sin cast the first stone."* Of course, they all dropped their stones and left. The Lord is saying for us to please Him in our moments, hearing and seeing what the Lord is doing in the moment and bring His will into the earth.

Next, the second part of the verse in Proverbs 16:7 states, **"He makes even his enemies to be at peace with him."** When a person believes and continues doing what God speaks, they become God's disciple, knowing

God's truth and then God causes things to work together for that person's good. Scripture states:

> "Then Jesus said to those Jews who believed Him, 'If you abide in My word, you are My disciples indeed. And you shall know the truth, and the truth shall make you free.'" ~ John 8:31-32 NKJV

Also:

> "And we know that all things work together for good to those who love God, to those who are the called according to His purpose."
>
> ~ Romans 8:28

THE VALUE OF RELATIONSHIP

When Adam disobeyed and sinned, he was disconnected from God and His Life and His thinking. Therefore, Adam was no longer hearing the *radio station with God's frequency.* Adam died, which means he lost the relationship with God that gave him kinship, authority, peace, power, God-life, favor and inheritance. The keys to assuring that you receive these things are getting the knowledge of God, love, faith and to walk in obedience. Faith comes from hearing God, believing what was heard and then becoming filled to abundance with it and acting on it. Obedience, such as forgiving, tithing, ridding self of previous priorities that were put before God, iniquities, and casting down any fear, keeps the *God flow* of *living water* moving in one through faith.

As we come into hearing God as a normal part of our day through obedience, prayer, meditation and diligence, God gives us His secrets. This is called revelation and it brings us into a deeper, more intimate, and powerful walk with God. As we come into this deeper walk with God, the things of the **supernatural** will begin to happen in our lives. When Jesus walked the earth, it was the norm for Him to heal the sick, cast out demons, work the miraculous and many other **supernatural** Kingdom of God things. The Lord will heal people through your prayers, give you spiritual insight into the gifts of knowledge, wisdom and discerning of spirits, etc. just as He did with and through Jesus also.

> "Most assuredly, I say to you, he who believes in Me, the works that
> I do he will do also; and greater works than these he will do, because
> I go to My Father."   ~ John 14:12 NKJV

In each of the 9 issues of life, God has a specific plan for you to come into being the "head and not the tail." This comes from you intentionally focusing on God's knowledge (His word) in each circumstance and coming into the secrets hidden in that word that has been reserved in heaven for you. "The secret things belong to the LORD our God, but those things which are revealed belong to us and to our children forever, that we may do all the words of this law" **(Deuteronomy 29:29).**

Impact of Iniquity and Generational Curses on a Person's Life That Cause Relationship Problems

As we consider the issue of relationships, my wife and I have done marriage counseling for over 40 years and can attest to the number of serious problems that have occurred with the root cause of iniquity that has led to generational curses from past hurts, abuses or lack, passing to descending generations.

> "But they that wait upon the LORD shall renew their strength; they
> shall mount up with wings as eagles; they shall run, and not be
> weary; and they shall walk, and not faint."   ~ Isaiah 40:31

The Lord showed me several years ago by revelation, as I meditated **Isaiah 40:31**, the word *wait* means to **"twist around."** The Lord further showed me that once He reveals something to you, as you continue meditating a *revealed saying* of God, He begins the process of *twisting His thoughts around* our thoughts until our thoughts disappear. In the following 3 illustrations two handkerchiefs are shown, one black and one white. As

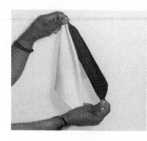

the twisting begins, soon the only color seen is one or the other: in this case, white. In spiritual terms, it means as we meditate God's word and we receive revelation, which is God speaking His secret *sayings,* our thinking on a matter change dramatically. In short, our thoughts disappear completely... or we lose our mind's previous perspective. This is called in **Romans 12:2,** the renewing of the mind. So, as our mind becomes renewed, we have God's thinking on issues of life.

> "For who hath known the mind of the Lord, that he may instruct him? but we have the mind of Christ."   ~ 1 Corinthians 2:16

There is an opposite to this wonderful revelation regarding iniquity and generational curses which has caused the passing down destructive, non-beneficial thinking patterns of our forefathers. In just the exact reverse of becoming one with Christ through the *twisting of His thoughts,* the opposite will also happen as the thoughts from the acquired thinking patterns from past generations causing failure are erased. Those thinking patterns may be fear, the inability to accomplish things or the inability to overcome poor self-esteem, etc. Therefore, the three pictures of the twisted handkerchiefs, once reversed, represent the *untwisting* of the iniquitous thinking that has caused the generational curses manifesting in our lives. The Lord's *revealed sayings* allows us to un-twist the thinking of our past generations through iniquity and generational curses until there is a separation of non-beneficial thoughts from our thoughts so we can discern what to get rid of, giving us God's Kingdom thinking in our issues of life.

The iniquitous thinking causes grief in the marriage bringing about marital problems, serious issues with the children and even divorce. The impact is not limited to marriages but to all persons. However, the Lord brought to our attention a diagram that very accurately displays the pain from one's past shown as an overflowing cup dispersing an acidic current that flows unto a plain destroying all vegetation and becoming a river that cuts a depression into the earth; as all river beds do. The picture then shows that the acidic flow coming out of the cup represents the results of the pain from the abuse or lack from the toxic relationship. That poisonous current comes from the iniquity in the person which causes the abuse or lack. It can be traced to a specific event or repeated events in the victim's life. It could be spiritual, mental or physical abuse. That abuse could come from physical pain afflicted on the victim, emotional trauma coming from an individual in the victim's life, whether they are present in the home or absent from it. Rejection is a major culprit and usually impacts the victim because of the absence of an individual that should be providing love, support or direction. As that current of abuse flows unto the plain creating the riverbed it destroys all in its path.

Next, the diagram shows the stopping of the abuse. That's a good thing, however the damage is already done and is impacting the victim's life. The old expression *into each life some rain must fall* causes monumental issues housed in the memory of the past. What we have explained to couples and individuals' is although the abuse, lack or rejection has ceased and often the victim has remarried, moved out of the abusive household, etc., as soon as problems arise elsewhere, the depression in the soul refills from the other non-related problem. Therefore, the new spouse, stepchild, or other new person in the picture, gets the blame, or worse than that, gets dumped upon by the victim. It's called *bringing one's old baggage* into the new relationship. We've especially seen this in blended families. A blended family is spouses coming into a new marriage and spouse number one has children and spouse number two has children and or a parent that comes along also. If there were unresolved issues in either situation, and there usually is, the problems are now multiplied. The issue is the depression in the plain caused by the riverbed of toxic hurts flowing in the victim's experiences from the abuser, has caused a hole or depression in the soul of the abused. Although the past pain ended 20 or 30 years ago, the video of it is still playing in the mind. Remember, "as he thinks in his heart, so is he?" This is where forgiveness and the renewing of the mind from the revelations of the *living word of God* restores the soul! Without the individuals submitting themselves to the process of this soul restoration, things will get far worse. Check the Index chapter to see the diagram and the scriptures once meditated that will bring the restoration of the soul.

Jayla's drawing of "Into each life some rain must fall,"[1] is a drawing of the damage to the soul from *toxic* relationships in the past that caused depression(s) in the soul that even after the toxicity ceased, the damage left a literal depression whereby future toxic relations caused a *replaying* of the past in the person's present, negatively impacting their life until the soul was restored by the Lord.

As a sidebar, one's relationship with God has a tremendous impact on their relationship with other people! I have heard that abused people, abuse. I would change that statement to, abused people that receive restoration of their souls, love others; but abused people who remain in that state are in danger because, "Looking diligently lest any man fail of the grace of God; lest any root of bitterness springing up trouble you, and thereby many be defiled;" **(Hebrews 12:15)**.

Offense is a thief preventing the Body of Christ from walking together in unity.

Obedience, love & forgiveness = Unity and God's Nature, Peace, and Power Manifested.

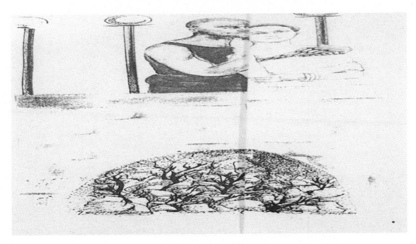

Dear Father,

I ask that you cause your people to receive your unconditional, overcoming, overwhelming love that is beyond their understanding; now just as they are. Father, that you give your care which is far beyond their caring, as you bring them into a place of giving you their time and praise and worship. Father, in return, I thank you for your covering and your blessing upon them from your love. Let them know that they are loved of you, they are loved of you, and I pray now that you cause that love to go beyond their understanding so that they receive and experience assurance. I thank you Father that this experience of your overwhelming love consumes their self-esteem and raises it to Christ-Esteem.

In Jesus name, amen.

SECTION III

←——————→

HEARING DIRECTION FROM GOD AND EFFECTIVE PRAYER

Speaking to, hearing and being led of God while moving steadfastly in that which He has purposed for you.

TRANSFORMING CHARACTERISTIC ~ VIRTUE ~

Being formed in the integrity of the character and righteousness of Christ's nature, yielding the power of God in you.

KINGDOM BENCHMARK ~ WISDOM ~

Knowing when and how to apply knowledge and understanding along with the product(s) they will manifest.

7

HOW TO MEDITATE
ON GOD'S WORD

"I am predestinated through His being bruised for my iniquities to being transformed by His thoughts into His image."
(Excerpt from: *Of God, I am*)

T his Book of the Law shall not depart from your mouth, but you shall meditate in it day and night, that you may observe to do according to all that is written in it. For then you will make your way prosperous, and then you will have good success." ~ Joshua 1:8 NKJV

"Blessed is the man Who walks not in the counsel of the ungodly, Nor stands in the path of sinners, Nor sits in the seat of the scornful; But his delight is in the law of the LORD, And in His law he meditates day and night. He shall be like a tree Planted by the rivers of water, That brings forth its fruit in its season, Whose leaf also shall not wither; And whatever he does shall prosper." ~ Psalm 1:1-3 NKJV

"Let the words of my mouth and the meditation of my heart Be acceptable in Your sight, O LORD, my strength and my Redeemer." ~ Psalm 19:14 NKJV

"Meditate on these things; give yourself entirely to them, that your progress may be evident to all."   ~ 1 Timothy 4:15

OVERVIEW OF MEDITATION

Definition: Meditate means to murmur, in pleasure or in anger. It further means to **muse, ponder, speculate, think, study, brood over,** and **contemplate.**[1] It is a **concentrated, repeated thinking** on specific items of thought. It requires **prioritization, intention,** and **time.** In the Bible, thoughts would be **spoken out, murmured** and even at times **hummed or put with music.**

Meditation on the word, statutes, precepts, commandments and testimonies revealed in scripture has not been suggested by God but **commanded.** All of the people used mightily in scripture did so; David and Solomon were good examples.

Hearing God is one of the most important things there is. **Proverbs 4:20** emphasizes this as the Lord says in **Isaiah 55:11:**

"So shall my word be that goes forth out of my mouth, it shall not return unto me void but it shall accomplish that which I please and it shall prosper in the thing whereto I sent it."   ~ Isaiah 55:11

What you hear from God will be extraordinary and **supernatural** in the results that it will bring forth. The prophets worked exploits in the earth due to the extraordinary things that they heard from God! Jesus did far greater things; again, based on what He heard from His Father.

It is God's provision and expectation for us to hear what He's directing us in so that we can know His will and ways. As we *hear Him accurately,* He causes His Kingdom to come in the earth. He watches over His word and causes its manifestation. God gives understanding of the hidden secrets within the written word (logos) when He sees our intention to do or obey whatever is revealed. People are not given revelation of God's secrets when He sees that the intent of their heart is not to follow the word. Example: Herkimer's heart is fixed on not forgiving Jane Doe or not giving a tithe to the Lord's purposes; therefore, God will not give him the secrets of Himself regarding good relationships nor financial prosperity to Herkimer. I have seen in ministry that there are those desirous of having good relationships and financial prosperity and they never reach either of those goals or any other goals because of their disobedience to the Lord's word. According to **John15:14-15**, God says if you love me, you'll do what I say and then I will call you friends and not servants. Jesus went on further to say that friends receive the things that the Father has told His Son. Those obeying God, prioritizing and seeking Him effectively, receive His *sayings* and achieve the **supernatural**!

GOD'S WORD IS ALIVE!

"For they are life to those that find them…"   ~ Proverbs 4:22a

"The Spirit gives life; the flesh counts for nothing. The words I have spoken to you they are full of the Spirit and life."   ~ John 6:63 NIV

"For the word of God is alive and active."   ~ Hebrews 4:12a NIV

Things that are alive grow, move, have communication processes and a will to bring functionality to its purpose and essence. The essence of a living object brings the basic, real, and invariable nature of its significant feature or features.[2] God's essence is light, life, love, peace, righteousness and joy. Part of the life of God is His expression of health and healing. There is no sickness and frailties in heaven. As an example, John or Jane Doe are presently suffering from a specific illness or physical incapacity; yet the Lord directs them to a scripture containing words regarding healing such as **1 Peter 2:24**:

"Who his own self bare our sins in his own body on the tree, that we, being dead to sins, should live unto righteousness: by whose stripes ye were healed."   ~ 1 Peter 2:24

Seeing that God's words are alive once a person hears God release a *saying* or a *rhema word* regarding a matter, that issue resolves itself speedily.

God's word must be received in the context of Jesus, who is the Alpha and the Omega; whose existence was before and at the ending of all events *(Revelation 1:11)*. Let us understand the word context: *the parts of a written or spoken statement that precede or follow a specific word or passage, usually influencing its meaning or effect.*[3] Jesus's spoken words therefore came from His knowledge, understanding and wisdom that He has before situations existed and also after they are resolved. He therefore knew 1,000, 2,000 or 3,000 years before an event occurred its resolution or ending. Therefore, as you meditate, contemplate, focus on God's words now with the expectation, belief, and intention to obey, He will show to you that which is hidden from the natural sight of man's intellect. God speaks a *saying* to you from the context of Himself which is far above our understanding and ways **(Isaiah 55:8-9)**. This definition of meditation was given to me on August 20, 2019 between 3:00 and 5:20am through what started as a dream and turned into awakened meditated thoughts and prayer for about an hour and a half.

In the opening chapters of this book I shared information relating to Adam's self-esteem, spiritual and intellectual status. It showed that before his fall, he moved with a unified relationship with God that gave him authority over everything in the sea, air and the earth. Adam was in charge! He had the thoughts and ways of God and his job was to restore order, replenish the void and give the *Light of God*.

"In the beginning God created the heavens and the earth. And the earth was without order, and empty; and darkness was upon the face of the deep. And the Spirit of God moved upon the face of the waters. And God said, **Let there be light, and there was light.**"

~ Genesis 1:1-3, emphasis added

In looking closely at these three scriptures, verses two and three reveal the following: the earth was without order, and an empty waste and darkness was upon it. God moved over all the earth and performed a *spiritual x-ray* of those circumstances, didn't approve of them and then thought the solution and spoke it in words... **"Let there be light."** As we go further, we find in verse five that the Lord called the "Light" Day, and the darkness was called Night... Verse 5b, **"And the evening and the morning were the first day."** As we go even deeper into the meanings of words, when God said, **"Let there be Light,"** in the Strong's Bible concordance, it gives the meaning of Light: *illumination, in every sense, including lightning, happiness, flood.*[4] On the other hand, *night* means: *a twist (away of the light), i.e. night; figuratively, adversity.*[5] This marked the first day. Therefore, when God spoke **"Let there be Light,"** it took away the lack of order, emptiness and darkness.

Imagine you're coming to my home for the first time at midnight and there is absolutely no illumination inside, and the furniture is in total disarray. I call you from the other side of the room and tell you to come quickly to me. Of course, you would stumble, stub your toes, fall and have a lack of confidence in moving toward me. The reason for this is simple: you can't *see*! Why not? There is no illumination. Now, I turn on the lights and you have illumination. Your first task would be to ascertain where I am in the house as I summon you to come quickly to where I am.

Next, you would begin to clear away the clutter in the path coming toward me. This is what happened when the Lord spoke, **'Let there be Light."** The results brought about order and provided *the way* to get rid of the void.

Going even deeper we find in verses 14-18, that the sun, moon and stars were made. The sun to give light in the day and the moon gave the sun's reflection of light in the night. We now see in verse 19, **"And the evening and the morning were the fourth day"** (Genesis 1:19, emphasis added). Therefore, the light coming from the sun and moon was not given until day four. Would you like to go a little deeper? We are given clues here that the *Light* in verses three and four did not come from the sun, moon and stars, as these were not made until day four and this *Light*, in verses 3 and 4, appears in day one. What is this light? Let's go further, we're getting warmer. The lack of order, emptiness and darkness in verse 2 were in existence because of the absence of light. However, this light did not, and I repeat again, *did not* come from the sun, moon and stars! Okay, so where did the light come from... it did some great things... but where is its origin? Verse three shows us clearly that it came out from God through His spoken word; **"And God said, Let there be light."** As we go even further into the context of the Bible, we find that when God speaks words from His mouth, illumination always comes.

"The entrance of thy words giveth light; it giveth understanding unto the simple" (Psalm 119:130, emphasis added). In John 1:1 the description of the "Light" is this:

> "In the beginning was the Word, and the Word was with God, and the Word was God. The same was in the beginning with God. All things were made by him; and without him was not any thing made that was made. In him was life; and the life was the light of men."
>
> ~ John 1:1-4

However, the *Light* that men receive from God and Jesus is internal not external. The *Light* comes from God's *Life* that is within Himself.

> "This then is the message which we have heard of him, and declare unto you, that God is light, and in him is no darkness at all."
>
> ~ 1 John 1:5

The *Light of God* comes from the *Life of God* and composes the Kingdom of God. This *Light* is found inside everyone that is hearing and following Jesus. When Jesus healed the ten lepers that came to Him it caused even the unbelieving Pharisees to acknowledge it and asked:

> "...when the kingdom of God should come, he answered them and said, The kingdom of God cometh not with observation: Neither shall they say, Lo here! or, lo there! for, behold, the kingdom of God is within you."   ~ Luke 17:20-21

There is a great gulf between verses 1 and 2 in Genesis 1. In verse 1, God had made the earth and everything that God made was in order and complete and full without confusion. There is no *darkness* in God. So, where did the lack of order, emptiness and darkness come from that is found in verse 2? **"And the earth was without form, and void; and darkness was upon the face of the deep"** (Genesis 1:2, emphasis added). It came from Satan.

When Satan was kicked out of heaven because of his rebellion against God along with a third of the angels he fell to the earth. This is found in four places in the Bible: **Isaiah 14, Ezekiel 28, Luke 10** and **Revelation 12.** We read in **Isaiah 14,** beginning in verse 12:

> "How art thou fallen from heaven, O Lucifer, son of the morning! how art thou cut down to the ground, which didst weaken the nations! For thou hast said in thine heart, I will ascend into heaven, I will exalt my throne above the stars of God: I will sit also upon the mount of the congregation, in the sides of the north: I will ascend above the heights of the clouds; I will be like the most High. Yet thou shalt be brought down to hell, to the sides of the pit."
>   ~ Isaiah 14:12-15

In these verses we are informed that when Lucifer, who was the archangel in charge of worship that ascended to God's throne, rebelled against God by wanting to exalt himself to God's level, was kicked out of heaven by God. When he got the boot out of heaven, he fell to the earth. Once in the earth he caused the disorder, emptiness and darkness that is described in Genesis 1:2, **"And the earth was without form, and void; and darkness was upon the face of the deep"** (emphasis added).

Another reference to this event is found in **Ezekiel 28** and **Luke 10**. Ezekiel describes the magnificence of Lucifer before his demotion along with the cause of his desire for elevation… pride. In Luke, Jesus describes seeing Satan fall from heaven to the earth, once again because of his pride and rebellion. The rebellion is further explained in **Revelation 12** as it showed the impact in the heavens as one third of the angels that had joined with Satan were also expelled from heaven to the earth. * (See the reference regarding Lucifer's fall from his first occupation and demotion to Satan in the index)

In reference to the light, we see even further as Jesus spoke regarding the *Light of God* in freeing the woman caught in the act of adultery who was about to be stoned by the religious leaders in John 8:12, "Then spake Jesus again unto them, saying, **I am the <u>light</u> of the world: he that followeth me shall not walk in darkness, but shall have the <u>light</u> of <u>life</u>"** (emphasis added).

As we venture back to Genesis 1, we see that the light came and destroyed the disorder, emptiness and the adversity of darkness or night. We see further in **Psalm 119:130**, that the entering in of God's word brings light and understanding to those without it. In both referenced scriptures in John we see that Jesus gave life which was the light of men and Jesus saves life (of the woman about to be stoned in **John 8**), by His word. Therefore, when His word enters us through His speaking it to us, *light*, *understanding*, and *life* are the results.

The purpose of meditation is to bring us into hearing God speak to us through His written and then His spoken *sayings* that come from them.

Those *sayings* come from God's thoughts and are *life* that gives *light* which is the essence and power of God. This, in turn, destroys all darkness which is that which did not originate in God. Therefore, fear, sickness, lack, poor relationships, etc., is destroyed by God's revealed *light* which is hidden in His word. It takes someone that has been born into the family of God that is walking in *right relationship* with Him through diligence and focus to find that light through meditation. Below, are a few methods that will assist you in *hearing God!*

Relationship with God and Meditation
<u>Elements to Hear Him</u>

To meditate effectively, hearing what the Lord wants to reveal to you, it's necessary to have a good relationship with Him. The following will establish that *good relationship*: commitment to God, prioritization of God, obedience, time, daily diligence, discipline, focus, setting the atmosphere in praise and worship and exercising the senses until the "habit" of meditation's elements are formed.

Meditation's elements are: 1. Getting a scripture. 2. Asking the Lord what it is He wants you to know. 3. Check the meaning of unknown words or words that the Lord will bring to your attention in the Bible concordance and dictionary. 4. Go over the given scripture(s) through comparing their meaning in the context that it's found in. 5. Take the time to *brood over* (think repeatedly) on the verse(s), *pray* (especially in the spirit), asking God the *meaning* and *application* of the given scripture(s) or thought(s) being meditated *until God speaks to you*. Now, you must utilize the same process regarding what the Lord speaks to you until you... 6. Come into actual belief of what you hear Him speak to you.

It is very important to understand that we don't come into **"<u>BELIEF</u>"** the moment we hear. It takes time to come into belief, for you must wash your mind of the thought or lack of thoughts that you are presently in. In short **you must unlearn some things before you learn another**. Getting results from meditation comes from **the Lord** *speaking to you* that which you will not find in the actual words you read or heard in the scripture verse(s). This is called receiving **revelation,** or *higher thoughts* from God Himself. The *higher thoughts* or **sayings** that you will receive are also referred to as a ***Rhema word.*** Rhema means a spoken word of light and life from God's mouth and custom-tailored to your specific circumstances.

Establishing a *right relationship* with God is among the 9 items that will be addressed. The right relation is included in obedience. The list below is the standard for obedience. The following show the major things the Lord addresses regarding it:

1. **Prioritize** the Lord and Walk in Love and Faith while abstaining from Idolatry.

2. **Prayer, Obedience, Forgiveness & Honor** the Lord while not testing Him with unbelief.

3. **Rid** ourselves of our "Heart problem;" Iniquity, while not grumbling and complaining.

4. **Get Established** in the Faith and move on to Maturity and Excellence.

5. **Display Christ's character** being Holy in Sexual Purity and Moral character.

6. **Train our children** in the things of God.

7. **Give** Tithes and Offerings.

8. **Be Diligent** as you come into God's Order and Attachment to your "Election."

9. **Win Souls** to the Lord and help in their Development

"My son, attend to my words; incline thine ear unto my sayings. Let them not depart from thine eyes; keep them in the midst of thine heart. For they are life unto those that find them, and health to all their flesh."   ~ Proverbs 4:20-22

"Let the words of my mouth and the meditation of my heart Be acceptable in Your sight, O LORD, my strength and my Redeemer."   ~ Psalm 19:14 NKJV

The first and one of the most important elements is in Proverbs 1:23, **"Turn you at my reproof: behold, I will pour out my Spirit unto you, I will make known my words unto you"** (emphasis added). Also, 2 Chronicles 7:14: **"If my people, which are called by name, shall humble themselves, and pray, and seek my face, and turn from their wicked ways; then will I hear from heaven, and will forgive their sin, and will heal their land"** (emphasis added).

God further speaks in Isaiah:

"Seek ye the LORD while he may be found, call ye upon him while he is near: Let the wicked forsake his way, and the unrighteous man his thoughts: and let him return unto the LORD, and he will have mercy upon him; and to our God, for he will abundantly pardon."
                                     ~ Isaiah 55:6-7

God is Holy and righteous, and as we repent, turn and seek His voice, He will forgive and speak to us His secrets and will.

<u>BENEFITS</u>

As we meditate on His word, the thoughts and precepts hidden within them appear. In short, the more we meditate God's word and the thoughts of God, the smaller the images and impact of our problems become, and the **larger the word's insights become**. In all the listed benefits that will be shared in the next few pages, I believe the greatest is being more fully in God's presence through the exercising of meditation and being obedient to Him. To meditate is to focus in a concerted manner whereby you magnify God's word to a point where you see (hear) things that have been hidden and missed by the casual reader or hearer of scripture.

METHODS

Take the scripture(s) God has laid on your heart and **memorize it** to realize its purpose. Initially, **set aside 15-20 minutes** in the early morning before getting into the "run of the day's activities," and give **concentrated thought** to the scripture. **Look up words** you may not understand. **Block out other thoughts,** problems issues etc., keeping your mind fixed on the scripture and your Heavenly Father. Use Bible dictionaries and concordances and use different Bible translations. Be open to the Lord's leading. He may lead you to pray in the Spirit, sing or sing in the Spirit*...He may lead you to other scriptures or Psalms...be open and continue. See the Meditation Exercise form given in chapter 7 of the Appendix and view the video on meditation on the website.

> "Therefore do not be unwise, but understand what the will of the Lord is. And do not be drunk with wine, in which is dissipation; but be filled with the Spirit, speaking to one another in psalms and hymns and spiritual songs, singing and making melody in your heart to the Lord,"   ~ Ephesians 5:17-19 NKJV

Another piece that will assist you greatly in meditation of God's word is to look at the surroundings of the word. Example: Tell me what you think of this man... He does not like to see children hurt. What are your thoughts?

Now, I'm going to take one word out of the sentence; tell me what you think of the man now... <u>He does not like to see children.</u>

_____

_____

Just by taking out one word, *hurt,* it changes the whole meaning of the sentence. You must meditate by looking at what is surrounding the scripture **in context**. That means reading the scriptures before and the scriptures that come after the verse! We have created a video on how to meditate. You can find it, along with other tools, on our website <u>www.guardyourheart.life</u> and click the icon, "How to MEDITATE."

Effective meditation brings about hearing the superior, highly elevated thoughts of God on matters that give you a superior, highly elevated advantage in every issue. Revelation knowledge gives light which destroys darkness. Effective meditation replaces thoughts that you had prior because you're being transformed by the renewing of your mind to far higher ones. Also, revelation knowledge is an advanced prophetic message from God that tells you things not only of the now, but of the future. What is the reverse of these two scriptures? Write your response below to each scripture.

> "My people are destroyed for lack of knowledge. Because you have rejected knowledge, I also will reject you from being priest for Me; Because you have forgotten the law of your God, I also will forget your children." ~ Hosea 4:6 NKJV

_____

_____

_____

_____

_____

_____

_____

"Where there is no vision, the people perish: but he that keepeth the law, happy is he."   ~ Proverbs 29:18

_____

_____

_____

_____

_____

Next, are more ideas that will help you to become successful at meditation.

STEPS TO SUCCESSFUL MEDITATION

1. **Make the decision** to do it

2. **Discipline** yourself, this is hard for the person who doesn't discipline themselves. **Just DO IT!**

3. **If You fail to PLAN, You plan to Fail. Set up a realistic plan** on a calendar to give time daily to do it.

4. **Keep the plan.** Get an accountability partner, set your clock or phone, whatever it takes, **do it!**

5. Get a **quiet place** at home and at work where you can do this without interruptions. This is important!

6. Now **memorize** the scripture to be meditated. Start off by breaking the scripture down in parts.

7. On the back of the MEDITATION TOOL # 1 there is a place for you to break the verse you're meditating into phases. You must **MEMORIZE** the verses that you will meditate word for word.

8. As you memorize the verse in phases, practice by **writing the verse** over and over while **speaking it aloud**. This is very important and is the reason you need a quiet environment. Turn off all distractions, the TV, radio, etc. You are training your brain and must do it repeatedly to **establish this habit**.

9. Use your phone to record yourself and then listen to yourself.

10. **Focus,** pay attention, think on what you're saying. **Focus, pay attention** and **think**! Over and over and over.

11. Put all the phases together and **speak** the whole verse being meditated. We will practice this in the on-site classes and in the on-line classes. Should you enroll in the classes you will find there are 3 sections to the course. Section 1 has 14 lessons and a review. Section 1 is "First Foundational Steps in God" (FFSIG), Section 2 is "Becoming Empowered in Christ" (BEIC) and has 12 lessons and a review. Section 3 is "How to go Through Tribulation Victoriously" (HTGTTV). It has 10 lessons and a review.

12. **This step is very important!** You must **believe** and **obey** the word of God as it is the **truth**! However, God is a person, He's a Spirit and He has a personality and you must establish a relationship with

Him. If you were not to believe a friend of yours it would have a detrimental impact on your relationship, this same thing applies to God. As you believe and obey you not only establish a good relationship, but you open the door for God to speak to you. Why would anyone tell you their secrets if they knew you would not believe and do what was revealed?

8

HEARING DIRECTION FROM GOD

"For I know the plans that I have for you,' declares the Lord, 'plans for welfare and not for calamity to give you a future and a hope."
~ Jeremiah 29:11 NASB ~

If the Lord knows the plans that He has for us, which includes our future, it stands to reason that we should go to Him to get direction for our lives. There is a way for us to be led of God while moving steadfastly in that which He has purposed for us.

Jesus Christ is our greatest example. He makes it clear several times in the scriptures that He heard from God and allowed Him to direct His life. Jesus said what He heard His Father say and did what He saw His Father do.

> "Then answered Jesus and said unto them, Verily, verily, I say unto you, The Son can do nothing of himself, but what he seeth the Father do: for what things soever he doeth, these also doeth the Son likewise. For the Father loveth the Son, and sheweth him all things that himself doeth: and he will shew him greater works than these, that ye may marvel. . . I can of mine own self do nothing: as I hear,

I judge: and my judgment is just; because I seek not mine own will, but the will of the Father which hath sent me." ~ John 5:19, 20, 30

"Trust in the Lord with all thine heart; and lean not to thine own understanding. In all thy ways acknowledge him, and he shall direct thy paths." ~ Proverbs 3:5

"I will instruct you and teach you in the way which you should go: I will counsel you with My eye upon you. Do not as the horse or as the mule which have no understanding. Whose trappings include bit and bridle to hold them in check, otherwise they will not come near to you. Many are the sorrows of the wicked; But he who trusts in the Lord, lovingkindness shall surround him." ~ Psalm 32:8-10

"For as many as are led by the Spirit of God, they are the sons of God." ~ Romans 8:14

HEARING FROM GOD AND KNOWING HIS WILL

Years ago, the Lord directed me to go to the hospital and pray with the sister of an individual who had just had the last rights of the Catholic church spoken over her. My initial reaction was really, Lord...they just gave-up on her the day before and I'm supposed to pray for her healing? It is God's full intention and provision that we come into that which we do not know in the natural realm; to come into the realm where: **"For as the heavens are higher than the earth, So are My ways higher than your ways, And My thoughts than your thoughts"** (Isaiah 55:9, emphasis added). The Lord told me as I crossed the threshold of the doorway into the hospital, the Lord spoke to me regarding the lady stating, *Do not look at her condition, look at me.* This caused faith to rise in my heart that wasn't there a few seconds before. As I went into her room, I found that she was in horrible shape. She'd had several strokes, pneumonia, her skin was as chalk, eyes were rolled back in their sockets not exposing the pupils and she was in a coma. The Lord reminded me... *do not look at her condition, look at me.* I confidently laid my hand on her forehead while telling those in the room, "I didn't come here as Postmaster, but as someone that hears God!" I prayed a 5-7 second prayer, assured the friends and family that she'd be just fine and left. The next week she walked into my office on a walker; the week after that she was on a cane and shortly thereafter, she was in total restoration.

There is no struggle in our walk after we've come into trusting the Lord! If we're struggling to obey, and do so completely, therein is the struggle that God wants to remove that will allow His rivers of life to flow out of us in the **supernatural**.

The bones in **Ezekiel 37** not only shook, not only had sinews and skin cover them, but the breath of God-life filled that which was dead and dry, and they lived. All of this was not known to Ezekiel as he was taking his walk past the valley of the dry bones. In the same manner, it is God's provision and intention that we come into knowing what we do not know, understand what we don't understand and receive the wisdom (strategies) of God to bring Heaven into our daily earth experience. Jesus stated in **Matthew 11** that John the Baptist was greater than any man that has opened the womb of a woman; this means John was greater than all the prophets from the past. Jesus then said that whoever is least in the Kingdom of Heaven is greater than John the Baptist...that happens to be us...**you!**

The real miracles in life are not people getting healed, delivered, or having blind eyes open...instead that which God waits for is our wills being surrendered to Him...completely. That's the real miracle! What avenue in the realm of God's Spirit are you on?

FAITH

Let's look at this thing called faith. Just what is it? Is it our speaking its definition perfectly? Hebrews 11:1, **"Now faith is the substance of things hoped for, the evidence of things not seen"** (emphasis added). **Romans 10:17,** "So then faith comes by hearing, and hearing by the word of God." <u>NO</u>, it isn't! Faith comes from our obedience to God through our being in His family and seeking Him diligently **until He speaks to our inner person.** That which He will speak will be something that we cannot do from our abilities or strength. He told Noah to build an Ark that would require 75 to 120 years to complete by a team of 8 people. In the meantime, God provided them with food, shelter, protection, means mockery and persecution from the townsfolk that gave strength, <u>supernatural</u> knowledge, understanding and wisdom. God then assembled the animals peaceably (the lion did not eat the lamb, etc.) and brought them from the 4 corners of the earth to one location.

The Lord told Abram to:

> "Now the LORD had said to Abram: "Get out of your country, From your family And from your father's house, To a land that I will show you. I will make you a great nation; I will bless you And make your name great; And you shall be a blessing. I will bless those who bless you, And I will curse him who curses you; And in you all the families of the earth shall be blessed." ~ Genesis 12:1-3

Abram, after thinking and meditating on it for a period, **received a rhema word from God or revelation,** then left his country, family and father's house and started traveling where he was unaware of, expecting God to show him. God did. As Abram traveled, he passed through Canaan and **God spoke to him again** telling him, "To your descendants I will give this land" (Genesis 13:7). There, west of Bethel, Abram built an altar to the Lord and began to call out to God. Relationship grew more intimate as he continued hearing, following and obeying the Lord.

There was a severe famine in Canaan, so Abram went south into Egypt. The Egyptians took Abram's wife Sarai as a trophy to Pharaoh after Abram had told her to not say that she was his wife, for his sake, and hers. Thus, she did, and God had Pharaoh bless Abram. **"He treated Abram well for her sake. He had sheep, oxen, male donkeys, male and female servants, female donkeys, and camels"** (Genesis 12:7B, emphasis added). God then struck Pharaoh and his people with great plaques. Pharaoh discerned that the plaques were from God due to Sarai having been Abram's wife and sent him out of Egypt with great wealth. Take note of God's original message to Abram, **"I will bless you And make your name great; And you shall be a blessing. I will bless those who bless you, And I will curse him who curses you"** (Genesis 12:2b-3a, emphasis added). Abram's name had become great amongst the Egyptians and he had become very blessed in favor with Pharaoh and Pharaoh gave him goods and servants. God had also placed a curse on Pharaoh due to Sarai and then stopped the many plaques once she was released back to her husband.

So, let's look at faith again. Abram **heard God** tell him to leave his country, people and father and go where He, God, would show him. **Abram did just** that after he received a *rhema word* and as he traveled, obeying in the first phase, God told him the land you're passing through belongs to your descendants (Canaan). Abram then went into Egypt and saw greater blessings that derived from Pharaoh, although he was cursed for taking Abram's wife initially.

Coming closer to our time and myself, about 18 years ago **the Lord told me** to start teaching a class. It started out as *First Foundational Steps in God* (FFSIG) and then grew to *How to Go Through Tribulation Victoriously (HTGTTV)*. These both came from a vision that **He showed me** in March of 1980. Later, about 11 years ago the Lord told me to start doing the class not only at various sites but to offer it online via the internet. I had absolutely no knowledge of doing this via the internet and therefore did not know where I was going nor what to do, but within one month of **His telling me** to do so, my daughter set up initial steps for the internet and a videographer joined our staff and began the initial filming and posting for the classes. Since then, one of our church members studied the field and set-up an interactive website for the church and classes. All these things have come about from **my hearing God, believing and acting on** what He said and **while** walking in unknown territory, the Lord has manifested that which I could not do in my own abilities, strength and power.

The **hearing God, believing** what He said and then **acting on** what was said…**is called faith.** Faith is evidence shown by the **action** that one takes from the unseen that was heard and believed from God's voice!

> "But without faith it is impossible to please Him, for he who comes to God must believe that He is, and that He is a rewarder of those who diligently seek Him." ~ Hebrews 11:6 NKJV

Your blessing will come as you come into hearing specifically what God has said to you.

Now, as stated in Chapter 7 on meditation, hearing from God one or a few times does not cause you to believe…you must meditate the initial thing(s) the Lord has said to you and that will cause an inner growth and processing within you until the belief and vision of God is developed. In Romans 12:2 it states:

> "…do not be conformed to this world, but be transformed by the renewing of your mind, that you may prove what is that good and acceptable and perfect will of God." ~ Romans 12:2 NKJV

Next, and this is crucial, you must act on that which you cannot see or feel in the natural realm...the acting on what God has said that you have come to believe, is **faith**. Faith pleases God (See **Hebrews 11:6**). The course **HTGTTV** takes you step by step into hearing God through meditation of God's word and revelations be they visions, dreams etc.

The bottom-line is having a relationship with God whereby you are hearing and hearing daily what God is speaking, "Give us this day our daily bread" **(Matthew 6:11)**. It is the foundation to having an effective prayer life and receiving God's intention and blessing in every issue of life.

SPIRITUAL INVENTORY

Give at least 3 things that stuck out in this chapter.

_____

_____

_____

_____

_____

_____

_____

_____

_____

Give at least 3 scriptures the Lord has given you from which you have received revelation secrets. . . "God's sayings." List your revelation also.

_____

_____

_____

_____

_____

_____

_____

_____

_____

_____

_____

_____

_____

_____

_____

9

PRAYER

The definition of prayer is the act of asking for a favor with earnestness; petition, supplication, entreaty; that which is asked; a solemn petition addressed to an object of worship. To the believer, prayer is the effective communication, speaking to and listening to Almighty God, our Father. In his teaching entitled, *Prayer*, Elder Morris Thomas of *Spiritual Aspects Ministries*, states, "Prayer is a communion or the means by which we enter into a conscious and intimate relationship with God. Prayer is indeed the very framework or essence of our relationship with God."[1]

In **Matthew 6:9-13** Jesus gives His disciples the model, or outline, for prayer. This same outline is to be used by us, His disciples, today:

1. Our Father:
   - ➤ We are to acknowledge God as our Father. This identifies us with Him in relationship and that we belong to Him. Therefore, as a loving parent, He provides for us.

2. Hallowed by they name:
   ➤ We are to reverence God by declaring His name is holy. It is separate and distinct from any other name.

3. Thy kingdom come:
   ➤ We petition God for His Kingdom to be revealed in the earth.

4. Thy will be done in earth as it is in heaven:
   ➤ We pray for God's will to be done. We want what He wants to be accomplished. The same things that are going on in heaven to be done in earth.

5. Give us this day our daily bread:
   ➤ We are to seek God every day for what He has for us. His direction and instruction for our lives. Just as we eat food daily, we should also seek what God has for us daily.

6. And forgive us our debts as we forgive our debtors:
   ➤ Confession is a must! Why? Because unchecked sin, leads us to further temptation and evil. It opens the door to Satan. Also, we must forgive anyone who has offended us, understanding that God can only forgive us to the extent that we forgive others.

7. And lead us not into temptation, but deliver us from evil:
   ➤ Again, we want to be aware of our weaknesses so that we are not tempted.

8. For thine is the kingdom, and the power, and the glory, forever:
   ➤ Acknowledging that God's Kingdom rules and God has all power and deserves all glory.

However, as we mature, we come to understand that there is a deeper side of prayer. Prayer, real prayer that is effective is far more than a one-way communication of us telling God what we need and want. He already knows. Instead, it is a two-way conversation between us and our Almighty Heavenly Father.

Prayer is the first internet that God set up in heaven available for downloading into our spirits and minds. As we pull up God's prayer website through praise, worship, study and looking to Him from our inner man (heart), we come into information, impartations, and the nature and power that are waiting to be transferred into the earth realm.

God is a Spirit and desires to fellowship with our spirit man. He wants to show us and to manifest in us the **supernatural** things of His kingdom.

"Likewise the Spirit also helpeth our infirmities: for we know not what we should pray for as we ought: but the Spirit itself maketh intercession for us with groanings which cannot be uttered. And he that searcheth the hearts knoweth what is the mind of the Spirit, because he maketh intercession for the saints according to the will of God." ~ Romans 8:26-27

"Howbeit when he, the Spirit of truth, is come, he will guide you into all truth: for he shall not speak of himself; but whatsoever he shall hear, that shall he speak: and he will shew you things to come." ~ John 16:13

"If my people, which are called by my name, shall humble themselves, and pray, and seek my face, and turn from their wicked ways; then will I hear from heaven, and will forgive their sin, and will heal their land." ~ 2 Chronicles 7:14

HAVING A RIGHT RELATIONSHIP WITH GOD

I remember my parents telling me stories of times when they were growing up that they had been rewarded or punished depending on their obedience or lack thereof with my grandparents. I also have fond and not so fond memories of my own good times and not so good times with my parents as I was growing up, dependent, once again on my obedience or lack thereof. I have fond memories in raising my own children, remembering the good and the not so good; and I have seen the same experiences of reward and punishment with my grandchildren as they are having the same experiences; all dependent on their obedience or lack of obedience. Can you relate to like experiences in your own life? God rewards us in like manner… **Isaiah 1:19,** "If ye be willing and obedient, ye shall eat the good of the land." Also:

> "Children, obey your parents in the Lord, for this is right. 'Honor your father and mother,' which is the first commandment with promise: 'that it may be well with you and you may live long on the earth.'"
>
> ~ Ephesians 6:1-3

We find God's expectations for us in this:

> "Blessed is the man Who walks not in the counsel of the ungodly, Nor stands in the path of sinners, Nor sits in the seat of the scornful; But his delight is in the law of the LORD, And in His law he meditates day and night. He shall be like a tree Planted by the rivers of water, That brings forth its fruit in its season, Whose leaf also shall not wither; And whatever he does shall prosper."
>
> ~ Psalm 1:1-3

God rewards our obedience with blessings and withdraws blessings from the disobedient. On the pages that follow, we will look at specific things that bring us into getting God's results in our prayer life and following His direction and leadings.

MATURITY

Maturity, in spiritual terms, means that one has come to a point where the unseen, the invisible to the natural eye and mind is seen in the Spirit and the spirit-eye is the norm.

> "...while we do not look at the things which are seen, but at the things which are not seen. For the things which are seen are temporary, but the things which are not seen are eternal."
>
> ~ 2 Corinthians 4:18

> "Now faith is the substance of things hoped for, the evidence of things not seen." ~ Hebrews 11:1

The bottom line to effective prayer and this is very, very, very, important... is hearing from God that which we did not know of before. Next, is the releasing of the resources of the Kingdom of Heaven, once again from that which we did not know before. An example of this is in **2 Kings 6**, as Elisha tossed a wooden branch into the water where an iron axe-head had sunk and then having the iron ax-head to swim up and attach itself to it. Secondly, was his knowing the secret plans of the Assyrian King plotting against the Israelites and then letting the king of Israel know so that he avoided the planned ambushes. Thirdly, Elisha released the resources of the Kingdom of Heaven, the angels, to smite the Assyrian army with blindness that was surrounding him and his servant at the city of Dothan.

All these are instances of hearing things that are unknown (the **SUPERNATURAL KNOWLEDGE** of God that is above our knowledge), then hearing and perceiving the (HOW and WHAT to do with that knowledge, which is **UNDERSTANDING**) and then receiving the WAY, WHY, WHEN and WHERE to release the unknown that has become known **(WISDOM)** from the kingdom of heaven into the earth.

"The secret things belong to the Lord Our God and those things that are revealed belong to us and our inheritance forever."

~ Deuteronomy 29:29

First, in having the iron axe head to swim, he displayed the **miraculous realm** of God's Kingdom over the natural elements in the earth. Next, in repeatedly discerning the secret plans of the Assyrian king against the Israelites, he moved in the kingdom of God **realm of revelation**. Lastly, in having the angels strike the Assyrian army with blindness, he moved in the **realm of the power** available in God's Kingdom for those moving in the Spirit of God in their inheritance. Remember Jesus' prayer blueprint for us is for His Father's Kingdom to come and His will to be done **"...in earth as it is in heaven"** (Matthew 6:10, emphasis added). In James 5:16, one finds that the effectual fervent prayer of a righteous man avails much. What makes prayer effective is knowing the will of God which is revealed because we are a friend of God as stated in John 15:14-15, **"You are My friends if you do whatever I command you. No longer do I call you servants, for a servant does not know what his master is doing; but I have called you friends, for all things that I heard from My Father I have made known to you"** (emphasis added).

Also, in John 16:13, **"Howbeit when he, the Spirit of truth, is come, he will guide you into all truth: for he shall not speak of himself; but whatsoever he shall hear, that shall he speak: and he will shew you things to come"** (emphasis added).

Our prayers must be diligently focused on what we are hearing from God, we must not allow our mind to get caught up with emotions or something that changes in the environment.

"For My thoughts are not your thoughts, Nor are your ways My ways," says the LORD. "For as the heavens are higher than the

earth, So are My ways higher than your ways, And My thoughts
than your thoughts."   ~ Isaiah 55:8-9

"Likewise the Spirit also helpeth our infirmities: for we know not
what we should pray for as we ought: but the Spirit itself maketh
intercession for us with groanings which cannot be uttered. And he
that searcheth the hearts knoweth what is the mind of the Spirit,
because he maketh intercession for the saints according to the will
of God."   ~ Romans 8:26-27

Things of the Kingdom of Heaven are hidden from us because we are
ignorant and infirmed in mind because of iniquity. The effective prayer
such as shown in the 13:26 minute You-Tube video-clip, "City
Transformation: Alomonga, Guatemala", brings us into a more enhanced
understanding through the Spirit of God via diligence and fervency, that
brings us to knowing that which we don't know at present. However, once
we know what we don't know in the natural mind, God gives us
understanding, what to do and how to do it. Then we get the strategies of
wisdom from God, that He wants to be ours. The Lord earnestly desires
us to get His results, as did Jesus; but we must first get His
SUPERNATURAL KNOWLEDGE, UNDERSTANDING and
WISDOM.

Now, let's get to the *real meat* of these situations regarding Elisha's
exploits mentioned in the prior paragraph. They were mighty, wonderful
and miraculous deeds! However, we have more power from a greater
inheritance! What am I saying and where am I coming from? In **Matthew
11** the story is told of how John the Baptist was thrown in jail and while
there, sent his disciples to Jesus asking, "Are you the Messiah that was to
come to the Israelites?" Jesus responded in verse 4-6 with, "Go and tell
John the things which you hear and see: The blind see and the lame walk;
the lepers are cleansed and the deaf hear; the dead are raised up and the

poor have the gospel preached to them. And blessed is he who is not offended because of Me" **(Matthew 11:4-6)**.

Jesus went on to tell His own disciples regarding John the Baptist that **"Assuredly, I say to you, among those born of women there has not risen one greater than John the Baptist"** (Matthew 11:11, emphasis added). What does this mean? There is no prophet or anyone else that has been born that is greater than John the Baptist. This includes Isaiah, Moses, Esther, Daniel nor Elijah…no one…. Born of a woman that was greater than John the Baptist! The exploits listed above including Elijah causing the rains to cease upon the earth for three and a half years…then caused it to rain again, were surpassed by John the Baptist. OK, you say that that is great, wonderous and marvelous, but after all it was Elijah the prophet doing these marvelous works! That's great and wonderful, John the Baptist was more powerful! But, here's the clincher… Jesus said: **"…but he who is least in the kingdom of heaven is greater than he"** (Matthew 11:11b, emphasis added). That's you and me also! We have been empowered and positioned to do greater things. But that's not all…Jesus said that we would do the same works as He did and greater works: **"Most assuredly, I say to you, he who believes in Me, the works that I do he will do also; and greater works than these he will do, because I go to My Father"** (John 14:12, emphasis added).

The issue with most believers is the **HBO**: Hearing, believing and obeying. We must give the time and prioritization to hear God. Believing takes more than hearing a word from God unto belief. We do not automatically believe; it takes concerted meditation over a period of focused concentration and the exercising of the mind to focus and continue listening to that which must come into the fullness of belief. This, in turn downloads the new belief system into our mind until it overwhelms and pushes out the old thoughts and ways by *KICKING OUT* the old belief system thoughts. Now, one must act on it…just do it! Herein is belief!

BELIEF

However, if distraction can set in, you lose IT!

BELIEF

At this point, you lose your image and therefore you no longer get the results you need.

Maturity is all about being prepared and being established. In 2 Chronicles it says,

> "So they rose early in the morning and went out into the Wilderness of Tekoa; and as they went out, Jehoshaphat stood and said, "Hear me, O Judah and you inhabitants of Jerusalem: **Believe in the LORD your God, and you shall be established**; believe His prophets, and you shall prosper."
>
> ~ 2 Chronicles 20:20, emphasis added

Everyone wants to prosper! Well to prosper you must first be established. Established means to be prepared whereby one becomes steadfastly set or skilled from training, so that things can be performed or accomplished. David's cup in Psalm 23 overflowed because it was established or complete... it had no holes or leaks in it. Had it holes or leaks, the blessings of God would have run out or not have been contained. So, it is with us. We must be established. Now note the scripture states believe in the Lord your God, and you shall be established. OK, believe what? Most Christians will quickly tell you that they not only believe in the Lord but love Him also. That's wonderful, but again I say believe what? It states what must be believed in to become mature or established in Hebrews:

> **"Therefore, leaving the discussion of the elementary principles of Christ, let us go on to perfection, (maturity) not laying again the foundation of repentance from dead works and of faith**

105

toward God, of the doctrine of baptisms, of laying on of hands, of resurrection of the dead, and of eternal judgment. And this **we will do if God permits.**"   ~ Hebrews 6:1-3, emphasis added

There are 9 foundational stones that are referred to in this verse. Once these are laid then we go on to the more mature things in God! These 9 foundational stones are followed by **Hebrews 6:4:**

"For it is impossible for those who were once enlightened, and have tasted the heavenly gift, and have become partakers of the Holy Spirit, and have tasted the good word of God and the powers of the age to come, if they fall away, to renew them again to repentance, since they crucify again for themselves the Son of God, and put Him to an open shame. For the earth which drinks in the rain that often comes upon it and bears herbs useful for those by whom it is cultivated, receives blessing from God; but if it bears thorns and briers, it is rejected and near to being cursed, whose end is to be burned."   ~ Hebrews 6:4-8

This is a very important passage of scripture as it follows the progression that has been provided and expected of God in verses 1-3. That progression is as follows:

FOUNDATION STONES

1.   Repentance From Dead Works

Repentance from dead words refers to our turning away from the errant thinking of those who believe that our doing good works, such as feeding the hungry, clothing the needy or providing shelter to the homeless and such the like, all being *good in our eyes*, gain favor with God. No, *good works* that are separate from *the WORK* that Jesus provided through His sacrifice of taking our sins, removing them by His blood and then His resurrection from the dead are completely meaningless to God! An example of a good work is in the spring of 2020, two of the HTGTTV students were led to procure diapers for those on aid or in financial lack. The time to procure the diapers ended up in the middle of the height of the coronavirus pandemic. The persons doing this were a married couple, both of which were dentists that had to close down their office, while paying their staff out of their own pocket. Needless to say, they were in a real fix; however, the Lord provided the finances for the continuing event, continuous supplies, along with a location to stock the diapers and large vehicles to transport the thousands of packages of diapers. It became an easy task and was far beyond the resources of the couple while giving glory to God and not themselves.

> "But we are all as an unclean thing, and all our righteousnesses are as filthy rags; and we all do fade as a leaf; and our iniquities, like the wind, have taken us away."   ~ Isaiah 64:6

> "For by grace you have been saved through faith, and that not of yourselves; it is the gift of God, not of works, lest anyone should boast."   ~ Ephesians 2:8-9

2.   Faith Towards God

Faith towards God equates to God's absolute requirement of faith to please Him and faith only comes by our actual hearing from God, believing what has been said and then acting in accordance without our *seeing something in the sense realm first.* **Hebrews 11:6** states that without faith, one cannot please God. In **John 20:29,** Jesus tells Thomas that the only reason he believed in Jesus' resurrection was because he *saw* Jesus with his eyes. Jesus said to him, "Blessed are they that have not seen, and yet have believed."

3.   Doctrine of Baptisms

Note- There are 4 Baptisms. The Baptism into Christ: this comes forth only after one has believed in the unseen shedding of the blood of Christ,

His death and then resurrection, within their mind, then Jesus cleanses them of their sin and then gives the new spiritual man new life through the total submergence of them into the life springs of spiritual waters, making them one in the Body of Christ. **Ezekiel 36:25-27** outlines this event while **John 3:3** gives the requirement of one getting into the Kingdom of God and **2 Corinthians 5:17** details what happened to the old spirit man of a person once they believe in Christ Jesus' work accomplished for them: **"Therefore, if anyone is in Christ, he is a new creation; old things have passed away; behold, all things have become new"** (2 Corinthian 5:17, emphasis added).

4.   The Baptism in the Holy Ghost

The baptism in the Holy Ghost gives the new spirit man the power to move in the new realm of spirit that they have been birthed into <u>supernaturally</u>. **Joel 2:28-29** prophesied that God would pour His Spirit out to man, **Luke 24:49** speaks to the being clothed upon with power per the prophecy's promise in Joel from the Father and finally **Acts 1:8**, the resurrected Jesus tells the disciples as He is ascending to heaven that the promise of power is arriving shortly but for them to wait in Jerusalem for its arrival.

5.   The Baptism in Water

The baptism in water was not only an event that gave an outer witness to the world of one's acceptance of Jesus **(Matthew 3:11)**, but gave an internal working of the Spirit as happened when the children of Israel were baptized unto Moses whereby the enemy was destroyed in their baptism unto him **(Exodus 13:21-22** and **14:21-31)**.

6.   The Fire Baptism

The Fire baptism causes a continual cleansing by the burning of all things of the flesh that would hinder the move of God by His Spirit through us **(Malachi 3:2** and **Matthew 3:10)**.

7.   The Laying on of Hands

The laying on of hands gave witness of God's Spirit through the believer that has been processed through the six prior foundations to come to a point of Christ-character and power to release the things of the Kingdom of God into and upon the earth (**Mark 16:15** and **Acts 1:8-9, Acts 10:38**).

8.   Resurrection from the Dead

This stone points to the knowledge and expectation of those who have continued faithfully in following the Spirit of the Lord to be raised from the dead even as had Jesus (**Acts 24:15, Romans 6:5, 1 Corinthians 15:21** and **Revelation 20:6**).

9.   Eternal Judgment

The final stone is the knowledge and belief in Eternal Judgment on those that have believed and followed the Lord and those who didn't (**1 Corinthians 15:52, 1 Thessalonians 4:13-18** and **Revelation 20:11-15**).

The point in raising these 9 foundation stones is this: with them being established in the lives of individuals, through the experience, understanding and living in them through the exercise of faith, one gains access into the deeper things of the Kingdom of God and its peace and power (these are covered in Section 1 of the HTGTTV course). This is evidenced through one flowing in the same works as did Jesus. Jesus said that we would do the same works as did He and greater works (**John 14:12**). Later, upon Paul reaching the disciples in Ephesus, obviously not seeing the power of the Spirit of God being exercised among them (he would ask the same question in some of the churches today):

"...'Did you receive the Holy Spirit when you believed?' So they said to him, 'We have not so much as heard whether there is a Holy Spirit.' And he said to them, 'Into what then were you baptized?'

So, they said, 'Into John's baptism.' Then Paul said, 'John indeed baptized with a baptism of repentance, saying to the people that they should believe on Him who would come after him, that is, on Christ Jesus.' When they heard this, they were baptized in the name of the Lord Jesus. And when Paul had laid hands on them, the Holy Spirit came upon them, and they spoke with tongues and prophesied."

~ Act 19:2-6

In the following 2 pictures, you see walls having been prepared to be painted with stripes. However, for the stripes to be straight and clear, many steps had to precede the paint. Measurements had to be taken and tape had to be applied to the wall. Once the walls were properly prepared, the paint could then be applied with good results. It would not have worked out had the painter simply used his best effort to estimate.

If the painter had used his best effort without the guidelines from the measurements that the tape was set to, the lines would not have the quality of excellence needed to produce the achieved results. God gives us *His guidelines* for the various issues in our lives that brings us to His standard.

PRAYER ASSISTANCE

A few years ago, I lost my cell phone while at a retail store. My wife and I thoroughly searched the vehicle and the house at least twice to no avail. We finally called to the retail store to see if anyone had turned in a phone. No one had turned in a phone. We therefore drove out to the store and

searched the parking lot and the areas in the store where we had traveled…
no phone. We went to the customer service office requesting if there had
been any phones turned in… there hadn't. We then went home and again
searched the vehicle and the house… no phone.

Later that evening, upon watching a Christian talk station I heard a
testimony from Pastor Jerry Savelle, how he and a pastor from Harlem,
New York had been interviewed regarding the **supernatural** intervention
of God. He stated that about 30 years prior he had been interviewing this
particular pastor and had stated that it must be challenging being a pastor
in Harlem due to the crime, etc. The pastor replied, "Not at all; we have
the Holy Spirit and the angels working with us." At that point the pastor
gave testimony how at the end of one evening service, the offering had just
been collected and two armed men came into the church and took the
money at gun point and ran toward the entrance door to escape. Upon
reaching the front door, the men came to a screeching halt, turned around
and ran back to the front of the church returned the money and accepted
the Lord. When asked why they had come back and turned in the money
and accepted the Lord, they stated upon approaching the front door they
saw two giant angels there, both pointing golden pistols at them! My wife
and my reaction to this testimony was "glory to God!"

Shortly thereafter, the Lord told me, *I'm looking at your phone.* I was
surprised at what the Lord had said to me, but not that He was looking at
the phone. I responded… *Father, I know that you see the phone, but I
want to see it too.* The Lord stated, *if you do what I tell you, you will.* I
responded, *Father, I will. What is it that you want me to do?* He let me
know that He would tell me at the appropriate time. (Now folks what's
really being talked about here in this story being shared is prayer.)

I went to bed around 10:30pm that evening and around 4:00am the Lord
awakened me and told me that He wanted me to come before Him in
worship with the song, "How great thou art!" I went to the place where I

pray and sang the song to the Lord. He told me to continue singing it (take note what is going on in the Spirit realm in this instance that I'm describing). After singing the song three or four times with the Lord stating, *sing it again*, I caught the hint that the Lord wanted me to continue singing the song until He told me to stop. This went on for 30-40 minutes and I really came into a focus on the Lord and really had shifted my focus from the phone to the glory and majesty of almighty God! At this point the Lord told me to begin singing in the same melody only now not speak English but sing in the spirit **(Ephesians 5:17-20)**.

I began worshipping the Lord, singing in tongues for the next 15-25 minutes. As I did this, I came to a point where I very boldly stated... "Satan I bind your every spirit that you have over whoever picked up my phone!" The Lord stopped me immediately stating, *I didn't tell you to bind any spirits! I have honest people out here and I sent your angel to get one and had them pick up your phone. Now tell your angel where you want the phone taken.* I was shocked!

Now, going back earlier in this chapter, it was stated that effective prayer needs at least 3 elements: 1. The **supernatural** knowledge of God that's beyond our knowledge. 2. The understanding of God that will give us the what and how to use the information that God gives. 3. The strategy of God that will give us the why, when and where to use the understanding that's been given to us to access the Kingdom of God and bring its results into the earth. My testimony continued... I told my angel to take the phone to a specific retail outlet that handles the type of phone that I had.

About 4 hours later my wife and I were on our way to corporate prayer at the church, it's 10:30am-12noon every Tuesday, and as I was driving I asked my wife to call the phone retail outlet to check on my phone. She did, and they stated that the phone had been turned in. After we opened the church, we had time to drive out to the retail outlet to retrieve my phone and get back in time before prayer started. Upon getting to the outlet I asked for my phone and was asked for identification as they retrieved my phone. The young man that was typing the information regarding the returning of the lost phone on his iPad, suddenly stopped and asked me... sir, I see that we have not yet contacted you regarding your phone being here so... how did you know to come here to retrieve it? I told him the Lord told me the phone was here... he stopped typing on his iPad... "What?" I repeated, "The Lord told me the phone was here." He handed me the phone with no further questions. We got to prayer early and really had a time of prayer!

The Power of Prayer as You Stand in Your Position of Unity

"Behold, how good and how pleasant it is for brethren to dwell together in unity! It is like the precious ointment upon the head, that ran down upon the beard, even Aaron's beard: that went down to the skirts of his garments; As the dew of Hermon, and as the dew that descended upon the mountains of Zion: for there the LORD commanded the blessing, even life for evermore." ~ Psalm 133:1-3

"Wherefore the rather, brethren, give diligence to make your calling and election sure: for if ye do these things, ye shall never fall: For so an entrance shall be ministered unto you abundantly into the everlasting kingdom of our Lord and Saviour Jesus Christ. Wherefore I will not be negligent to put you always in remembrance of these things, though ye know them, and be established in the present truth." ~ 2 Peter 1:10-12

In **Psalm 133**, the value of unity is explained and how it is compared to the precious ointment, which represents the Spirit of God that was poured upon the head of Aaron. The Holy Spirit being poured upon the head represents God's thoughts and anointing upon one that impacts the entire body as it flows downward. This is possible because the body has no breaks, or is one, unified. In this place of unity and in the thoughts of God, the blessing is commanded. That blessing is the restoration of eternal life. There is power, peace and love in unity! This, therefore, has a tremendous benefit in prayer. **Amos 3:3, "Can two walk together, except they be agreed"** (emphasis added)? Also, unity's results show in, **Matthew 18:19**:

> "Again I say unto you, That if two of you shall agree on earth as touching any thing that they shall ask, it shall be done for them of my Father which is in heaven. For where two or three are gathered together in my name, there am I in the midst of them."
>
> ~ Matthew 18:19-20

Note… because believers are unified, in agreement, the power of Christ is released! What this looks like in the church is when believers are one with the vision of the church body; that is, they are not only in attendance but in the will of the Father as He has released His vision and purpose for the local assembly. This means the prayers of individuals who are one with that given vision in the body, are far, far more effective.

It must also be noted that as you are attached faithfully to your position or calling that the Lord has given you, the anointing of God passes via impartation unto you. In **Matthew 6:33**:

> "But first and most importantly seek (aim at, strive after) His kingdom and His righteousness [His way of doing and being right—the attitude and character of God], and all these things will be given to you also." ~ Matthew 6:33 AMP

One cannot strive for the purpose of God's Kingdom and His righteousness if they have not sought after and attached themselves to the *position* or *election* that God has for them. It states in 2 Peter 1:10, **"…brethren, give diligence to make your calling and election sure"** (emphasis added). As an individual places God's priority as their priority,

God does the same with them; for we reap what we have sown. Years ago, as a husband, father, assistant pastor, evangelist, teacher and Postmaster of a large metropolitan area with 2,500 employees, I maintained the responsibilities of my calling in God. I had been seeking advancement in my natural career and the Lord spoke very clearly to me regarding the desired advancement by saying, *You have taken care of my business, I shall take care of yours.* I was not only promoted but blessings flowed in many dynamic ways! It pays tremendous dividends in prayer to be unified in the Body of Christ and connected faithfully in your calling.

SECTION IV

HEALING AND HEALTH

Inheritance benefits necessary to fully work God's
Kingdom expression in the earth.

TRANSFORMING CHARACTERISTIC
~ KNOWLEDGE ~

Repentance from dead works, faith towards God, the
four baptisms, laying on of hands, resurrection of the
dead, and eternal judgment

KINGDOM BENCHMARKS
~ PRAYER AND FASTING ~

Effective two-way communication with God with
discipline manifesting multiplied results.

10

COMING INTO
HEALING & HEALTH

You have just left the retirement party of a dear friend. As you approach the coat rack, you notice that the person in front of you has just put on your new cashmere coat someone recently gave you as a gift. You say, "Excuse me, but you have my coat," and they respond that the coat is theirs. At this point you both notice that there is another coat that is the exact replica of the coat they have on, and a closer examination shows that although identical, it is slightly worn. Then you state to the individual that in the inner pocket you have a set of keys and in the bottom inside right sleeve have your initials embroidered in it. The key check was sufficient proof, but the initials made it conclusive that the coat is yours. The individual removes the coat embarrassed and apologetic and hands it to you. You receive the coat which is yours, put it on and it is so comfortable and fits you to the T, after all you had it custom tailored. The coat belongs to you, was purchased for you as a gift, has your belongings within in it along with your name in the inner right sleeve… undoubtedly, indisputably, yours! You had absolutely no intention of leaving without it!

Just like in the example with the coat, our health and healing is ours also. They were purchased for us by Jesus' stripes that He took on His way to Calvary. He intentionally bore each stripe, all of them, as part of His portion in order for us to receive our portion... complete health and healing!!!

> "Surely he hath borne our griefs, and carried our sorrows: yet we did esteem him stricken, smitten of God, and afflicted. But he was wounded for our transgressions, he was bruised for our iniquities: the chastisement of our peace was upon him; and with his stripes we are healed."
>
> ~ Isaiah 53:4-5

> "When the even was come, they brought unto him many that were possessed with devils: and he cast out the spirits with his word, and healed all that were sick: That it might be fulfilled which was spoken by Esaias the prophet, saying, Himself took our infirmities, and bare our sicknesses."
>
> ~ Matthew 8:16-17

> "Who his own self bare our sins in his own body on the tree, that we, being dead to sins, should live unto righteousness: by whose stripes ye were healed."
>
> ~ 1 Peter 2:24

The scriptures above tell us clearly that Jesus has already taken care of our healing. The New Testament scripture, **1 Peter 2:24,** uses the past tense verb "were" which clarifies the fact that it is already done. If it's already done, its already ours – we just have to claim it!

The Lord has given me revelations regarding our health and being healed and healed now; before we can see it or feel it. I have received miraculous wonderful healings in my own body on a number of occasions. Once I was healed instantly of a bleeding ulcer in my stomach. (The doctor searched for what had been found a week earlier but could not locate it... also told me that he did not believe in the miraculous). In 1999 I was healed of stroke level blood pressure. In 2011, I was healed of a condition causing me extreme pain in my core and groin area which prevented me from lifting my feet more than one inch above the ground without episodes of horrific pain. In 2015 I received healing from a spine injury that had been verified by x-ray from a doctor showing damage to the bottom four vertebrae causing the nerve endings to be exposed to the muscle. In each of these healings of health episodes I received a spoken word from God's mouth to my heart, through meditation on His word, believing it, and then speaking it to my condition. In the last instance, it came through an impartation of either the gift of healings, miracle or an impartation of the gift of faith, through my wife's anointing. Healing is your *coat* benefit that belongs to you NOW!

"I walk in His peace through His being chastised and have healing and divine health because of the stripes He received."
(Excerpt from "Of GOD, I Am," My personal meditation)

Again, the Lord has given me revelations regarding our being healed and healed now… before we can see it or feel it. In coming into healing or any other issue, a major thing to enact in our lives is to repent of any sin. Take note:

> "If my people, which are called by my name, shall humble themselves, and pray, and seek my face, and turn from their wicked ways; then will I hear from heaven, and will forgive their sin, and heal their land." ~ 2 Chronicles 7:14

Did you see the second to the last statement? It states… turn from their wicked ways… that means to repent and walk in obedience. In the case of my being healed of stroke-level blood pressure, I had to humble myself, forgive and then pray for the wellbeing of an individual who had wronged me.

The Absolute Need of Repentance in Our Healing Package

Repentance is major... *very* **major.** In **Hebrews 4:12** it states:

> "For the word of God is living and powerful, and sharper than any two-edged sword, piercing even to the division of soul and spirit, and of joints and marrow, and is a discerner of the thoughts and intents of the heart."
>
> ~ Hebrews 4:12 NKJV

Psalm 66:18 states that **if we regard iniquity in our heart, the Lord will not hear us.** Also, in **John 15:14, if you love the Lord, you obey the Lord** and from that, **John 15:15 tells us, Jesus reveals the things that His Father has revealed to Him, to us.**

> "God is not a man, that He should lie, Nor a son of man, that he should repent. Has he said, and will He not do? Or has He spoken, and will He not make it good?"
>
> ~ Numbers 23:19 NKJV

There are specific things that prevent God from answering your prayers; here are some of them: **unforgiveness, not being holy, ignorance, disunity, not tithing** and **not being diligently connected to your calling.**

Let's look at the first one, unforgiveness. In a model for prayer in **Mark 11:22-26**, the Lord makes it very clear if you do not forgive others, the Lord will not forgive you and He makes mention of this often. In **Matthew 18**, it talks about Peter coming to Jesus and asking Him how often should a brother sin against you and you must forgive him till seven times in a day? The Lord Jesus made it very clear, not seven times in a day but seven times seventy you must forgive! Forgiveness is critical if you want to be heard and responded to by God.

Another critical issue holding us back is sexual sin. You cannot be in sexual sin and expect God to answer your prayers. **1 Peter 1:15-16** states that

God is Holy, therefore we must be holy. Your body is the temple of the Holy Spirit, and the Lord states that we are not to be conformed to the world but have our mind renewed so that we may prove what is good, acceptable and the perfect will of God. Sexual sin such as fornication and adultery are the only sins that ties the body to the deed.

Next, unity as shown in **Psalms 133**, talks about how beautiful it is for brethren to dwell together in unity because whatever state of mind I'm in, that will reflect my behavior, for by my actions, my heart is revealed. Therefore, if I'm against a brother or a sister in the body of Christ, it's against Christ and is not unity! **Psalms 133** states when we are in unity then we can command the blessings of God into our situations. We can declare a thing because we agree with God Himself.

Next is the tithe, which is 10% of your gross earnings including any increase you receive. This is a real genuine issue in the Body of Christ as it relates to being obedient to God. The Lord says so clearly in **Malachi 3:8a**, "Will a man rob God?" The religious leaders responded to God, what do you mean? Hey, we're your special chosen ones, and we're good people! We're good people so how do we rob you? The Lord responded, "You rob me in not giving your tithes and offerings." He said repent, turn from this, because you are against the ordinances of God and the bottom line to the tithe is it's really a relationship issue with the Lord. The Lord says if you love me, you'll do what I tell you to do so that love causes you to obey. A tithe is 10% of your gross so if you made $100,000 this year, a tithe would be 10% of that or $10,000 that's the bottom line. Then the Lord says to give an offering also with the tithe. The offering is whatever you decide to give of your own free will, that's whatever is in your heart. Now let's get to that, your heart is whatever is in the center of your mind and the Lord loves a cheerful giver.

"But this I say: He who sows sparingly will also reap sparingly, and he who sows bountifully will also reap bountifully. So let each one

give as he purposes in his heart, not grudgingly or of necessity; for
God loves a cheerful giver." ~ 2 Corinthians 9:6-7 NKJV

We had one person that was in the church years ago and they heard from
God, but they did not tithe. They were very adamant about it and went so
far as to say that God had told them that they didn't have to tithe! My
wife asked, *Lord, Father, you told us that we had to tithe so why would
you tell the other individual that they did not have to?* The Lord's response
was, *I love a cheerful giver.* He went on to say that He told this person
that they did not have to tithe because they did not do so willingly. So, the
Lord's attitude is if you don't do it willingly, keep it. I gave an illustration
while giving a sermon one day; I asked my wife in front of the congregation
to give me a kiss, which she willingly did. I then said, give me a kiss very
grudgingly, and of course she wouldn't give it to me, nor did I want it. So,
it is with the Lord, He wants us to give willingly not grudgingly.

"If you are willing and obedient, You shall eat the good of the land;
But if you refuse and rebel, You shall be devoured by the sword;"
For the mouth of the LORD has spoken." ~ Isaiah 1:19-20 NKJV

The next point is diligence. We have talked about this before, but the
bottom line is **Hebrews 11:6**:

"...without faith it is impossible to please Him (God), for he who
comes to Him must believe that He is, and that He is a rewarder of
those who diligently seek Him."

~ Hebrews 11:6 NKJV, brackets added

The Lord wants us to be diligently connected to our calling.

Although there are other things aside from these, repentance that's talked
about in **2 Chronicles 7:14**, turn from their wicked ways, is me and you
repenting of our ways to come into God's ways. At this point, we agree
with God and the Lord says in **Amos 3:3**, two cannot walk together except

they be agreed; we must be on the same page with God and repentance is extremely vital and important! One last point in summary of hearing from God: in the beginning, Adam heard from God continually...until he disobeyed...disobedience cut off the hearing from God. Obedience, due to Jesus, cuts it back on. **Romans 5:19, "For as by one man's disobedience many were made sinners, so by the obedience of one shall many be made righteous"** (emphasis added).

TESTIMONIES OF HEALING

The Lord gave me an illustration relating to our meditating His word in the daytime which I understood, but I questioned how I would meditate in the night while asleep. He showed me this scripture:

> "He will not allow your foot to be moved; He who keeps you will not slumber. Behold, He who keeps Israel Shall neither slumber nor sleep."   ~ Psalm 121:3 NKJV

My wife was out of town ministering for a few days and had prepared my meals and had frozen them. When I got home late, as was my routine at that time, all I had to do was to thaw and warm them. On one specific day I had gotten home and placed the frozen dinner in the microwave to thaw. While this was happening, I drove to the gas station to fill-up, getting back home about 15 minutes later. The meal thawed in the microwave by the time I returned home leaving me to only warm it for a minute or two. The Lord said to me that while I was not consciously watching the food thawing in the microwave is the same process that occurs while I was away getting the gas for the car. He said that my spirit man is made in the similitude of His Spirit and does not sleep nor slumber but is always alert. He told me when I put scripture on my mind before going to sleep, those scriptures are *microwaved* by my spirit and served to my consciousness already warmed up... **"O taste and see that the LORD is good"** (Psalm

34:8, emphasis added). Please take note of the underlined boldened words as they give the way to healing.

The Benefits of Praying in Tongues as it Relates to Hearing from God and Healing

I have also learned through God's leading me by the Holy Ghost something that I had read many times in scripture as a major benefit to hearing from God. In **Romans 8:26-27** we are told that because of the iniquitous state of our minds we do not know what to pray for but as we pray in tongues, the Holy Spirit prays through us the perfect will of God! In **Isaiah 28:11-12,** the Lord instructs that with stammering lips and another tongue, He will speak to us. The verses go on to state that God will speak to us words that give us **"...rest wherewith ye may cause the weary to rest; and this is the refreshing..."** (Isaiah 28:12b, emphasis added). The first rest refers to the comfortable state of matrimony or marriage. The marriage of course is to the Lord; now that is comfort and security with peace of mind! The second rest means (to dwell, stay, let fall, place, let alone, withdraw, give comfort, etc.):—cease, be confederate, lay, let down, (be) quiet, remain....bottom-line cease all concerns from the status one has obtained. The last part of that scripture states that **"and this is the refreshing."** Refreshing means to come to rest **suddenly**. When Jesus spoke to the roaring seas "peace, be still," (Mark 4:39) the waves died down to calmness quickly. The **suddenness** came about from a far superior presence coming onto the scene.

After experiencing several miraculous healings, I was diagnosed with prostate cancer and scheduled for surgery in July of 2011. My mind stated that seeing that I know personally of healing through the stripes of Jesus and getting a personal word from the Lord I had absolutely no intention of going through with the surgery until the Lord spoke to me on that day to go through with it. I was ironing a shirt that morning and the Lord spoke to me through a song that I had not heard in maybe 20 years. The song was by the Winans', "Ain't no need in worrying what the night is going to bring, it'll be all over in the morning." In those words, the Lord told me that the night refers to darkness. Darkness was not the absence of sunlight but the absence of revelation from the *light of God*. Darkness references fear. Fear of what the surgery could bring, fear of what could happen in my body, fear of the interruption to my normal life and fear of the unknown. The morning represented the *light of God* which comes from His speaking direction, comfort, peace, and power. **Psalm 119:130, "The entrance of thy words giveth light, it giveth understanding unto the simple"** (emphasis added). I would soon find out what the Lord meant by light.

Successful Initial Results from Surgery

I was prepped for surgery and before I knew it, it was over. There I was in my hospital bed with reports from the doctor saying everything went great. I felt great; in fact, I was up very early walking down the hallway... maybe too early. I was released from the hospital went home once again in great shape! Praise the Lord! Ain't no need to worry what the night is going to bring; it'll be all over in the morning." Obviously, the morning had come, I felt great!

Two or three days after my hospital release, everything went south!

Suddenly I could not raise my feet 1/2 inch above the ground without horrendous pain! Not only was there pain... it was multiplied... and I couldn't walk! I could not raise my feet! My wife had to put me in a chair with wheels and roll me around the house. I was almost totally helpless. Did I say that there was pain? There was pain that the local drugstore pain medications did absolutely nothing to remedy. The pain got so bad that I had to go back to the hospital. I couldn't even make it down the three back steps because I could not change elevation levels due to something out of order in my groin area. After getting down the first step I had two steps to go that I could not navigate. She had to back the car into the backyard as close to the back steps as she could and have me fall over on her so she could carry me to the car. That is the way I experienced my first trip to emergency for re-hospitalization.

Once getting to the hospital, the nurses picked me up and placed me in a wheelchair. While I was hospitalized, I remember my surgeon bringing me into a room with three other surgeons. They thought I was unconscious under the anesthesia, but I was very much aware and awake. I kept my eyes closed and witnessed the conversation between the surgeons. My doctor said, "I've done this operation thousands of times, something went wrong and this man is in horrendous pain." At that point I asked, "So what did you do wrong?" Well at that juncture they got me out of that room very, very, quickly.

A couple days later I was released from the hospital with a walker and pain medication that was supposed to be extremely strong. It did nothing for the pain. Unfortunately, once home, there was no change. I was re-hospitalized again and finally after a few more days, released. The pain did not go away, and I could only be rolled around in a chair with wheels. I could not walk anywhere, nor could I go anywhere. Lord, Lord, Lord, what about, *It'll be all over in the morning?*

Through all this, the Lord kept me assured that *by His stripes, I was healed!* I agreed, kept my focus on His word and His presence. I went to church that first Sunday only to find out that was a big mistake. I almost passed out mounting the stairs… I counted each one… 7. I should have never entered the sanctuary with a walker not in the pain that I was in, plus I could do nothing… I could not walk well. I could not give my usual resounding, "Amen!" I couldn't bring a message, and in my mind, I was a very poor example of victory. At the end of the service, one of the deacons came to me and stated, "Pastor Lloyd, your job is to take care of us however, if you don't take care of yourself, how will you take care of us? Stay home and take care of yourself until you are better, so you can take care of us." This was wisdom and I followed his counsel. The next couple of Sundays I was at home meditating, mending, hearing the Lord clearly and healing.

Getting Out of the House to Reclaim My Life

Did I mention that I could not drive? Okay, I could not drive. Lord, Lord, Lord, when is the morning? Over the next couple of Sundays that I was at home, my wife would leave me in a chair at the table with my Bible and a writing pad and she would leave for services. I felt everything was on her... at least that is what the accuser whispered, and I had to shut the devil up! I had the best of times getting before the Lord in prayer, praise, worship, study, meditation while getting focused on hearing what the Lord was saying, and He did speak.

God's Confirmation at the Restaurant

My darling wife decided to get me back into a more normal scenery by taking me to a restaurant. I refused to have her pull up to the front entrance of the restaurant and let me out close to the front door. I had her park the car in the parking lot and go in and reserve a booth for us... after all, I am the man and I am not helpless (Just stupid, filled with pride and in need of a healthy portion of wisdom)! Let me stop right here for a meditation revelation. **"Pride goeth before destruction, and an haughty spirit before a fall" (Proverbs 16:18, emphasis added).**

DESTRUCTION: Now, let us pair that scripture, just like what is done in some restaurants; a drink is paired with a meal. Here is the scripture:

> "Who forgiveth all thine iniquities; who healeth all thy diseases; Who redeemeth thy life from destruction; who crowneth thee with lovingkindness and tender mercies."   ~ Psalm 103:3-4

Both words in **Proverbs 16:18** and **Psalm 103:4** have similar meanings. So simply put, my pride prolonged my illness, just as it does many others.

I was walking with the walker in pain, very slowly to the restaurant entrance. Once I got halfway to the door from the car, it began to rain. Now, of course I cannot rush as I was doing the best I could. Once getting into the restaurant and folding up the walker and putting it under the table, I could not order for about 20-30 minutes as I was in pain and totally exhausted.

An older couple came in probably in their 80's and they set to the right of where Pat and I were sitting. About a half-hour later the gentleman came over and spoke a word to Pat and I from the Lord. The word concerned growth and direction of the church. We had never seen him before and to our knowledge he had never seen us. His word was confirmation. We told him that we were pastors and he spoke well. This then was a confirmation we said. Indeed, it was. At that point, he laid hands on me and begin to pray and rebuke every negative report that came from the hands of doctors. I must add that he could not see the walker, nor had he seen me come in because we came in probably 30 to 45 minutes before he did. After that day I graduated from the walker to a cane. I went back to work. Walking was still a challenge and very painful. I needed to use the banisters when going upstairs to my office to lift myself to take any pressure off the groin area. However, *the morning had begun to dawn!*

A short time later while sitting upstairs at my desk in my home office, I remember the Lord telling me, *meditate* **1 Peter 2:24**. My response...*Father, I already know that scripture by heart,* and the Lord responded with, *You know the scripture intellectually, but it has not been revealed to you by my Spirit.* As I took the prescription from the Lord: *meditate 1 Peter 2:24:*

> "Who his own self bare our sins in his own body on the tree, that we, being dead to sins, should live unto righteousness: by whose stripes ye were healed."   ~ 1 Peter 2:24

I did so over the next four or five days, day and night. As I prayed in the spirit while doing so, the Lord spoke to me **suddenly**, *Seeing that you are dead to sins, you're dead to the penalty that came with them!* **Suddenly,** I saw a picture of Adam, before his sin and the fall, without any sickness, pain, and misery. **Suddenly,** I had understanding that sin is the support by which sickness, disease, etc. could lay upon, but without sin there was no support for it!

Let me put it this way… I just placed an ink pen on the desk in front of me and it lays there supported. As I remove the desk, the pen falls to the floor because it has no support.

The Lord showed me this: *seeing that you are dead to sins, you're dead to the penalty (support) that came with them.* I then spoke from the wisdom that derived from the understanding which was the fruit of the knowledge I had received from meditating the word as the Lord had instructed me to do. I spoke health and healing to my body and then moved as I could not do before. I did feel a small amount of discomfort, but nothing like the pain that had been in the past. I then spoke directly to the adversary, "You're a liar I have no pain because I was healed by the stripes of Jesus!" The minor discomfort **suddenly** disappeared… peace be still! *Ain't no need in worrying what the night is going to bring, it'll be all over in the morning.*

In **Proverbs 1:23**, the Lord tells us, as we repent, He pours His Spirit out upon us. His Spirit makes His word known unto us or understood. Many Christians quote, "by His stripes, I was healed," without getting any results; they need the understanding of the knowledge which only comes through the Spirit of God. **Joel 2:24-28** states how the Lord will pour His Spirit out upon all flesh in the last days… We are in them now! If you have not received the gift of the Holy Spirit with the evidence of speaking in tongues, I exhort you to ask the Lord to explain the gift to you and then ask Him if He wants you to benefit from receiving it.

Now, we are further told in **1 Corinthians 2:8-16, 1 Corinthians 14** and **Jude 1:17-20** that the Spirit of God will show us things that our eyes have not seen, nor ears heard and that have not entered our hearts. He states that we are to walk in love and to desire spiritual gifts; while letting us know that as one prays in tongues, they are praying the secrets of God but do not understand what's being prayed because they are speaking in *unknown tongues*. This is not different languages that can be interpreted by man as it happened on the day of Pentecost in Acts 2. However, at this point the Lord tells us in **1 Corinthians 14,** to ask Him to give us the interpretation of the secrets we are praying in the *unknown tongues* so that our intellect can receive understanding also. Often a fresh look at instructions cause a *eureka experience* of knowledge and understanding that comes as we suddenly see how something works that was not understood with the prior mind. We have been promised the mind of Christ and can have it for the asking.

CUTTING OFF STINKING THINKING

"For as he thinketh in his heart, so is he:"   ~ Proverbs 23:7a

"Death and life are in the power of the tongue: and they that love it shall eat the fruit thereof."   ~ Proverbs 18:21

In **Proverbs 4:20-24,** the Lord tells us to pay attention to His words and keep them in the midst of our hearts. They are not to depart from our eyes and we are to pay close attention to whatever God will speak out of those written words to our minds. The Lord then says that those spoken words are life to those that find them and health to their flesh. He finally tells us to get rid of a "froward" mouth and "perverse" lips are to be put far from us. The "froward" mouth is a mouth that is filled with distortion and crookedness, gossiping, causing division, confusion and distraction. Such a mouth will not conduct the thoughts nor intentions of the Lord. Next, "perverse" lips are those that are willfully determined or disposed to go counter to what is expected or desired; contrary. Therefore, God says that you **are** healed; perverse lips will say that you're not for a zillion different reasonings that are opposed to God. Stay away from those sorts of thoughts!

In **Luke 1**, Zacharias' negative speaking caused his speech to be cut off completely until he believed and acted in faith. The angel from the Lord appeared to him while he was executing his priestly office of burning incense and told him that his prayers had been heard and that he and his wife Elisabeth would have the child that he had been praying for. He responded with perverse lips in stating:

> "And Zacharias said unto the angel, Whereby shall I know this? for I am an old man, and my wife well stricken in years. And the angel answering said unto him, I am Gabriel, that stand in the presence of God; and am sent to speak unto thee, and to shew thee these glad tidings. And, behold, thou shalt be dumb, and not able to speak, until the day that these things shall be performed, because thou believest not my words, which shall be fulfilled in their season."
>
> ~ Luke 1:18-20

This is the epitome of *stinking thinking!*

In James 3 we learn more about our tongues that need control. In verse 3:

> "Behold, we put bits in the horses' mouths, that they may obey us; and we turn about their whole body. Behold also the ships, which though they be so great, and are driven of fierce winds, yet are they turned about with a very small helm, whithersoever the governor listeth. Even so the tongue is a little member, and boasteth great things. Behold, how great a matter a little fire kindleth! And the tongue is a fire, a world of iniquity: so is the tongue among our members, that it defileth the whole body, and setteth on fire the course of nature; and it is set on fire of hell. For every kind of beasts,

and of birds, and of serpents, and of things in the sea, is tamed, and hath been tamed of mankind: But the tongue can no man tame; it is an unruly evil, full of deadly poison." ~ James 3:3-8

This really puts much more emphasis on the need for the Holy Spirit to be given the rule of our natural tongues to God. I believe this had an impact on Paul as he states I thank my God that I pray in tongues more than ye all.

The two scriptures of **Proverbs 18:21** and **23:7a,** say it all...we are what we think and death and life, or the bad life or the good life are all in our mouths. What comes out of our mouths is really what we speak, or *prophesy* will happen in our lives. Those that speak *not well* will be not well, or sick. Those that speak well...will be.

The Necessity of Being on the Offense Regarding Success and Healing

The Lord tells us that it's necessary that offenses come (**Matthew 18:7** and **Luke 17:1**) however we are to deal with offence according to God's word and forgive whomever the offense came from. Therefore, offense has three critical areas:

1. The Lord says for us to forgive, (**Matthew 5:44-48** and **Matthew 18:21-35**)

2. The Lord says that because of offence many who are unforgiving become bitter which causes division in the Body of Christ.

3. In natural warfare it would be rather silly, even foolish if the enemy did not take shots at us or try to harm us. We need to understand that the enemy is not man but Satan and his demons. Therefore, the Lord says we are not ignorant of his devices. Satan will come after us and against us because the thief has come to steal, kill and destroy (**John 10:10**). Also, "for the accuser of our brethren is cast down,

which accused them before our God day and night." (**Revelation 12:10**) He is the author of every lie and a murderer; so why are we so troubled by someone coming against us with offence which is being directed by the enemy. We are not ignorant of the enemy's devices, or at least we shouldn't be. (**2 Corinthians 2:11**)

Now a perfect example of this is Joseph, Jacob's son in **Genesis 37-50**. Joseph had been beat up and thrown in the pit by his brothers, due to their jealousy and hatred of him. He was eventually sold off into slavery which ended up being an Egyptian slave. However, it states, "but God was with him." So, although he was sold into slavery and found himself on Potiphar's Plantation, God was with him in favor and Potiphar saw that he was blessed of God because of Joseph. He, therefore, placed Joseph in charge of his entire plantation and Joseph ran it because everything was in his hand. Now Potiphar's wife began to lust after Joseph while Potiphar was absent, and she came after him sexually and he denied her. She continued trying and she therefore lied and said Joseph tried to rape her. Of course, Potiphar placed Joseph in jail, but God was with Joseph and he ended up running the jail. As he was running the jail pharaoh's butler and baker fell out of favor with pharaoh and they were placed in the jail. Joseph noting their sadness, asked what the problem was. They both, the butler and baker told Joseph, of a dream that troubled them. Joseph went on by the favor of God and interpreted their dreams. For the butler, he told him that favor was going to bring him back into Pharaoh's service and things would go well with him. However, Joseph not having gotten over the offense of his brothers beating him up and throwing him in the pit and eventually selling him into slavery, told the butler when you come in to renewed favor with Pharaoh don't forget about me because I'm innocent. My brothers did me wrong and Mrs. Potiphar lied on me. The problem here is:

1. Joseph had not forgiven his brothers nor Mr. and Mrs. Potiphar. So, he was still living in the darkness of the offense.

2. Joseph was depending on man and not God...big problem!

Therefore, Joseph remained in jail for two full years, until he got over the offenses and forgave his brothers and the Potiphars. Once Joseph trusted completely in the Lord, God forgave him and gave Pharaoh two dreams that of course he could not interpret along with any of his counselors and officers. At that point, the Lord brought to the memory of the butler that there's a guy in jail by the name of Joseph who interprets dreams. Pharaoh had Joseph released from jail and Joseph interpreted the dreams and gave the wise counsel of God regarding what should be done because of the dreams. Pharaoh and his counselors and officers were so impressed with God's wisdom in Joseph regarding the actions to be taken per the two dreams' interpretation, that Pharaoh made Joseph the prime minister of Egypt!

God had known from the beginning of the offenses that would come against Joseph by men and had made the plan for Joseph to overcome them. Therefore, in spite of the offences Joseph took over the plantation and the prison and became prime minister of Egypt. From that status, Joseph helped the entire world and therefore had influence over the entire world. This was God's plan from the beginning; once forgiveness reigned in Joseph, Joseph reigned in Egypt. God uses our offences not to be stumbling blocks but stepping-stones for us as He did with Joseph. So, it is with us... offenses are stepping-stones not stumbling blocks as we forgive and do well to those that have offended us as God has directed.

"Ye have heard that it hath been said, Thou shalt love thy neighbour, and hate thine enemy. But I say unto you, Love your enemies, bless them that curse you, do good to them that hate you, and pray for them which despitefully use you, and persecute you; That ye may be the children of your Father which is in heaven: for he maketh his sun to rise on the evil and on the good, and sendeth rain on the just and on the unjust. For if ye love them which love you, what reward have ye? do not even the publicans the same? And if ye salute your brethren only, what do ye more than others? do not even the publicans so? Be ye therefore perfect, even as your Father which is in heaven is perfect." ~ Matthew 5:43-48

All things are possible as long as we believe!

Several years ago, in the post office we had a measurement for overnight first-class mail arriving at its destinations timely. The measurement was taken care of by an outside company that would place bundles of mail in the blue drop-off collection boxes every day. We call that seeded bundled mail. How it worked was like this, let's say you had 35 seeded pieces of mail in those bundles and that mail was going to various zip codes. This mail going to the particular zip codes was due to be delivered overnight. The destination end point of that mail would be "seeded mailer recipients" and they would report in that they had received the mail at a particular date to the off-site company that the post office had hired to do the measurement. Well, the goal in those days was to have 93% of the mail that was supposed to be overnight to arrive on time. These mailers would report how many pieces were missed in a particular bundle so if you had 35 pieces in a bundle that was dropped in the blue collection box and 35 made it then that would be 100%. However, if you had two pieces that missed that got there in two days or more then you would have 94.28%. If three pieces failed overnight delivery you would have 91.48%. The goal was **93.00%** and at the end of 9 months activity or three quarters of the year, we had arrived at 92.60. That was not good and there were seven districts in the Great Lakes Area. We were the only District that was failing. The seeding was done 6 days a week so if you had gone 9 months and you had a score of 92.60, you had basically 26 days each month. Look for the chart for chapter 10 with the given calculations at www.guardyourheart.life.

Row A was the accumulation for the entire year which gave us a **92.60%** which was failing. The four executives, of which I was one, were summoned to the area headquarters for a very serious meeting in which we were informed that it was the Area's total expectation that we would not fail! Each executive had to give their strategies for accomplishing the year end goal of **93.00%**. It was a very stressful meeting and as we were beginning to give our goals we were asked very harshly…"Show us your strategies to accomplish that which you've failed to do all year… or are you expecting divine intervention?!"

Row B shows an improvement for the month as compared to the months before, but we were still not meeting the goal of **93.00%**. We had already begun meeting with the top leadership in the district bi-weekly, going over every process, dotting I's and crossing t's. At the end of each meeting the Lord told me to assure our District manager and the top leadership that we were going to make it! That was very inspirational and gave much needed assurance to all.

Row C shows that we finally had surpassed the goal with a **93.35%**. However, this score was just for the month and still left us year to date with a failing score at only **92.695%** for the year.

We increased the intensity of our meetings with the top leadership in the district bi-weekly still going over every process and doting I's and crossing T's. At the end of each meeting the Lord told me to assure our District manager and the top leadership that we were going to make it! That was very inspirational and gave much needed assurance to all, but we would need almost a miracle turn around for the last month. The top leadership in the district were not very inspired and were rather downtrodden despite my confidence in the Lord. The last month's bi-weekly meetings were not good.

Row D shows greater improvement, but it was not enough. With two weeks to go, I showed the Lord that if we got a **100.00%** each of the remaining 12 days, we could not cross over the **93.00%** year to date goal... *So dear Lord, I must have missed it regarding your telling me to tell everyone in these bi-weekly meetings that we were going to make it.* The Lord responded with, *Say that you're going to make it.* I reasoned with the Lord... *Father, I know you know the math far better than myself, but even with a daily 100% we can't make it now...* the Lord said, *Say what I've told you to say and at each meeting.* I did as the Lord told me and each meeting became worse than the one before.

Row E shows the end of the year came and our final score was for the entire year was a **92.7625%**. Before that meeting began I was paid a visit by the manager over the East and West side of the city of Detroit that reported to myself and they congratulated me on my great faith in God and assured me that they had great respect and even love for myself and honored my leadership..."But boss, please do not say that we're going to make it. The other leaders in the district have come to us and told us that they think you're losing it with these proclamations of we're going to make it... the year is over, and we've failed!" I did not return a message to the two senior managers that reported to me, but they got the feeling that I had not changed. The Lord once again told me to repeat my message... *We made it,* at the end of the meeting. The district manager was so angry with me that he walked out of the conference room and slammed the door behind him. The rest of the top leaders in the district refused to speak to me nor make eye contact.

Approximately two weeks after that last meeting the top leaders in the district accompanied me and the District manager to a yearly Combined Federal Campaign to raise money for charities. The District Manager was the chairperson for the Combined Campaign of federal agencies and was making a speech at the podium when I received a pager notification. I went to the phone and called my secretary who went on to tell me that the company that did the seeding measurements for the postal service had sent out a notification stating that they had discovered an error in their seeding scores and had taken a specific seeding out of the prior year's scorings. The Detroit district's new score was a **93.14%** for the year... **we had made it, after all!**

So, my point in bringing up this issue is this: I heard the Lord say, *"Speak, we made it,"* although my intellectual mind could not comprehend, and it made no sense to me... I obeyed and spoke it by faith. My intellectual mind could not grasp it... bottom line, we made it. The Lord changes things as only He can do! This is all inclusive, which of course is referring to your health and healing also!

SPIRITUAL INVENTORY

Give at least 3 scriptures the Lord has given you from which you have received revelation secrets. . . "God's sayings." List your revelation also.

_____

_____

_____

_____

_____

_____

_____

SECTION V

←——→

EDUCATIONAL PREPARATION

Acquired learning to meet and contribute to the spiritual, social and economic environment that you are a part of.

TRANSFORMING CHARACTERISTIC
~ TEMPERANCE ~

Walking confidently in God's presence through pleasant or adverse environments.

KINGDOM BENCHMARK
~ CHARACTER ~

Effective two-way communication with God with discipline manifesting multiplied results.

11

PURSUIT OF EDUCATION

G od has a definite plan for each of us to get educated in schools, in the trades, by experiences, professions and talents. The purpose for us becoming educated in various areas is so that we can not only benefit society, but more importantly, the kingdom of God, as worthy examples to be looked to by all.

The following are just a few examples of people God used mightily to bring His will to pass in the earth:

- Moses had to be trained and educated in governing. He had the responsibility of leading over 3 million people for 40 years.

- Abraham had become trained and educated in accounting, governing, cattle and sheep herding, along with management of land cultivation.

- Joseph had also become trained and educated in accounting, governing, cattle and sheep herding, along with land cultivation.

- Paul was in government via the Temple and was a tent maker by trade.

- Jesus, who is King of kings and Lord of lords in the kingdom of God, was trained and educated as a carpenter by His earthly father.

OVERVIEW OF EDUCATIONAL PREPARATION

In this chapter education is defined as:

1. the act or process of imparting or acquiring general knowledge, developing the powers of reasoning and judgment, and generally of preparing oneself or others intellectually for mature life.[1]

2. the act or process of imparting or acquiring knowledge or skills, as for a profession.[2]

3. a degree, level, or kind of schooling:[3]

4. the result produced by instruction, training, or study[4]

Instruction, schooling, learning. EDUCATION and TRAINING imply a discipline and development by means of study and learning. EDUCATION is the development of the abilities of the mind (learning to know): *a liberal education*.[5] TRAINING is practical education (learning to do) or practice, usually under supervision, in some art, trade, or profession: *training in art, teacher training*.[6]

EDUCATION and CULTURE are often used interchangeably to mean the results of schooling. EDUCATION, however, suggests chiefly the information acquired. CULTURE is a mode of thought and feeling encouraged by education. It suggests an aspiration toward, and an appreciation of high intellectual and esthetic ideals:[7] *The level of culture in a country depends upon the education of its people.*

In short, to educate, means to bring to the light.

"The entrance of Your words gives light; It gives understanding to the simple."   ~ Psalm 119:130

"For we did not follow cunningly devised fables when we made known to you the power and coming of our Lord Jesus Christ but were eyewitnesses of His majesty. For He received from God the Father honor and glory when such a voice came to Him from the Excellent Glory: "This is My beloved Son, in whom I am well pleased." And we heard this voice which came from heaven when we were with Him on the holy mountain. And so we have the prophetic word confirmed, which you do well to heed as a light that shines in a dark place, until the day dawns and the morning star rises in your hearts; knowing this first, that no prophecy of Scripture is of any private interpretation, for prophecy never came by the will of man, but holy men of God spoke as they were moved by the Holy Spirit." ~ 2 Peter 1:16-21 NKJV

In the scriptures we find that people who God used to perform mighty acts were very proficient in specific areas of "natural work experiences." Remember, man was told by God that he would have to earn his living by the sweat of his brow because of the fall of Adam. There are scriptures pertaining to how God blesses the wise in understanding, while causing their natural work to prosper and provide for them. (See the 9 scriptures given for Educational Preparation in the Issues of Life Tool # 4.)

Take note of the reference in the scriptures: **Jeremiah 29:11** says: **"For I know the thoughts that I think toward you, saith the LORD, thoughts of peace, and not of evil, to give you an expected end"** (emphasis added). We see that in Jeremiah the Lord speaks very specifically that He has a specific *end in mind for all of us.*

"Brothers and sisters, in the name of our Lord Jesus Christ we order you not to associate with any believer who doesn't live a disciplined life and doesn't follow the tradition you received from us. You know what you must do to imitate us. We lived a disciplined life among you. We didn't eat anyone's food without paying for it. Instead, we worked hard and struggled night and day in order not to be a burden to any of you. It's not as though we didn't have a right to receive support. Rather, we wanted to set an example for you to follow. While we were with you, we gave you the order: "Whoever doesn't want to work shouldn't be allowed to eat." We hear that some of you are not living disciplined lives. You're not working, so you go around interfering in other people's lives. We order and encourage such people by the Lord Jesus Christ to pay attention to their own work so they can support themselves. Brothers and sisters, we can't allow ourselves to get tired of doing what is right. It may be that some people will not listen to what we say in this letter. Take note of them and don't associate with them so that they will feel ashamed. Yet, don't treat them like enemies, but instruct them like brothers and sisters."   ~ 2 Thessalonians 3:6-15

In **Thessalonians 3,** it is made very clear that we are not to be *busy bodies,* instead we should work and add value. When I worked in the Postal Service as the Postmaster of Detroit and in other like positions I made a point of assuring that my managers and postmasters were proficient in math, oral and written communication skills (they had to know the difference between to, too and two along with there, their and they're, no and know as an example) and were thoroughly knowledgeable of contractual issues and their execution along with professional social etiquette.

Spiritual Education Development: <u>History in the USA</u>

EDUCATION SUGGESTS chiefly the information acquired. CULTURE is a mode of thought and feeling encouraged by education.

Now, let's define **development: the act or process of developing;** growth; progress: expansion, elaboration, growth, evolution; unfolding, opening, maturing, maturation.[8]

A very interesting fact and important to note is that this country's first university, Harvard, was established to assure that ministers of the gospel be raised up and educated to propagate the spreading of the truth to the country and world. Therefore, regarding educational preparation the origins of Harvard Divinity School and the study of theology can be traced back to the very beginning of Harvard College, when an initial fund of 400 pounds from the General Court of Massachusetts Bay Colony established the College in 1636. The founders of Harvard recorded their reasons for establishing this center of learning: "After God had carried us safe to New England and we had builded our houses, provided necessaries for our livelihood, reared convenient places for God's worship, and settled the civil government: One of the next things we longed for and looked after was to advance learning and perpetuate it to posterity; dreading to leave an illiterate ministry to the churches, when our present ministers shall lie in the dust." [9]

Because of the founders' desire to perpetuate a learned ministry, preparation for religious learning and leadership continued to hold a position of importance as Harvard grew. Harvard Divinity School itself was established to ensure that "every encouragement be given to the serious, impartial, and unbiased investigation of Christian truth." The Divinity School was the first nonsectarian theological school in the United States.

Becoming Established in the Faith
Leads to Prosperity

"So they rose early in the morning and went out into the Wilderness of Tekoa; and as they went out, Jehoshaphat stood and said, "Hear me, O Judah and you inhabitants of Jerusalem: Believe in the LORD your God, **and you shall be established**; believe His prophets, and you shall prosper."   ~ 2 Chronicles 20:20, emphasis added

"You prepare a table before me in the presence of my enemies; You anoint my head with oil; **My cup runs over.**"

~ Psalm 23:5, emphasis added

149

Everyone that I have met in my life, as far as I can recollect, had the desire to prosper. The definition of *prosper* is **to be successful or fortunate, especially in financial respects; thrive; flourish;** it means **to make successful or fortunate.** Its root comes from being made happy. The causative factor of prosperity is skillful and prudent understanding (Prudent = careful in providing for the future).

Satan's plan is to prevent you from becoming educationally prepared so that he can steal, kill and destroy. This is to get you to sidestep Jesus' plan for you to have life and have it in abundance. However, the Lord has provided His blueprint for building our prosperity. In **Psalm 23:5,** David's cup ran over; it could not *run over* if it were filled with holes or not established. So, it is with us in things concerning spiritual matters.

In chapter 10, I introduced the 9 foundation stones that cause us to become ***established in the faith,*** that would then provide a person with a cup without holes so that it can *run over* with God's blessings. The holes represent a person not having the knowledge and experience of a foundational stone's benefit in their life. David stated in **Psalm 23** that his *cup runs over.* Otherwise, a person would be able to maintain the blessings of God flowing into their life without them leaking out because their life is structurally sound or established. If you are not **established in the full truth** of believing in God, you will not prosper! Look at the 3 cups

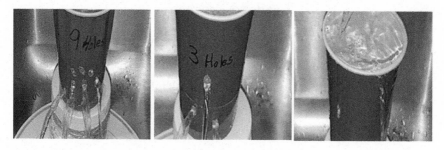

pictured. The first cup has 9 holes, the second has 3 and the last has no holes (it's established; therefore, it can be filled so that it can *run over*).

Along with the 9 foundation stones, there are 9 Christ characteristics that pair-up to *establish our cups within us*, enabling us then to run over in the *abundant life* of Christ which is His prosperity.

> "Beloved, it is my wish above all things that you may prosper and be in health, even as your soul prospers." ~ 3 John 1:2

Our Blueprint to Follow Diligence, Faith & Virtue

Everything that is built must come from a design. Every vehicle, home, building, article of clothing, shoes and even the toothbrush that we use, all have intricate, and exact designs that they are created from. The victorious life that has been made available to us in Christ Jesus promotes our self-esteem to Christ-esteem, turns ignorance of direction in life, to hearing direction from God and promote us to effective prayer. This is opposed to dejection, gloominess and being melancholy. All these life characteristic outcomes are what Jesus came to give us in the "**abundant life**" that He spoke of in **John 10:10**. Jesus tells us:

> "The thief does not come except to steal, and to kill, and to destroy. I have come that they may have life, and that they may have it more abundantly." ~ John 10:10 NKJV

Note the scriptural reference below that drives the transformation.

> "And beside this, **giving all diligence**, add to your faith virtue;" ~ 2 Peter 1:5, emphasis added

The Lord underlines that the first characteristic to begin the kingdom of God results in our lives is DILIGENCE... in fact the scripture states... "**giving all diligence**." Jesus spoke in **Mark 4:30-32** and **Matthew 17:20** and **John 8:31-32** of the necessity and power of **diligence**.

> "And he said, Whereunto shall we liken the kingdom of God? or with what comparison shall we compare it? It is like a grain of

mustard seed, which, when it is sown in the earth, is less than all the seeds that be in the earth: But when it is sown, it groweth up, and becometh greater than all herbs, and shooteth out great branches; so that the fowls of the air may lodge under the shadow of it."   ~ Mark 4:30-32

"And Jesus said unto them, Because of your unbelief: for verily I say unto you, If ye have faith as a grain of mustard seed, ye shall say unto this mountain, Remove hence to yonder place; and it shall remove; and nothing shall be impossible unto you."
                                                         ~ Matthew 17:20

"Then said Jesus to those Jews which believed on him, If ye continue in my word, then are ye my disciples indeed; And ye shall know the truth, and the truth shall make you free."   ~ John 8:31-32

These scriptures point out that in the Kingdom of God there is DILIGENCE of character and for us to get said results we must be diligent... continuous, focused, having a manifestation of character of not giving up or quitting! This is why we have prepared classes to educate people in the disciplines that will produce DILIGENCE in the *How to go Through Tribulation Victoriously* (HTGTTV) course that is available on the website www.guardyourheart.life. DILIGENCE of character gets you God's results in your life.

"And beside this, giving all diligence, add to your faith virtue;"
                                                ~ 2 Peter 1:5, emphasis added

Next, diligence is added to faith. Bottom line... "Faith comes from hearing and hearing by the word of God" (**Romans 10:17**). We must hear, in our spirit, the voice of God! We must do more than read it... more than hear the minister exhort on it... more than hear the DVD or CD teaching on it, and more than hear someone else's testimony regarding the great move of God in their lives! You must give the prioritization and time to God to meditate day and night on what His word says, focus, concentrate, repeat it and think on it while asking God what it IS He is saying to YOU!

"And beside this, giving all diligence, add to your faith virtue;"
~ 2 Peter 1:5, emphasis added

VIRTUE means excellence. How have you applied yourself to your studies, reading, seeking God, while meditating His word? It is looking up words that you are not aware of, reading some of the resources listed, calling other believers and comparing notes… come on already… what you sow, you will reap! What is it that you really want to get from the Almighty, who happens to be your Heavenly Father?

Our Enabling Power, Knowledge, Temperance, and Patience

"…and to virtue knowledge; And to knowledge temperance; and to temperance patience; and to patience godliness;"
~ 2 Peter 1:5b-6, emphasis added

I have found through seeking the Lord and praying in the spirit that in *2 Peter 1*, there are two different word meanings for the word KNOWLEDGE. In verse 2 it's listed twice, once in verse 3, once in verses 5 and 6, and once in verse 8. However, in all the verses except 5 and 6, its meaning is to have information or recognition. In verses 5 and 6, its meaning broadens to "certify, declare, give to understand and has its meaning ratcheted up to receiving secrets and revelation from God." The Lord spoke the following regarding the different levels of knowledge:

From having *knowledge* in the desert of the need for water when one is thirsty, to the *hope* when water is seen, to the *experience & benefit* of drinking it!

KNOWLEDGE in verses 5 and 6 come in alignment with **graduating from the knowledge** that there are benefits in the Kingdom of God **to the experience** of having them. It's a far better reality to receiving healing than knowing that it exists.

TEMPERANCE is self-control. When speaking of this it means through the power of God you can get mad and not lose control by cursing or hitting someone. You can be lied on and not end up disliking the person. The Lord speaks in **1 Corinthians 14:40**, "Let all things be done decently and in order." He causes and empowers this to come off the page of the Bible into **reality** in our daily lives... now this gives Kingdom results!

PATIENCE is the strength to be calm in the storm. The reason we can be calm is because we've received assurance from God by revelation knowledge, experience and confidence that all is and will be well. Note the references below:

> "And when the servant of the man of God was risen early, and gone forth, behold, an host compassed the city both with horses and chariots. And his servant said unto him, Alas, my master! how shall we do? And he answered, Fear not: for they that be with us are more than they that be with them. And Elisha prayed, and said, LORD, I pray thee, open his eyes, that he may see. And the LORD opened the eyes of the young man; and he saw: and, behold, the mountain was full of horses and chariots of fire round about Elisha."
>
> ~ 2 Kings 6:15-17

> "And when neither sun nor stars in many days appeared, and no small tempest lay on us, all hope that we should be saved was then taken away. But after long abstinence Paul stood forth in the midst of them, and said, Sirs, ye should have hearkened unto me, and not have loosed from Crete, and to have gained this harm and loss. And now I exhort you to be of good cheer: for there shall be no loss of any man's life among you, but of the ship. For there stood by me

this night the angel of God, whose I am, and whom I serve, Saying, Fear not, Paul; thou must be brought before Caesar: and, lo, God hath given thee all them that sail with thee. Wherefore, sirs, be of good cheer: for I believe God, that it shall be even as it was told me."   ~ Acts 27:20-25

God's Results in Us (His Kingdom Come), Godliness, Brotherly Kindness & Charity

I foresee God's results as an outcome of our being formed in the character of Christ. It states in **Amos 3:3**, "Can two walk together, except they be agreed?" Again, as I have sought the Lord diligently and in the spirit; He has revealed to me that the scripture does not say, *can two walk together except they agree*. Rather, it states clearly, *"except they be agreed!"* There is a huge difference between the two words of **agree** and **agreed**! Agree means to have a mutual mental assent to do. AGREED means to have **become by action** and transformation to not only the same mental assent but having done what was agreed to… **to have become it**.

The character of Jesus is found in the 9 Christ characteristics. We find that in part of His nature, **He is diligent, faithful, with excellence of revelation knowledge, self-controlled, patient, Godly (Holy), with extreme kindness in LOVE.** As we become transformed by His Spirit and our obedience, we walk with Him and become yoked together… AGREED!

Therefore, the character of **Godliness (Holiness)** means to **demonstrate character as one is consecrated to God** and His purposes through His revealed will. Well, Jesus is all of that. As we become the same, we put

155

away lying, unforgiveness, fornication, adultery, stealing, jealousy, not tithing, disobedience, while adding diligence, revelation knowledge, power, self-control and patience.

Next, **BROTHERLY-KINDNESS** has been displayed as Jesus continuously walked in compassion as He traversed the earth.

> "And Jesus went forth, and saw a great multitude, and was moved with compassion toward them, and he healed their sick."
>
> ~ Matthew 14:14

> "And Jesus, moved with compassion, put forth his hand, and touched him, and saith unto him, I will; be thou clean."
>
> ~ Mark 1:41

Through the ability we have received from Jesus by the power of the Holy Spirit we can do as He did.

Lastly, **CHARITY** which is the nature of the highest love or Agape, which is the love of God or Christ for humankind. It is the love of Christians for other persons, corresponding to the love of God for humankind. It is the unselfish love of one person for another without sexual implications; brotherly love. This love can be summed up with only one scriptural reference:

> "For God so loved the world, that he gave his only begotten Son, that whosoever believeth in him should not perish, but have everlasting life." ~ John 3:15

As we end this portion focusing on getting established, let's look at the scriptural information given after these Christ characteristics:

> "For if these things be in you, and abound, they make you that ye shall neither be barren nor unfruitful in the knowledge of our Lord Jesus Christ. But he that lacketh these things is blind, and cannot

see afar off, and hath forgotten that he was purged from his old sins. Wherefore the rather, brethren, give diligence to make your calling and election sure: for if ye do these things, ye shall never fall: For so an entrance shall be ministered unto you abundantly into the everlasting kingdom of our Lord and Saviour Jesus Christ. Wherefore I will not be negligent to put you always in remembrance of these things, though ye know them, and be established in the present truth." ~ 2 Peter 1:8-12

There are 7 things I would like to draw your attention to:

1. if these things be in you, and abound

2. make you that ye shall neither be barren nor unfruitful in the knowledge of our Lord Jesus Christ

3. if ye do these things, ye shall never fall:

4. brethren, give diligence to make your calling and election sure

5. so an entrance shall be ministered unto you abundantly into the everlasting kingdom of our Lord and Saviour Jesus Christ.

6. put you always in remembrance of these things

7. and be established in the present truth.

Please see the chart showing the 9 Foundation Stones, 9 Christ Characteristics, 9 Issues of Life and the 9 points of the *Of God, I am Meditation*, on the website of www.guardyourheart.life.

NATURAL EDUCATIONAL DEVELOPMENT

The importance of education in getting a good job is critical! Education is a major criterion on a job application because it tells the employer your level of training, your level of skills (discipline, focus, maturity of character and diligence) and it also impacts quite often your pay rate. The world has become more advanced in technology therefore, we must increase our educational level, so that our skills match the need and advancement. Also, what you sow is what you reap; so, the more you put into education equates to the more you get out of it in benefits and the less you put into it is the less you get out of it in your results in life. Therefore, the more you put into it the greater your pay will be and benefit package and the greater your satisfaction. Everything is advancing, cell phones, TVs, computers, medicine, automobiles, services, delivery companies and retail outlets. Everything is on the move forward with greater results being expected and received. No one can get what tomorrow requires via the rapid advancements that are fueled by greater and more extensive education requirements by staying where the needs were yesterday. If one continues to learn they continue to grow.

In many promotion packages there will be the question of what organizations away from the job you belong to and what leadership role(s) you have been a part of. The purpose is to see what you have displayed and accomplished outside the job as an indicator of what value you will add in the new assignment that you're striving for. There is also the search for what advancements and improvements you have sponsored in other venues as they determine what you'll do in the one you're striving to attain. Education is a major indicator as to what you have been willing to invest in yourself. What you've self-invested is what you'll invest in the company you're seeking to be hired into or promoted upward in. I always told my employees that the only thing constant is change; we must educate ourselves to move with the change. The Lord is forever progressing toward His original intent in mankind for us to be fruitful, multiply, replenish the earth and have dominion over all things. He therefore is constantly calling us to come into greater light by faith through love to advance toward His **"higher calling in Christ Jesus."**

Around 2005, there was a teenage young lady that was struggling to advance, her average grades (C to C+), and in the middle of my message that Sunday morning, the Lord had me to pause and call her out by name and inform her that she would obtain above a 4.00 (A+) grade point average in that present year. She was shocked in hearing that message, as were her parents, the congregation and I must admit, myself also. At the year's end she obtained a 4.16 grade point average. She had never done so well before. The Lord states in **Deuteronomy 28:13:**

> "And the LORD will make you the head and not the tail; you shall be above only, and not be beneath, if you heed the commandments of the LORD your God, which I command you today, and are careful to observe them."   ~ Deuteronomy 28:13 NKJV

Also, in **3 John 1:2**, "Beloved, I pray that you may prosper in all things and be in health, just as your soul prospers" (NKJV).

When God says we are to be the "head and not the tail," He is not referring to church services or ministry only. When He states that, it is His desire that we prosper in all things and be in health according to how we think in our minds. Again, He's not referring to church services nor ministries alone, but in everything we do in life inclusive of the education we obtain that drives the accomplishments in our lives.

> "Therefore David inquired of the LORD, and He said, "You shall not go up; circle around behind them, and come upon them in front of the mulberry trees. And it shall be, when you hear the sound of marching in the tops of the mulberry trees, then you shall advance quickly. For then the LORD will go out before you to strike the camp of the Philistines." And David did so, as the LORD commanded him; and he drove back the Philistines from Geba as far as Gezer."   ~ 2 Samuel 5:23-25

In those days before David went into warfare, as the scripture points out above, the Lord would move by His Spirit and they would listen for the rumbling in the tops of the mulberry trees to know when to move into battle. Can you hear the moving of the mulberry's branches? God's move is to be in our individual and corporate lives to advance, to meditate and study His word, move into the deeper things of the Spirit of God, to desire spiritual gifts but rather that we prophesy (**1 Corinthians 14:1**).

The Spiritual and Natural Legacy We Invest and Multiply Towards our Future Generations

I was one of the first in my immediately family to receive a four-year college degree and then continue advanced studies in Postal management to go into an executive position. My wife received a four-year degree in speech pathology and then went on to receive a master's in counseling. We both have continued studies in the ministerial field in marriage counseling and other ministerial disciplines while pastoring a church and providing advanced teaching in the **supernatural** elements of the Kingdom of God (we're seeing the miraculous manifest in services and meetings).

Our daughter has received a bachelor's degree in computer science with math as her major. She went on to take her master's in teaching instruction and strategies, is presently an assistant principal in high school after finishing courses in educational administration. She's the acting Superintendent of her school district. She also has received a license in real estate and has several entrepreneurial businesses. Our son-in law has a master's degree in engineering, a second MBA in business administration, while being in an executive position in a top 100 corporation and has begun a business in producing and sponsoring Christian musical artists. Our son has taken business classes and started a trucking company. We have four grandchildren, and all are doing extremely well in school, one has a bachelor's degree in engineering and math with a 3.70 GPA with two total scholarships, one for academics and the other for volleyball, three others have 3.70 and 4.0+ GPA's in high school. All have accepted the Lord Jesus Christ as their Savior and are advancing in the Kingdom.

Education, spiritual and natural, is a topic that is discussed at the dinner table, with visits to our home, pleasure excursions that the family takes and is a normal expectation of our family values. At present, there is one joint family corporation and it is growing. "A good man leaves an inheritance to his children's children, But the wealth of the sinner is stored up for the righteous" **(Proverbs 13:22)**.

> "Now this is the commandment, and these are the statutes and judgments which the LORD your God has commanded to teach you, that you may observe them in the land which you are crossing over to possess, that you may fear the LORD your God, to keep all His statutes and His commandments which I command you, you and your son and your grandson, all the days of your life, and that your days may be prolonged. Therefore hear, O Israel, and be careful to observe it, that it may be well with you, and that you may multiply greatly as the LORD God of your fathers has promised you—'a land flowing with milk and honey.' "Hear, O Israel: The LORD our God, the LORD is one! You shall love the LORD your God with all your heart, with all your soul, and with all your strength. "And these words which I command you today shall be in your heart. You shall teach them diligently to your children and shall talk of them when you sit in your house, when you walk by the way, when you lie down, and when you rise up. You shall bind them as a sign on your hand, and they shall be as frontlets between your eyes. You shall write them on the doorposts of your house and on your gates." ~ Deuteronomy 6:1-9

The Lord has a full expectation from each of us that we are to lead the way for our children and future generations… a major portion of our leading the way is in education both spiritually and naturally: "Train up a child in the way he should go and when he is old, he shall not depart from it" **(Proverbs 22:6)**.

SPIRITUAL INVENTORY

Give at least 3 scriptures the Lord has given you from which you have received revelation secrets. . . "God's sayings." List your revelation also.

_____

_____

_____

_____

_____

_____

_____

_____

_____

_____

_____

_____

_____

_____

SECTION VI

←——————→

VOCATIONS

There are two vocations that pertain to each individual.
The first refers to being effectively connected in your
position in Christ's Body. The other is where you
earn a living.

TRANSFORMING CHARACTERISTIC
~ PATIENCE ~

Hearing, trusting, and believing God while continuing to
follow Him and expecting His results.

KINGDOM BENCHMARKS
~ CALLING & ELECTION ~

Calling is the invitation of God to you to take your
assignment plan. Election is your becoming qualified
for this position.

12

VOCATION IN THE
BODY OF CHRIST

E ach person that has received salvation and been engrafted into the kingdom of God has been given a vocation in the Body of Christ by God our Father.

In **Jeremiah 29:11** the Lord tells us that He has an expected end for each of us. We have been called by God for a specific purpose. A calling is the invitation of God to you to take your assignment plan.

We have to be patient when it comes to our calling and expected end. The transforming characteristic relating to our spiritual call is patience. We have to hear, trust and believe God while continuing to follow Him and expect His results.

So, the question you have to ask yourself is, "Am I connected with God in my purpose in life and am I making advancements?" There are three specific steps that we must take to find vocational prosperity.

PUT GOD FIRST

You must put God first. You do this by placing Him in the number one spot in your life. You have to love Him and build your calendar around

Him in your time, tithes, offering and energy.

"But seek ye first the kingdom of God, and his righteousness; and all these things shall be added unto you." ~ Matthew 6:33

"And thou shalt love the Lord thy God with all thy heart, and all thy soul, and with all thy mind, and with all thy strength: this is the first commandment." ~ Mark 12:30

GET EQUIPPED

Secondly, you must get spiritually equipped. If you are not a part of a good Bible teaching church, you are in the wrong place. You must be attached to a good Bible teaching church that not only **talks** the word but **walks** it as well. This is important because you must submit yourself to the Pastor and leadership of the church. This is the order of God and He has given specific anointing for your equipping. If you are not currently attached to a local congregation, pray and ask God where He will have you to go to receive what He has already planned for you.

"And he gave some, apostles; and some, prophets; and some, evangelists; and some, pastors and teachers; For the perfecting of the saints, for the work of the ministry, for the edifying of the body of Christ:" ~ Ephesians 4:11-12

FIND YOUR POSITION

One of the best ways to find your position in the Body of Christ is to volunteer! Yes, volunteer. Every church has a variety of ministries. Each ministry of the church is considered a ministry of helps and most positions, if not all, are unpaid. So, when we join any of these ministries, we are actually volunteering our time to the Kingdom, volunteering our time to God. As we do this, we will be drawn to certain positions and the Lord will begin to draw us where He wants us. When this happens, you should learn the position, be faithful in it, and labor to bear fruit and help win souls.

> "Till we all come in the unity of the faith, and of the knowledge of the Son of God, unto a perfect man, unto the measure of the stature of the fullness of Christ: That we henceforth be no more children, tossed to and fro, and carried about with every wind of doctrine, by the sleight of men, and cunning craftiness, whereby they lie in wait to deceive; But speaking the truth in love, may grow up into him in all things, which is the head, even Christ: From whom the whole body fitly joined together and compacted by that which every joint supplieth, according to the effectual working in the measure of every part, maketh increase of the body unto the edifying of itself in love."
>
> ~ Ephesians 4:13-16

> "Ye have not chosen me, but I have chosen you, and ordained you, that ye should go and bring forth fruit, and that your fruit should remain: that whatsoever ye shall ask of the Father in my name, he may give it you." ~ John 15:16

How are Callings, Vocations or Elections Related?

Calling: The invitation of God to a select position of service in the body of Christ.

Vocation: This word has the same meaning as Calling.

Election: the *(divine)* selection of God. This comes after you have proven yourself to be diligent and faithful while it causes a godly anointing upon you in the specific endeavor that spills over in other activities in your life.

> Romans 11:29 For the gifts and calling of God are without repentance." ~ Romans 11:29

> "Let every man abide in the same calling wherein he was called."
>
> ~ 1 Corinthians 7:20

In the two scriptures above, we see that all those who have come into salvation have received an assignment and gifts in the assignment, once they adhere to it. Jeremiah was told by the Lord:

> "Then the word of the LORD came to me, saying: "Before I formed you in the womb I knew you; Before you were born I sanctified you; I ordained you a prophet to the nations."   ~ Jeremiah 1:4-5

What we need to learn from this is that God has already planned our life's calling and vocation before we were birthed from our mother's womb. In verse 6, Jeremiah spoke from a lowered self-esteem based on what he saw in his own abilities saying, "Then said I: 'Ah, Lord GOD! Behold, I cannot speak, for I am a youth'" (Jeremiah 1:6). The Lord went on to correct him in verse 7 by telling him not to say what he thought of himself, but instead told him that his destiny was to go where He, God, would send him and to say whatever he was given to say. He was further told not to be afraid of men's faces because He, God, would be with him to deliver him and then God touched His mouth, which means Jeremiah was empowered through the anointing of God to do the things he was about to be told. The greatest thing for Jeremiah and **YOU** was the next statement and action of God: **"Behold, I have put My words in your mouth"** (Jeremiah 1:9b, emphasis added). He was told that he had been placed over the nations and kingdoms, "...to root out, and to pull down, and to destroy, and to throw down, to build, and to plant" (Jeremiah 1:10b).

Progressive Development to One's Calling

Take note of the progressive stages below. Everyone is given *called to giftings* of the Lord. In the parable that follows, the Lord gave *talents*:

> "For the kingdom of heaven is like a man traveling to a far country, who called his own servants and delivered his goods to them. And to one he gave five talents, to another two, and to another one, to

each according to his own ability; and immediately he went on a journey."   ~ Matthew 25:14-15

We must, however, diligently apply those *giftings* by doing just as the good servant who had received 5 talents in verse 16, "Then he who had received the five talents went and **traded with them**, and made another five talents" **(Matt.25:16, emphasis added)**. **Traded with them** means he went and obtained natural education, be it in college, other courses of higher learning or some skilled trade avenue. The bottom line is, just as with the good servant, we must also add skills, exercises, etc. to that which the Lord has given us from the outset, in order to convert it to Kingdom use. If you added a skill to yourself–that's good, but if it does not convert to *kingdom currency*, it's a waste and a dead work.

The Preparation: Before we were formed in the womb, God already had determined what our skill sets would be and what purpose they would be used for. "Before I formed you in the womb I knew you" **(Jer.1:5a)**. Also see **Ephesians 1:5 & 11**.

The Calling (Invitation and Introduction): As a little boy, I was delighted in organization. I remember being in the bathroom for probably an hour to an hour-and-a-half planning the planting and growing of my spring garden. My mother came storming in, her patience having run out plus needing to use the lavatory herself. I had sheets of 8 ½" x 11" paper all over the bathroom floor, bathtub, sink, etc. Mom quickly dealt with my private office bathroom conversion plan. I was filled with a drive to organize because I had a natural penchant, a natural calling to organize things that would grow and produce results; in this case it was vegetables and fruit even as a little boy.

The Exercising: As I grew older, in college, my field of interest was education, so I took a degree in education via teaching. It is necessary for us to add natural learnings to enhance the things given us in the spirit.

Examples in the scriptures are Moses, Abraham and Joseph, just to name a few, who added accounting, agricultural expertise, animal breeding and care, business education, principals of warfare and governing to utilize God's spiritual giftings. In my position as a letter carrier I began developmental training for the new carriers. I'd had a bad experience because of the inadequate training that I received as a new carrier and became determined to assist others as they entered the field. I changed the initial training of two-three days of haphazard, non-standardized training that was being given to the new carriers to a full week of documented, thorough experiences that mirrored the actual duties and responsibilities that the carrier would experience. Also, while yet being a letter carrier, I finished my requirements for a bachelor's degree in education.

The Image (Receipt of the Vision): I began to teach a Bible study on my route on Thursdays at 7pm. After I had received the baptism in the Holy Spirit, I began to witness to people on my route regarding the Lord and I saw many get saved, healed etc. My plan was to send them to the church that had a thorough Bible study program that my wife and I had taken the year before. The people told me that they had no intention of going to the study at the church and that they wanted me to teach them. Of course, I told them no way that was going to happen... but the Lord told me that He wanted me to teach them. I told the Lord that I didn't know what to teach them, but the Lord said to start out with 3 subjects. He said teach them what the word of God is and where it came from, then teach them how faith comes and show them how to pray. So, I began what I thought would be three or four weeks, that ended up being 15-20 years and going far beyond Thursdays after my route.

In March of 1980, the Lord showed me the first vision of my life. I saw the world in deep darkness (spiritual darkness/the absence of the knowledge of the Lord) while skyscrapers exploded, and rubble fell into the streets. At this point the Lord spoke again and said the skyscrapers were exploding and falling due to them being built from the *world system that was coming to destruction.* Upon driving away from the rubble on a road that kept getting more and more narrow until only the left tires of the car would fit on the road. The Lord spoke again and said:

> "Enter by the narrow gate; for wide is the gate and broad is the way that leads to destruction, and there are many who go in by it. Because narrow is the gate and difficult is the way which leads to life, and there are few who find it."   ~ Matthew 7:13-14 NKJV

At this juncture we got out of the car as we were far out into the wilderness and saw a church building in the woods. Upon mounting the stairs, I noticed two things: it was made from one stone and that stone was red. The Lord went on to tell me that those that were in this church were standing on the Rock by doing the word that the Lord spoke and red represented the blood of Jesus that cleansed them of all sin. I did not enter the church, for the Lord whisked me away in the Spirit and I found myself back downtown floating above the continuing exploding skyscrapers. I then entered one of the buildings, a church, through the glass domed ceiling. I was not hurt nor did the glass break as I passed through it like light. The church was huge and very well decorated inside. As I looked around the building I noticed, again two other things: it was not made of Stone nor was it red. I looked through the ceiling, as it was glass, and stated within myself, *I can see right through it,* the Lord responded *right, I can see right through it.* It exploded at that point, as did the other structures. The Lord again whisked me away whereby I was instantly out at the wilderness church floating above it and looking at the oceans of people flooding into the building through the roof. The Lord spoke yet again to me and said, **teach them how to go through tribulation.** In 2003, the Lord instructed me to begin teaching the course, *How to Go Through Tribulation Victoriously (HTGTTV).*

The Image Transfer in the Body of Christ

In 1976 I assisted a group of believers to begin the **Central Detroit Full Gospel Businessmen's Fellowship** group that had monthly breakfast, lunch or dinner meetings. At each meeting someone would share their testimony and then invite participants at the meal to accept the Lord, receive the baptism in the Holy Spirit and have other needs met through prayer.

My wife and I began working with the teenagers at our church as ministry. At work I began to be promoted over and over and once again saw the need to teach the supervisors, managers and then postmasters how to progress to results, through seeing the image of success before it manifested. I began motivational speaking whereby I was sent all over the country to speak. All of these were part of my calling. A major thing that I would do regarding the image of something, would be to bring people to the front and tell them "I'm going to ask you to do something very simple, will you do it?" Of course, the person I brought to the front would say, yes. I would then say something under my breathe where they could not hear me, then quickly ask them in front of the crowd "you said that you would do what I asked and you didn't do it." They would become defensive and of course confused and then I repeated the same exercise twice. The 4th time, I would speak aloud so they could hear and of course seeing that they heard my request, such as "hand me the ink pen" or "the coffee cup," they having the image of what I said in their mind, could easily look for the object and pick it up and hand it to me.

It's all about one having the image of what they are seeking in their mind. Once the individual, any individual, sees it in their mind, they can achieve it. This includes operational tasks, marriages, healing, forgiveness and anything else. "As a man thinks (images) in his heart, so is he" **(Proverbs 23:7A**, brackets added). I would teach, "You must have the image of a thing before you can do it." Then the Lord took those things and put it in the spirit realm… you must have the image before you can do it. Write the vision, make it plain on tables so that men may run when they read it (**Habakkuk 2:2**).

God's Calling is Part of our Kingdom Inheritance

In the three scriptures below, we see further that we have a hope and glory in our calling and inheritance. The glory refers to benefits in our *Christ* inheritance that are beyond our natural thinking and abilities. Paul even refers to the prize of the *high calling* of God in Christ Jesus. It is meant for us to understand that there is a maturing in this calling just as there has been a maturing in our natural body once we are born as an infant… our bodies grow physically and mentally into maturity.

> "The eyes of your understanding being enlightened; that ye may know what is the hope of his calling, and what the riches of the glory of his inheritance in the saints,"   ~ Ephesians 1:18

> "There is one body, and one Spirit, even as ye are called in one hope of your calling;"   ~ Ephesians 4:4

> "I press toward the mark for the prize of the high calling of God in Christ Jesus."   ~ Philippians 3:14

The three scriptures below, point us to our calling being holy and heavenly and not natural. We are further exhorted to be very diligent and purposeful as we consider and pursue becoming mature and perfected in the elements and cause of our calling. A promise of never failing is attached to our life efforts as we put God in priority.

> "But seek ye first the kingdom of God, and his righteousness; and all these things shall be added unto you."   ~ Matthew 6:33

"Who hath saved us, and called us with an holy calling, not according to our works, but according to his own purpose and grace, which was given us in Christ Jesus before the world began,"

~ 2 Timothy 1:9

"Wherefore, holy brethren, partakers of the heavenly calling, consider the Apostle and High Priest of our profession, Christ Jesus;"

~ Hebrews 3:1

"Wherefore the rather, brethren, give diligence to make your calling and election sure: for if ye do these things, ye shall never fall:"

~ 2 Peter 1:10

The scriptures below in Corinthians point us to the differences in gifts, administrations and operations, but it is the same God working in all of us that are born again and know Jesus as our Lord. These scriptures go on further to describe the specific gifts (9) and then point out that though there are different gifts in the body of Christ, God works all of them together for His purposes. This illustration comes to mind as this is described: In the game of baseball, once a hitter hits the ball that is pitched by the pitcher into the far outfield and it rolls to the furthest part of the outfield, the outfielder retrieves it and throws it to an infielder, who then catches it and throws it to the catcher behind home plate to try to prevent a run from scoring. Several different players (9) in different positions are in the game all working together for the same purpose... to win. So, it is in God's Kingdom through the church body... there are different persons in different positions all working together in cooperation to win God's game. In baseball the outfielder does not retrieve the ball at the outer fence and then run all the way to home plate to try to tag the runner out. They use the skills (callings) they have with the skills and *callings* of the other teammates.

"Now there are diversities of gifts, but the same Spirit. And there are differences of administrations, but the same Lord. And there are diversities of operations, but it is the same God which worketh all in all. But the manifestation of the Spirit is given to every man to profit withal. For to one is given by the Spirit the word of wisdom; to another the word of knowledge by the same Spirit; To another faith by the same Spirit; to another the gifts of healing by the same Spirit; To another the working of miracles; to another prophecy; to another discerning of spirits; to another divers kinds of tongues; to another the interpretation of tongues: **But all these worketh that one and the selfsame Spirit, dividing to every man severally as he will.** For as the body is one, and hath many members, and all the members of that one body, being many, are one body: so also is Christ. For by one Spirit are we all baptized into one body, whether we be Jews or Gentiles, whether we be bond or free; and have been all made to drink into one Spirit. For the body is not one member, but many." ~ 1 Corinthians 12:4-14, emphasis added

How does God make Provision for Your Calling?

God's callings to each of us were completed from the foundation of the world. He states very clearly that all His works were finished from the time the world was founded. We were preordained to do specific things in His callings as the scriptures listed below will show. Those blueprints that God gave for each of us are hidden in the *spiritual DNA* found within us and come to light as we pursue His will in our lives. As we discover the anointing, which is within us, it opens the doors as does an electronic eye does to a remote door as one approaches it… it suddenly opens up for our entrance into the room without our hand's effort or strength.

"And on the seventh day God ended his work which he had made; **and he rested on the seventh day from all his work which he had made.**" ~ Genesis 2:2, emphasis added

"For we which have believed do enter into rest, as he said, As I have sworn in my wrath, if they shall enter into my rest: **although the works were finished from the foundation of the world.**"
~ Hebrews 4:3, emphasis added

"For we are his workmanship, created in Christ Jesus unto good works, **which God hath before ordained that we should walk in them.**" ~ Ephesians 2:10, emphasis added

What are the Small Things that You are to Become Faithful in?

As you begin to get God's word diligently into your heart and do what He will lead you to do, He has promised to direct your path as you trust Him. (See **Proverbs 3:5-6**) You will discover as you attach yourself in consistent fellowship with other believers seeking God's direction in their lives along with the work He has called them to do that which attracts you in His work. As you begin to work in that area and seek God, He will open more up to you and begin manifesting His anointing on the things you are called to do while blessing your efforts in other activities. He will bless it in such a way that you will not only have unequaled successes, but you will see confirmation of that which He purposes in your life. Remember, Potiphar saw the great success Joseph was having in the natural work on his plantation, success that Potiphar had never seen the likes of before and it states in Genesis 39:

"And his master saw that the LORD was with him and that the LORD made all he did to prosper in his hand. So Joseph found favor in his sight, and served him. Then he made him overseer of his house, and all that he had he put under his authority. So it was, from the time that he had made him overseer of his house and all that he had, that the LORD blessed the Egyptian's house for Joseph's sake; and the blessing of the LORD was on all that he had in the house and in the field. Thus he left all that he had in Joseph's hand, and he did not know what he had except for the bread which he ate." ~ Genesis 39:3-6

From Calling to Election with the Gifts Making Room for You

"Wherefore the rather, brethren, give diligence to make your calling and election sure: for if ye do these things, ye shall never fall:" (**2 Peter 1:10,** Also take note of verses 1-11 in 2 Peter 1). Ephesians 4 says:

"I therefore, the prisoner of the Lord, beseech you that ye walk worthy of the vocation wherewith ye are called, With all lowliness and meekness, with longsuffering, forbearing one another in love; Endeavouring to keep the unity of the Spirit in the bond of peace." ~ Ephesians 4:1-3

As we have discussed earlier in this chapter that God has summoned or *called* each believer to a specific task, job or position in the Body of Christ. As we look at the context of the two scriptures above, we see that once a person shows diligence, obedience and an exercising of the characteristics of Christ, they become eligible in being promoted to, or chosen for the *called to* position. They become *elected.* There are many persons that run for the office of president of the United States but there is only one that becomes elected. It states in **Matthew 22:14,** "For many are called, but few are chosen." We discover in the context of this scripture many had been invited to (or called to) the wedding of the King's son, but none had honored the invitation. The King increased the wedding invitations to many more persons, but then it was found one had come in inappropriately

177

dressed and was cast out into outer darkness because of it. So, it is in the Kingdom of God, we must put on the *spiritual garments within the inner man* in order to be appropriately attired and *exercised* to be able to run the race necessary to find oneself *elected* to that which God has called us. See the following references for greater understanding: **1 Corinthians 9:22-27, Hebrews 12:1-3, Ephesians 4:22-24, 2 Timothy 2:1-7** and **Hebrews 5:11-14.**

As one becomes exercised as they "seek ye first the Kingdom of God and His righteousness," the Lord equips them with the spiritual enablement to be effective in the spiritual realm of which we are engaged. The Lord's enablement includes the fruit of the Spirit (**Galatians 5:22-23**), the gifts of the Spirit (**1 Corinthians 12:4-11**), the armor for spiritual battle (**Ephesians 6:10-18**) and the characteristics of Christ (**2 Peter 1:1-12**), along with the 9 Foundation stones that cause one to become *established* so that they move deeper into the **supernatural** things within the Kingdom of God. The Lord also provides development of the members of the Body of Christ through the 5-fold ministries of the Apostle, Prophet, Evangelist, Pastor and Teacher as shown in **Ephesians 4:7-16.** The Lord, through His leading via the Holy Spirit, causes us to be further enabled for Kingdom work through using our Spiritual gifts which pave the way for us as we are led of His Spirit. "A man's gift maketh room for him, and bringeth him before great men" (**Proverbs 18:26**). Through these gifts, God gives abilities and favor that are beyond the natural abilities of mankind.

As I look back on my walk with God, I am reminded that as I grew in my relationship and prioritization of God in my life, the Lord had people in the 5-fold ministry of His Kingdom pray and prophesy over me, assist in my development and mentor me. At the same time the Lord showered me with blessing, favor and promotion in my natural job and in my personal life. My wife and I began counseling and developing couples through the

Power of 2 marriage ministry. Through these various activities we were blessed as the Lord began to manifest His gifting of prophesy, faith, healing, discerning of spirits and words of wisdom and knowledge. We also saw the gifting of government; ruling, helps, ministry and administration come into operation. These giftings greatly enhanced our natural careers, hers as a speech pathologist and then high school counselor and mine as a supervisor, superintendent and executive in the Postal Service (See **1 Corinthians 12, Romans 12:1-13**). In short, as we took care of God's business, He took care of ours regarding the blessings of health, relationships, finances, natural promotion in the workplace and favor according to **Deuteronomy 28:1-15**.

> "And the LORD shall make thee the head, and not the tail; and thou shalt be above only, and thou shalt not be beneath; if that thou hearken unto the commandments of the LORD thy God, which I command thee this day, to observe and to do them:"
>
> ~ Deuteronomy 28:13

We have seen our gifts make room for us and bring us before great men. God has the same blessing for our future endeavors and for all others who make the decision to put God first in their lives and seek His righteousness… the invitation is to all that "make their calling and election sure."

Vocation Whereby You Earn a Living

In the Bible we find that particular people whom God used to perform mighty acts were very proficient in specific areas of *natural work experiences*. In **Genesis 3:19** man was told by God that he would have to earn his living by the sweat of his brow because of the fall of Adam.

There are several scriptures pertaining to how God blesses the wise in understanding, while causing their natural work to prosper and provide for them.

The Lord, very simply, guarantees us success and prosperity as we put Him first in our lives and activities. Early on in my career I'd been taught this principal by the Lord. I adhered to it vigilantly and in turn, the Lord true to His word, blessed my activities at home, in the family and at work. I was promoted to an area that yielded for more responsibility and in it found a sudden lapse in the success I had been experiencing. I remember going to the Lord one late evening while leaving work and I said to the Lord the following: *Father, I have done as your word says, I have sought Your Kingdom first and that which I believe is right with you. I work in the church children's ministry, while loving as best as I know how and give tithe and offerings...why have things gone south...where is the success you stated in Psalm 1?*

> "Blessed is the man that walketh not in the counsel of the ungodly, nor standeth in the way of sinners, nor sitteth in the seat of the scornful. but his delight is in the law of the Lord; and in his law doth he meditate day and night. And he shall be like a tree planted by the rivers of water, that bringeth forth his fruit in his season; his leaf also shall not wither; and whatsoever he doeth shall prosper."
>
> ~ Psalm 1:1-3

About a week or two after this prayer, I had left work one Friday and rushed to the church with my wife as we assisted the pastor and a few other workers prepare the church for a weekend speaker. I was upstairs in the balcony getting the machines ready to record the speaker. While there the Lord spoke very plainly to my heart... *son, you have taken care of my business, I will take care of yours!* Very soon after that success blossomed in my endeavors and I found myself promoted again to an even higher level with unmatched success (**2 Thessalonians 3:9-18**)!

How to Find Your Call in the Body of Christ and Where You Earn a Living

Now that you have become aware of the truth of the matter that God has a specific call for your life… how do you come into it? First, **become faithful in the small or little things** and God will make you ruler over great things (**Matthew 25:21**). It would make no sense whatsoever to give an individual one million dollars to invest if they don't know how to use one hundred dollars. God is the top priority planner in the universe. It is He who tells us to first seek His Kingdom and what's right and then everything else will be added unto us. Along the path of discovery of that which you could not imagine in your wildest imaginings or dreams are the revelations that only come through diligence. **Diligence is far more than a word.** It is a process of continued focus which through it causes that which was purposed by God in you, to develop unto its full power and ability the unseen purposes of God's faith released in you. Walt Disney could not have imagined Disney World through his first sketches of Mickey Mouse. Thomas Edison had not an inkling of a two-mile-high scooping of a city's lights shining in the night from his first of hundreds of attempts at the electric light. Orville and Wilbur Wright could not see the earth from the moon in their first attempt at Kittyhawk, North Carolina in 1903.

It has been my experience that as it states in Matthew 6:33 when one seeks God's kingdom first and what's right with Him, you are given the direction regarding your position in the Body of Christ or where you earn your living, or in anything else. As you perform in that position the Lord knows the thoughts, He thinks toward you being thoughts of peace and not of evil to give you His expected end in the matter. That end will be far beyond anything you can dream of as you seek to do it as unto Him (**Colossians 3:23**). When you are faithful over the little things, God makes you master over much. You do not have to strive, struggle, or sweat as He will enable you to do all things through Christ who will strengthen you.

SPIRITUAL INVENTORY

Give at least 3 scriptures the Lord has given you from which you have received revelation secrets. . . "God's sayings." List your revelation also.

_____

_____

_____

_____

_____

_____

_____

_____

_____

_____

_____

_____

_____

_____

_____

_____

SECTION VII

←——————→

FINANCE$

God's resources turned toward His purposes. Are
you in control or are you being controlled in
financial matters in your life?

TRANSFORMING CHARACTERISTIC
~ GODLINESS ~

Love-forgiveness, humility, holiness, taking off flesh and
putting on spirit and righteousness.

KINGDOM BENCHMARK
~ POWER ~

God's will in the earth expressed through you
in and beyond any and all obstacles.

13

FINANCES

Finances, finances, finances! Are you in control or being controlled in financial matters in your life? Being broke is not funny, nor is it fun. But as much as being broke now is bad, being broke later is worse. What are you doing to make sure you won't be in the same financial position forever? Even if your financial position is good, you have to plan to be a blessing.

Let's look at a few questions and then a few scriptures to give us God's direction. Do you think God is poor? Do you think God is aware of your financial condition? Do you think God wants you to be blessed with more than you have now?

The first scripture we're going to look at is in the book of Psalms. **Psalm 24:1** says, "The earth is the Lord's, and the fullness thereof; the world, and they that dwell therein." This scripture shows us the reality that the whole earth and everything in it belongs to God.

"But thou shalt remember the LORD thy God: for it is he that giveth thee power to get wealth, that he may establish his covenant

185

which he sware unto thy fathers, as it is this day."

~ Deuteronomy 8:18

"Beloved, I wish above all things that thou mayest prosper and be in health, even as thy soul prospereth."   ~ 3 John 1:2

Okay, now let's review the 3 scriptures above on the matter. **Psalm 24:1** shows the reality that the whole earth and all that's within it belongs to Almighty God. Then it states that "the world," which refers to the systems of the earth, such as the land ownings, banking structure, all businesses outside of the church, educational, industrial, entertainment industries and the like are also in His charge along with all those that are within them.

Deuteronomy 8:18, gives a conditional blessing of God that as one keeps Him in the forefront of their mind, acknowledging Him in their financial matters with the intention to first support the gospel message going out to the world; God favors them with **"power to get wealth."** That **power** is composed of the **knowledge** regarding the steps or beneficial tools that lead a person into getting finances or resources and favor that will yield more money than is needed. Next, the Lord gives that individual understanding of financial matters to cause a growth in them. (Remember, understanding = the HOW and WHAT to do with one's knowledge to get the desired results in a matter) Lastly, **"the power to get wealth"** = **wisdom** or strategies (which is the WAY, WHERE, WHEN and WHY to utilize the understanding to yield the benefit needed in the specific issue one is dealing with) In the case of finances, the benefit needed is wealth.

Look at **3 John 1:2**. In the beginning of this chapter as it gives the utmost plan and desire of God's will for His people to have an abundance and to be in total health. However, it states that your health and finances will prosper only "as your soul prospers." Your soul is your mind it prospers when it's flourishing with the thoughts of having health and wealth. Therefore, it is dependent on how you invest in God's thoughts regarding them. We are what we think… "For as he thinketh in his heart, so is he" **(Proverbs 23:7A).**

In 1994 my wife and I did a two-year lease on a Lincoln Continental. In December we decided because we really liked it, we would purchase it instead of getting another two-year lease on a 1996. I therefore, set about making plans over the next 13 months to double and sometimes triple the monthly payments and when we received our income tax returns in March to add an additional $3-4,000 towards the payments. Our goal was by December of 1995, to make the last payment and own the car. In January of 1995, upon my return home from work, my wife informed me that before getting out of bed that morning, the Lord spoke to her and said: *you can pay the car off now.* She asked how that could be and the Lord had her to go and pull out our budget book. As she did that the Lord showed her how to make certain financial adjustments, etc.

When I got home that evening, she told me what the Lord had said to her. I told her that we could pay off the car according to the plans we had made back in December by increasing the monthly payments. She then took me to the budget book and showed me what the Lord had shown her. Bottom line… we paid off the car that month. Interesting note, the people at the dealership were so accustomed to leasing vehicles that when we gave them the balance of what was owed on the car, it took them about a half hour of making calls, etc. to find out how to conduct the purchase.

I must add to this testimony **Deuteronomy 8:18**, "And you shall remember the LORD your God, for it is **He who gives you power to get wealth**, that He may establish His covenant which He swore to your fathers, as it is this day" (NKJV, emphasis added).

Pat and I have put God's agenda first in our lives and we were about the business of getting people saved and developed in their inheritance in Christ Jesus. At that time, we were not Pastors and had a young family, with very busy careers, but God's covenant was our top concern. Covenant = The agreement between God and the Israelites and the church, whereby God promises to protect, favor and bless us if we take His message and purpose of it, to bring people to Him.

Examples of God's Power of Wealth to Proclaim His Covenant

Please note the financial points in the parable of the talents:

"For the kingdom of heaven is like a man traveling to a far country, who called his own servants and delivered his goods to them. And to one he gave five talents, to another two, and to another one, to each according to his own ability; and immediately he went on a journey. Then he who had received the five talents went and traded with them, and made another five talents. And likewise he who had received two gained two more also. But he who had received one went and dug in the ground, and hid his lord's money. After a long time the lord of those servants came and settled accounts with them. "So he who had received five talents came and brought five other talents, saying, 'Lord, you delivered to me five talents; look, I have gained five more talents besides them.' His lord said to him, 'Well done, good and faithful servant; you were faithful over a few things, I will make you ruler over many things. Enter into the joy of your lord.'..."Then he who had received the one talent came and said, 'Lord, I knew you to be a hard man, reaping where you have not sown, and gathering where you have not scattered seed. And I was afraid, and went and hid your talent in the ground. Look, there you have what is yours.' "But his lord answered and said to him, 'You wicked and lazy servant, you knew that I reap where I have not sown, and gather where I have not scattered seed. So you ought to have deposited my money with the bankers, and at my coming I would have received back my own with interest. So take the talent from him, and give it to him who has ten talents. 'For to everyone who has, more will be given, and he will have abundance; but from him who does not have, even what he has will be taken away."

~ Matthew 25:14-21, 24-29 NKJV

The *faithful servant* was rewarded not only with 100-fold gain of 5 additional talents, but also received the talent that was not used by the unfaithful, wicked and lazy servant, along with a future that would have "many more things and the blessing of the joy of the Lord." It states in verse 16, "Then he who had received the five talents went and traded with them, and made another five talents" (Matt. 25:16 NKJV). He "traded with them" came about because of the mindset of the faithful servant, who ended up with 100% more. Take note, the gifting was, "to each according to his own ability." What this means is the one who was given 5 talents had a thinking pattern that went out and obtained whatever education that was necessary whether it was formal in a college or university, or trade or classes or learning that were available through whomever had the abilities. The one who had received 2 talents had followed the same course as the one with 5 but had not yet attained to the same level. The one who had received the 1 talent, received also according to his ability. This means that he took the gifting from God that had been received and sat on it. In essence, he received salvation and did not attach himself to the ushers, choir, praise and worship team, liturgical dance, audio-visual-media, mercies-benevolent team, administrative assistant, secretary, deacon, trustee, welcoming committee, teachers, books and library, building and grounds, nursery, pantry, kitchen, baptismal, leadership, budgets and business, communications, missions, follow-up or prayer, or any other assignment or ministry... instead they sat in the pew year after year.

Now, back to the person with the 5 talents that went out and traded with them to obtain 100-fold. As the Lord saw the intentions of their heart to gain more for advancing the purpose of the covenant, and to be about the business of God in winning souls to the Lord and taking an active role in the development of them He acted on their behalf with blessings. Look at Jesus at the age of 12 in the temple asking questions and answering the Pharisees and Sadducees. He was asked by His parents why was He doing this, His response: **Luke 2:49,** "And He said to them, 'Why did you seek Me? Did you not know that I must be about My Father's business?'" Those persons in the Body of Christ who are intentionally working in their lives to bring forth God's covenant whether at their natural job, in the neighborhood, school etc. God makes sure they have the needed finance$ for whatever activity is required.

THE PURPOSE OF WEALTH

Genesis 1:1, "In the beginning God created the heavens and the earth." It is a simple statement of truth that God made the heavens and the earth.

> "So God created man in His own image; in the image of God He created him; male and female He created them. Then God blessed them, and God said to them, "Be fruitful and multiply; fill the earth and subdue it; have dominion over the fish of the sea, over the birds of the air, and over every living thing that moves on the earth."
>
> ~ Genesis 1:27-28

God gave man stewardship over the earth to be fruitful which means to increase. The increase was referring to the *gifted state* that man was in before sin entered his reality. Adam thought and moved, acted as did God, **supernaturally.** He moved in **supernatural** gifts as the norm as did Jesus thousands of years later. Jesus was called the second Adam. To multiply was a matter of additions to the race being brought forth. To fill the earth and subdue it is to remake that which Satan and his demons had destroyed. Adam, before the fall, had the God-ability to do this. Adam also had dominion which was also the norm; man had control overall. **Psalm 24:1** says, "The earth is the LORD's, and all its fullness, The world and those who dwell therein." Truth, for the last scripture, the earth belongs to God, therefore, it is legal for Him to give it to whomsoever He wishes. His word states that it's His decision to give it to those who are in proper alignment with Himself. This means people who are hearing from God and doing His word, are in a covenant relationship. OK, that's out of the way; the earth is the Lord's.

The next issue is He's given mankind a task. Replenish and take dominion. Bring in the Kingdom of God! "Our Father, which are in Heaven, Hallowed is your name; Your Kingdom come Your will be done on earth as it is in Heaven" **(Matthew 6:10)**. He has given us the authority and power to get rid of sickness, poverty, poor self-esteem and poor relationships, and has given us the keys to the kingdom that whatever we bind on earth is bound in heaven and whatever we loose on earth is loosed in heaven. **Malachi 3:6**, "For I am the LORD, I change not; therefore ye sons of Jacob are not consumed." For the gospel of God's covenant with man to be sent out to all the world requires God's vision, strategies and finances. Well, God gives to those who remember Him in the fullness of His word. Those that have His word, through revelation come into knowledge, understanding and wisdom. "I wisdom dwell with prudence, and find out knowledge of witty inventions" **(Proverbs 8:12)**. When an individual has the mindset to do the will of God toward the gospel, God gives the… "power to get wealth to establish His covenant as He sware unto our fathers…" **(Deuteronomy 8:18)**.

THE LAW OF THE WEALTH TRANSFER IN ACTION:

The Joseph Case

In **1 Corinthians 10**, God admonishes us through several examples in reference to the Israelites when He delivered them from Egyptian bondage while giving them the wealth of Egypt. It's shown in **1 Corinthians 10:5,**

"Nevertheless, God was not pleased with most of them; their bodies were scattered in the wilderness. Now these things occurred as examples to keep us from setting our hearts on evil things as they did."

The Israelites made the following errors: they became boisterous idolaters, while becoming immoral sexually and God destroyed 23,000 in one day. They rebelled against Him. Many were killed by snakes. Some murmured and complained so the Lord sent the angel of destruction to wipe them out. Therefore, God reminds us to take note of things recorded in scripture to show us His way and to remember:

> "These things happened to them as examples and were written down as warnings for us, on whom the culmination of the ages has come. So, if you think you are standing firm, be careful that you don't fall! No temptation has overtaken you except what is common to mankind. And God is faithful; he will not let you be tempted beyond what you can bear. But when you are tempted, he will also provide a way out so that you can endure it."
>
> ~ 1 Corinthians 10:11-13

Joseph, as I have shown in other chapters, not only enhanced the wealth of the Egyptian empire, but greatly increased it as the nation's surrounding them poured their wealth into Egypt in order to survive by purchasing food. Therefore, our question should be, how does Joseph's testimonies apply to ourselves and our situations?

The Daniel Case

Daniel's story starts in Jeremiah. Jeremiah prophesied about the people of Judah. For 70 years, Jeremiah prophesied:

> "This is what the LORD says: When Babylon's 70 years are over, I will come to you. I will keep my promise to you and bring you back to this place. I know the plans that I have for you, declares the

LORD. They are plans for peace and not disaster, plans to give you
a future filled with hope." ~ Jeremiah 29:10-11 GWT

Daniel, Shadrach, Meshach and Abed-Nego were four of the captives taken into Babylonian captivity. However, through their walking in their Kingdom inheritance God released His giftings in them so that they eventually ran the Babylonian kingdom with Daniel as the prime minister. In time, Persia succeeded in conquering Babylon and their king, Cyrus. God had Isaiah prophesy about Cyrus 150 years before he was born and 200 years before the temple of Jerusalem would be rebuilt. He prophesied:

"Who says of Cyrus, 'He is My shepherd, And he shall perform all My pleasure, Saying to Jerusalem, "You shall be built," And to the temple, "Your foundation shall be laid."'" ~ Isaiah 44:28 NKJV

The children of Judah were returned to Judah and Jerusalem along with the treasures of the Temple. Daniel went on to reign as the prime minister of Persia also while setting up universities and taught of the Messiah (Jesus) that would be born in the land of the Jews. The "wise men" came from the land of Persia due to Daniel's influence because of his vast knowledge, understanding and wisdom. At the time of Jesus' birth, there would be a caravan of (magi) wise men, from Persia, that saw the star in the East and then traveled to Jerusalem to seek the new King of the Jews. It had been prophesied that He would be born after the appearing of the bright star in the heavens. (The caravan was more like 100-200 men bringing 3 diverse types of gifts: gold, frankincense and myrrh.) Daniel and his companions along with others of the covenant oversaw great wealth in order to build the universities of the Persian empire. The magi that were trained in them would impact the entire culture of Persia to maintain the beliefs in order to send a caravan for a trip that took 3-4 years to complete.

"Now after Jesus was born in Bethlehem of Judea in the days of Herod the king, behold, wise men from the East came to Jerusalem, saying, "Where is He who has been born King of the Jews? For we have seen His star in the East and have come to worship Him." When Herod the king heard this, he was troubled, and all Jerusalem with him. And when he had gathered all the chief priests and scribes of the people together, he inquired of them where the Christ was to be born."

~ Matthew 2:1-4 NKJV

The star that had shown up in the East for the wise men two years prior to their arriving in Jerusalem, for it required this amount of time for them to gather the materials needed and venture to Jerusalem. As soon as they had received the message of where the King would be born, they departed from Persia. As they departed, the star reappeared and led them to the *house*, not manger, where the young child was. After they had given the gifts the Lord warned them in a dream not to return to Herod but to go back to Persia using a different route.

Let's consider: 1. The trip and sojourn in Egypt by Joseph and Mary with the child Jesus was financed through the gifts that the wise men had brought. 2. The wise men brought the gifts because they had knowledge of what the bright star appearing in the East represented, that the King of the Jews and savior of the world had been born. 3. The wise men not only had knowledge of the meaning of the star seen in the East, but through the teaching and spiritual impartations of Daniel they had become avid believers in this newborn King. "The earth is the Lord's and fullness thereof; the world and all they that dwell therein" **(Psalm 24:1)**. This not only refers to the material possessions in the earth belonging to God but also the political realms even of the non-believing nations belonging to the Lord also.

"Have you not known? Have you not heard? Has it not been told you from the beginning? Have you not understood from the

194

foundations of the earth? It is He who sits above the circle of the earth, And its inhabitants are like grasshoppers, Who stretches out the heavens like a curtain, And spreads them out like a tent to dwell in. He brings the princes to nothing; He makes the judges of the earth useless. Scarcely shall they be planted, Scarcely shall they be sown, Scarcely shall their stock take root in the earth, When He will also blow on them, And they will wither, And the whirlwind will take them away like stubble."   ~ Isaiah 40:21-24 NKJV

The Present Case

As one ventures through the scriptures, you can't help but notice that there are many other men and women, who were totally committed to God and His purpose of reaching lost mankind with the news of God's plan of redemption for the world. God provided wealth for these people for them to carry out His purposes. There was Moses, Ruth, Esther, Jeremiah, Elijah, Elisha and many more inclusive of people in our time period. In this section we will break down wealth and its transfer to individual cases. I repeat at this time what I began this chapter with, Finances...are you in control or being controlled in financial matters in your life? Let's look at a few questions and then a few scriptures to give us direction, God's direction, in this area. Answer the following by putting a check mark in either of the given blanks....

Do you think God is poor? Yes____No _____ Do you think God is aware of your financial condition? Yes____No _____ Do you think God wants you to be blessed with more than you have now? Yes____No _____

As we consider this, it comes down to **Matthew 6:33**, "But seek first the kingdom of God and His righteousness, and all these things shall be added to you." As we go after God's Kingdom as a priority in our lives along with the righteousness that comes with it, everything else, every other issue of life, is provided for. There is a need to be very clear on these two principles: The **Kingdom of God** and **righteousness**.

The term Kingdom of God is used 68 times in ten New Testament books, whereas the Kingdom of Heaven is found 32 times only in the book of Matthew. In **Matthew 19:23** Jesus tells the rich young ruler that it's hard for a rich man to enter the Kingdom of Heaven. Then in the next verse Jesus says it is easier for a camel to go through the eye of a needle than for a rich man to enter the Kingdom of God. The terms are used interchangeably. The Kingdom of God is <u>supernatural</u>. It is not my joining a church and being there on Sunday and other days. Let's look at how the terminology Kingdom of God or Kingdom of Heaven was used in the scriptures. Firstly **Matthew 12:28** says, "But if I <u>**cast out demons by the Spirit of God**</u>, surely the <u>**kingdom of God**</u> has come upon you" (NKJV, emphasis added). As well:

> "Now it came to pass, afterward, that He went through every city and village, preaching and bringing the glad tidings of the **kingdom of God**. And the twelve were with Him, **and certain women who had been healed of evil spirits and infirmities**—Mary called Magdalene, out of whom had come seven demons, and Joanna the wife of Chuza, Herod's steward, and Susanna, and many others who provided for Him from their substance."
>
> ~ Luke 8:1-3 NKJV, emphasis added

> "But when the multitudes knew it, they followed Him; and He received them and spoke to them about the **kingdom of God**, and **healed those who had need of healing**."
>
> ~ Luke 9:11 NKJV, emphasis added

> "The centurion answered and said, "Lord, I am not worthy that You should come under my roof. But only speak a word, and my servant will be healed. For I also am a man under authority, having soldiers under me. And I say to this one, 'Go,' and he goes; and to another,

'Come,' and he comes; and to my servant, 'Do this,' and he does it." When Jesus heard it, He marveled, and said to those who followed, "Assuredly, I say to you, I have not found such great faith, not even in Israel! And I say to you that many will come from east and west, and sit down with Abraham, Isaac, and Jacob in the **kingdom of heaven**." ~ Matthew 8:8-11 NKJV, emphasis added

So often when the terminology of Kingdom of Heaven or Kingdom of God is used it is referring to one or several <u>supernatural</u> events occurring. An elderly sister about the age of 85, came to me in a motorized wheelchair and asked if I would pray for her to walk again. I was about to stretch my hand to place on her head or shoulder to pray, when the Lord stopped me and told me to ask her if she believed it was His will that she walked again. She stated, "I hope so." I then asked her to recite the Lord's prayer. When she got to the place where it states, "Thy Kingdom come thy will be done on earth as it is in Heaven," I stopped her and asked, "Mother when you get to heaven will you see anyone in wheelchairs?" She thought for a few seconds and replied, "No, there won't be." I asked why not? She thought for a few more seconds and responded, "Why, it's the Kingdom of God!" I shared a few other scriptures with her to give her further clarity and build her faith then I asked her again, "Mother, do you believe that it's God's will for you to walk again?" She responded with a sound and strong yes! I then laid my hand on her forehead and prayed for a few seconds... she stood up for a moment and then sat back down. On Monday or Tuesday of the next week she phoned my house and left a message on the answering machine. Upon my return call to her she excitedly proclaimed, "Pastor, I just want you to know that I walked from my living room to my kitchen, and I haven't walked in eight years since I had a stroke!"

The **Kingdom of God** that Jesus tells us to seek first is not being in a church service, nor serving as an usher or any other functioning position within the church. All those positions are good and needed and necessary.

However, the **Kingdom of God** is <u>supernatural</u>, and this is what Jesus told us to seek **FIRST**, the <u>supernatural</u>! Now, let's get back to what seeking God's Kingdom and righteousness really is. After this, He told us to seek His **righteousness**. What is that? OK, let's look at what it isn't. It is not what we wear on the outside. It's not what we carry that looks Christian, such as a large embroidered covered Bible or cross on a necklace or bracelet or watch, etc. It's not us dressing in white nor wearing or not wearing jewelry nor our hair looking any particular way. In fact, it's nothing that can be seen on the outside at all. Instead, it's the inner man of the heart:

> "Do not let your adornment be merely outward—arranging the hair, wearing gold, or putting on fine apparel—rather let it be the hidden person of the heart, with the incorruptible beauty of a gentle and quiet spirit, which is very precious in the sight of God."
>
> ~ 1 Peter 3:3-4 NKJV

As mentioned in chapter 3, **righteousness** comes from our hearing God, believing what has been said and to do that which was said. The first time that it is spoken of is in Genesis 15:4:

> "And behold, the word of the LORD came to him, saying, "This one shall not be your heir, but one who will come from your own body shall be your heir." Then He brought him outside and said, "Look now toward heaven, and count the stars if you are able to number them." And He said to him, "So shall your descendants be." And he believed in the LORD, and He accounted it to him for righteousness."
>
> ~ Genesis 15:4-6 NKJV

> "And when he was demanded of the Pharisees, when the kingdom of God should come, he answered them and said, The kingdom of God cometh not with observation: Neither shall they say, Lo here! or, lo there! for, behold, the kingdom of God is within you."
>
> ~ Luke 17:20-21

OK, let's review. To seek the **Kingdom of God** first, means what?

If you said to seek after the **supernatural** things of God to manifest in your life for an example and witness of God, you're correct.

Next question: What is righteousness?

If you said to hear God, believe what you've heard from God, then to do it, you are correct again! As a person truly sets their life to consistently seek first God's Kingdom and His righteousness, they will shift their priorities in life to learn of Him, hear from Him and follow Him. These things will change the inward man of our hearts. There will not be a problem in learning to hear God, learn of Him, pray, repent, give and serve. God, by His Spirit, will also lead us to get ourselves in order spiritually, physically, sexually, educationally in relationships and financially.

Now, seeing that we are referring to FINANCE$ let's go a little deeper. Just as there are testimonies of healing, relationship restorations, miracles and deliverances, God's desire is for us to have testimonies in our FINANCE$ also. The scriptures below refer to the tithe which is one tenth of the total monies increase that we come into. God has instructed His people in the Old and New Testaments to give a tithe and offering to Him. Those that obey are protected from Satanic attack due to their being under God's umbrella of His covenant; those that do not, aren't.

In 1977, my wife and I were busy being about the things of the Kingdom of God (we still are) and we had schedules filled with ministry items that were growing with more needs and responsibilities. Those things and schedules related to bringing people into the knowledge of the salvation that Jesus brought to the world and then getting them rooted and grounded in the doctrines of the 9 foundation stones found in **Hebrews 6:1-3**. My wife and I had a 4-year old daughter and a son that was on the way. She was a speech pathologist, a Sunday school teacher, was part of a women's ministry that traveled and sponsored weekend retreats for ladies bringing them into the deeper things of God. We both worked as the sponsors of the teen ministry of about 30 young people at the church. She also had speaking engagements for various women ministry programs. I was a letter carrier and working on finishing my requirements for a teaching degree while being over the children's church, weekly Bible studies on my route after work and had just assisted a group of brothers in initiating the central Detroit Full Gospel Businessmen's fellowship. We were slightly busy.

My wife had cried out to the Lord telling Him that something on her calendar had to go. The Lord answered her cry and stated, *Quit your job.* My wife responded with, *No Lord, I meant one of the ministry responsibilities.* The Lord's response was, *Quit your job.* He then confirmed it with me... and she quit her job. I might add to this that we had a new home we had just purchased, so there was a house now to consider; I had just purchased a new car and although our home was a duplex, and we rented the upstairs, the Lord had just moved on us to allow a person who was out of work and ill to move in without making any payments... free. Oh, by the way, my wife had a better salary than I. We had major financial issues; I quickly put my new car of 2-3 months up for sale and it sold in 2 days, but we still had monumental financial concerns. We expected that a financial breakthrough was going to manifest any day; seeing that the Lord had told her to quit her job, but it didn't. I found quickly that you could only "rob Peter to pay Paul" once, then Paul had a major attitude.

Well, we were about to find out what living by faith looked like and learn... really learn, the meaning of: "Trust in the LORD with all your heart, And lean not on your own understanding; In all your ways acknowledge Him, And He shall direct your paths" (**Proverbs 3:5-6** NKJV), "The LORD is my shepherd; I shall not want" (**Psalm 23:1** NKJV) and:

> "Not that I speak in regard to need, for I have learned in whatever state I am, to be content: I know how to be abased, and I know how to abound. Everywhere and in all things I have learned both to be full and to be hungry, both to abound and to suffer need. I can do all things through Christ who strengthens me."
>
> ~ Philippians 4:11-13 NKJV

We learned how to seek God's direction, hear His voice and follow it despite what things looked like. We learned how not to worry, but trust God, how to pay off all our bills, how to buy a new car after going from 2 paychecks to 1, how to get rid of credit card debt and pay off our new home early, while giving our tithes and offerings with joy. We saw what the favor of God will do for you through other people and circumstances and I began to get promotion after promotion after promotion.

Just a few testimonies that happened during this time and there are numerous ones. One lady purchased a piano for our daughter, purchased new carpet for the entire home and another gave two large bags of expensive clothing for the children. Another person sent us a check for $200.00 (that would be $3,000.00 with today's inflation) and stated, "The Lord said send this to you and for you to use it for things you want not need." We had begun to purchase meats and poultry in bulk because it was less expensive, so we purchased a large freezer to hold the food. My wife was at the meat market using a flyer that she had for a year or so and the butcher/owner of the market was so amazed that she still had that *old flyer* that he gave her a discount on the meats and filled her cart with free chicken.

I can go on and on with testimonies on finances. During all this time, the Lord through those testimonies had us to begin counseling couples regarding various marital problems, financial included. There ended up being so many couples in need of help that we could not fit them all in our schedule, so we began marriage seminars. Another very important thing we learned was how to live through the guidance of a budget. I give an example of budgeting on the website. They might look complicated, but it is a discipline that you must and can master to come into financial success.

THE STAR OF FINANCIAL PLANNING
S. (Situation) T. (Task) A. (Action) R. (Results)

Situation

1. Tithes & Offerings: Come out of the curse into the Blessings of God. **(Mal.3:6-10, Gen. 14, Mt. 23:23, Heb. 7)**

2. Bring your budget from disrepair to REPAIRED

3. Quit spending more than what's coming in

4. Get another or better job

5. Go back to school if needed

6. Check for the best and beneficial banks, credit unions, **Investments,** CD's and money market accounts

7. Budgets (balanced) must have a record of what is coming in and being spent monthly

8. Get educationally prepared...1st. spiritually (must have spiritual knowledge/finances) then naturally

9. Requirement to **work in unity** as husband & wife & for singles having an accountability person

10. Set financial goals...short (1-2 years) and long term (5-7 years)

11. Establish future planning, establish a family legacy

12. %, decimals, interest rates, learn how to calculate compounding interests, etc.

13. Have a financial library of books, CD, DVD's, teaching and go to financial seminars

14. Follow-up regarding goals...follow-up, follow-up, follow-up, follow-up, follow-up, follow-up, follow-up!

15. Go to a class regarding financial planning of known Christian leaders that have a testimony of faithful service bringing people to salvation and leading and building people in Kingdom knowledge, coupled with an abundance of wealth in their personal financial portfolios.

16. Walk in **2 Chronicles 7:14**

Task

1. Teaches you to have a balanced budget

2. Teaches you what your net worth is, and how to figure it out to improve your lot in 12 months maximum. (of course, the Lord will teach you to lessen the 12 months)

3. Educational materials provided through handouts and websites

4. Given Pre-Test/Post-Test strategies

5. Taught beneficial compounding interests in savings and investments vs. credit card interest rate traps

6. Shown mathematical calculations in teaching.... KNOWLEDGE, UNDERSTANDING & WISDOM!

7. Surveys of where they are and where they're going

8. Shows how to invest

9. Shows how to go into business, how to get franchises, purchase property and become landlords

10. Show how to buy a home vs. renting

11. Shows the need to have tax strategies, IRA's, etc.

12. Shows how to pay off cars, homes, etc. and how to pay for the future ones in cash (show the advantages)

Action

1. Per the items above, things (issues, subjects) must be taught piece meal...If you were to eat an elephant, you'd do it one bite at a time.

2. Show how to have a Balanced Budget

3. Show and give examples of the Leading of the Spirit of God being matched with personal or family financial plans

Results

1. Should have knowledge of their monthly, quarterly/yearly cost of living

2. Have a Balanced Budget

3. End of Year (EOY) Financial goals done at the beginning of each year

4. The Leading of the Spirit of God being matched with the personal or family financial plans

5. Children of the household having a positive work ethic and being taught financial strategies also to enhance the family's legacy

Tracking and Disciplining Your Finance$

Please see the budgets provided on the website www.guardyourheart.life. They, along with the video presentations, will walk you through populating a very thorough budget, then balancing it out to a zero balance by the end of a month. **There are other budgets that will show you how to eliminate debt, pay for everything in cash and begin developing wealth.**

SPIRITUAL INVENTORY

Give at least 3 scriptures the Lord has given you from which you have received revelation secrets. . . "God's sayings." List your revelation also.

_____

_____

_____

_____

_____

_____

_____

_____

_____

_____

SECTION VIII

←——————→

LEGACY

Your influence on family, friends and everything you touch.

TRANSFORMING CHARACTERISTIC
~ BROTHERLY KINDNESS ~

Loving, corrective actions with believers.

KINGDOM BENCHMARK
~ VISION ~

The operation plan of the Kingdom of God's
blueprint in your life.

14

LEGACY:
AN OVERVIEW

L egacy is defined first as: Law. A gift of property, especially personal property, as money, by will; a bequest. Secondly, legacy can be defined as anything handed down from the past, as from an ancestor or predecessor. Thirdly, legacy is something achieved that continues to benefit or detract, after a person dies, ie. an accomplishment, feat or influence that continues having an effect.[1] (McMillan dictionary)

Legacy…what are you leaving behind to family, friends and associates? (This is not limited to $) When we hear, believe and obey the Lord's direction for ourselves, He measures it as righteousness. We then do the word of His righteousness and it becomes **FAITH** which pleases Him (see **Hebrews 11:6**) Now, we add to this diligence, steadfastness and continuance…this guides us into truth.

> "If ye continue in my word, then are ye my disciples indeed; And ye
> shall know the truth, and the truth shall make you free."
>
> ~ John 8:31-32

This, in turn, makes us the Sons of God. He now gives His Sons, favor, the anointing which yields His power of His Spirit to fulfill the **supernatural** calling He has predestinated for those in Son ship. Those Sons are summoned up into the *Calling* of the Kingdom of God in every Issue of Life. This *calling* has an **Elected Place of Position** filled with the Knowledge, Understanding, Wisdom, Favor, Love, Peace, Joy and Power of friendship with God through having a *right relationship* with Him.

Daniel 11:32b says, "...but the people who know their God shall be strong, and carry out great exploits" (NKJV). These exploits that God has predestinated us to fulfill, come from *knowing Him and being strong*. They are not only for family, friends and associates, but are for the whole world to observe the *works of God* and come unto Him... this is His legacy in each of us.

Joseph provided a legacy for his mother, father, brothers and those who were related to them. He also provided for all the Egyptians and the nations surrounding them. His examples provided for instruction and a legacy of faith for the entire world. Daniel, Esther and many others spoken of in the scriptures have done the same...it's now up to us to follow in their footsteps of obedience, faith, love, along with the knowledge, understanding and the wisdom of God that they walked in.

God Established the First Legacy

"Then the word of the LORD came to me, saying: "Before I formed you in the womb I knew you; Before you were born I sanctified you; I ordained you a prophet to the nations."   ~ Jeremiah 1:4-5 NKJV

"For whom He foreknew, He also predestined to be conformed to the image of His Son, that He might be the firstborn among many brethren."   ~ Romans 8:29 NKJV

"For we who have believed do enter that rest, as He has said: "So I swore in My wrath, 'They shall not enter My rest,'" although the works were finished from the foundation of the world."

~ Hebrews 4:3 NJKV

"For we are His workmanship, created in Christ Jesus for good works, which God prepared beforehand that we should walk in them."   ~ Ephesians 2:10 NKJV

Please note the 4 scriptures listed. You will note three general themes **1.** "*Pre* - such as: before, formed, foreknew, and beforehand" **2.** Along with an action that the Lord had taken, such as: "knew, sanctified, ordained, were finished, conformed, created in, prepared," and finally **3.** There is a destination point to a specific purpose that God intended for the *chosen people* of God. What has been shown to me is that God did a work in each of us before our spirit man was joined to our bodies in the womb. Let's go further with this: Jeremiah, Joseph, Esther, and Daniel already had been ordained and given the prophet DNA in the spirit, with a specific task and election before coming into their body. They had already gone to classes in the spirit realm of heaven and had graduated at the top of the class; all selected or predestined to God's purposes, graduated at the same level... excellence. When Jeremiah had suffered persecution for speaking the word of God, he became weary in his natural man and decided that he'd no longer be a spokesperson for the Lord; note what happened:

"Then I said, "I will not make mention of Him, Nor speak anymore in His name." But His word was in my heart like a burning fire Shut up in my bones; I was weary of holding it back, And I could not."

~ Jeremiah 20:9 NKJV

What had happened to Jeremiah is the Kingdom of God *pre-destination* kicked-in and the timing for the specific work to happen manifested in the chosen vessel in the earth. The predestined word in Jeremiah said the time is now, forget your natural limitations and speak, declare, prophesy what is in the wind now. Jeremiah went forward with the word of the Lord at the specific time and place that it was to have happened, and every word that came forth from his mouth came to pass.

Jesus was at the wedding with His mother when she came to Him and said, "They have no wine." Jesus responded, "...'Woman, what does your concern have to do with Me? My hour has not yet come.' His mother said to the servants, 'Whatever He says to you, do it'"" **(John 2:4-5 NKJV)**.

Just as the Roman centurion had stated, again by revelation, while placing a demand of faith on the Kingdom of God:

> "Lord, do not trouble Yourself, for I am not worthy that You should enter under my roof. Therefore I did not even think myself worthy to come to You. But say the word, and my servant will be healed. For I also am a man placed under authority, having soldiers under me. And I say to one, 'Go,' and he goes; and to another, 'Come,' and he comes; and to my servant, 'Do this,' and he does it."
>
> ~ Luke 7:6b-8 NKJV

This did not begin in the natural world but in the spirit realm before the centurion was formed in his mother's womb. There are Kingdom works, **supernatural** works, that you have been predestined to accomplish, through obedience, in this end-time. Those works are beyond what you can think in your intellect because they are not at all intellectual, but spiritual. **Ephesians 2:10B** says, "For we are His workmanship, created in Christ Jesus for good works..." (NKJV). But as it is written:

> "Eye has not seen, nor ear heard, Nor have entered into the heart of man The things which God has prepared for those who love Him." But God has revealed them to us through His Spirit. For the Spirit searches all things, yes, the deep things of God."
>
> ~ 1 Corinthians 2:9-10 NKJV

Therefore, God has selected for you an action that He took and *set you aside* for and then a *destined position* for a *specific task* to be accomplished in your life.

God's legacy restores even if we leave our inheritance.

As we look at the meaning of the word Legacy, that which has been left for one's family and world, which continues to benefit or detract, understand that God's legacy has the lasting power to continue to impact, as He's yet present. An excellent example of this is the story of the prodigal son in **Luke 15**.

The story relates how a father had two sons and one of them came and asked if he might have his inheritance before the father had passed. The father gave the son his inheritance and the son left and went to a faraway country where he spent his inheritance quickly through sin and foolish wasteful living that he had not learned from his father. After the son spent all his money a severe famine hit the land and he had to go and find employment with a citizen of that land. He was hired to feed the swine. This speaks of the issue of educational preparation in a prior chapter. Apparently, he didn't prepare himself educationally or complete his education while yet with his father, so now in a different land he could only find employment in a lesser job.

As he labored in this lesser position of feeding the swine, "And he would gladly have filled his stomach with the pods that the swine ate, and no one gave him anything" (**Luke 15:16** NKJV). At that point he came to his right mind and said that his father's servants eat far better than what he was doing, and at present, he was starving. He stated to himself that he would repent and return to his father's house and confess to his father that he had sinned and was no longer worthy to be called a son, and plead to be just hired as a servant.

"And he arose and came to his father. But when he was still a great way off, his father saw him and had compassion, and ran and fell on his neck and kissed him. And the son said to him, 'Father, I have sinned against heaven and in your sight, and am no longer worthy to be called your son.' "But the father said to his servants, 'Bring out the best robe and put it on him, and put a ring on his hand and sandals on his feet. And bring the fatted calf here and kill it, and let us eat and be merry; for this my son was dead and is alive again; he was lost and is found.' And they began to be merry."

~ Luke 15:20-24 NKJV

There are those in the Body of Christ that have been saved and after receiving benefits from the Lord, have backslid, left fellowship with God and other believers and went back out into the world with greed, sexual sins, and other worldly behaviors, placing other things before the Lord. Even now, the Lord has compassion (love and forgiveness) and has open arms calling you to come back to Him. He is forgiving, patient and more than willing to bring you back into His fellowship, dust you off and clean and restore you to His inheritance.

The Spiritual DNA Component that Causes Legacy

It is through "Faith" that all those that heard, believed and then did the will and purposes of God leave an impact on those coming after them. Faith is the current that travels through an electrical wire causing the power that brings forth the *functioning end result* such as light, the running of a dishwasher or hair dryer, etc. That current is what makes the wire *live*, giving God's purposed destiny.

"So, shall My word be that goes forth from My mouth; It shall not return to Me void, But it shall accomplish what I please, And it shall prosper in the thing for which I sent it."   ~ Isaiah 55:11 NKJV

The power within the electrical wire comes from whatever the generating force is, be it a dam, windmill, lightning, etc. In the Kingdom of Heaven, the generator is God's will and purpose, the wire is whatever expanse there is in the heavens or earth for God needs no *wire*, and the believers are the *instruments*.

"Behold, I have created the blacksmith Who blows the coals in the fire, Who brings forth an instrument for his work; And I have created the spoiler to destroy. No weapon formed against you shall prosper, And every tongue which rises against you in judgment You shall condemn. This is the heritage of the servants of the LORD, And their righteousness is from Me," Says the LORD."

~ Isaiah 54:16-17 NKJV

In these two verses of Isaiah the Lord tells us that He has created circumstances in our lives that cause a heating-up to burn off things within us that do not benefit His Kingdom purposes, such as sin and fear. As those things are burned-off of us, He makes us the *instrument* that is perfect for the circumstances surrounding us to bring about His word through our behavior manifesting the light in the darkness surrounding us. This is His legacy living through God's revealed word in us and none of the weapons that Satan uses against us will have success. Anything said against us, we will be given the knowledge, understanding and wisdom of God to destroy it.

The real bottom-line here is God had Jesus pay too great a price to allow any sin or sins that we could commit to override that price. Therefore, nothing can separate us from so great a legacy that is through the love of God and the blood of Christ Jesus! This is the spiritual DNA component that causes our legacy from God, the Love and power of the blood of Jesus.

In the natural I was a letter carrier, dissatisfied in my position, with other *business ambitions and abilities*. I had therefore decided to quit my job and go into business for myself. At that specific time, I was attending college at a local university studying in the field of education. I was married and had two small children, my wife was a speech pathologist whom the Lord had directed to quit her job and stay home to be with our children. Therefore, my plan of quitting was causing some anxiety, despite my confidence that I would be able to provide adequately for my family.

I was very determined to take the steps of going into business for myself, but my wife was troubled by my decision and had said to the Lord, *Father, I support Lloyd in his endeavors, but I have no peace with his decision, so would you show me your direction and will regarding this issue?* Later that evening, while she was reading a book, the Lord showed her a vision that appeared on the pages of the book that she was reading. She saw me working in the post office in a supervisory position, speaking to a lady regarding the Lord. When I arrived home that evening, she informed me, "It is not the Lord's will for you to quit the post office, because He showed me a vision of you today while I was reading a book, and you were ministering to a lady in the post office." I reminded her that I already do this, and that she is a part of it, for we taught Bible studies on my route at 7pm every other week. She went on to tell me that in the vision, I was not in a letter carrier's uniform, but instead was dressed in a tie and jacket, as I was the lady's supervisor. At this point, I believed the vision she had received and asked, "OK, what should I do now?" She responded, "I don't know." I decided not to quit, and I waited and believed that the Lord would provide further direction. About a month later, my manager approached me and asked if I would replace one of the supervisors who was about to go on an assignment.

This was the beginning of my management experiences in the post office that continued to expand until I became Postmaster for the city of Detroit and 15 other cities surrounding it. In this capacity, the Lord gave and anointed me with favor, witty inventions and success that was unparalleled in the post office at that time. Because of the great success, I was requested in various cities throughout the country to assist them in coming into success.

In 2003 I had decided, please note, *I had decided,* to retire from the post office as I had 35 years of service which equated to receiving a full retirement. My wife and I also had no bills, so I felt that I could retire and give all my time to the pursuit of God's purposes in my life. Regarding legacy, the Lord spoke the following, *Did I say you could retire?* I was somewhat surprised, as I hadn't thought that I had to ask if I could retire.

Don't forget the following scripture, "Trust in the Lord with all thine heart; and lean not unto thine own understanding. In all thy ways acknowledge him, and he shall direct thy paths" **(Proverbs 3:5-6)**.

I then told the Lord, *Father, I've already informed my superiors that I was going to retire, and I've made the announcement.* He told me to simply cancel it and inform them that I had changed my mind. I then stated, *but they will say that I am usually so sure in my decisions, so why then am I changing this one?* The Lord then told me, *tell them that I said you were not to retire.* It happened just as I have written.

Later that year I was contacted by the president of one of the Postmaster associations regarding coming to speak at their 100th year anniversary convention. I asked how he knew me, and I was told that he was in the audience when I had spoke at an Iowa state postmasters meeting and felt that I was the one that should do the motivational address for the convention. God gave a rousing successful meeting and at the last of the two speaking engagements, I asked one of the participants of the meeting where she was from. I saw her walking in the hotel lobby with one of the programs that I had handed out to the audience on the **Metamorphosis of Success**. She went on to tell me that she was not a postmaster and in fact did not work for the post office at all. She said that she was laying in her bed that morning and the Lord told her that she was to come to the hotel to hear a message that was for her. She obeyed, came to the hotel and went to the various venues of speakers until she arrived where I was speaking. The Lord showed her, *this is where I want you to be.* At that point of sharing with me, she picked up the program handout that I had provided the audience, smiled and waved it at me and said, "I got what I came for!"

Eight years later, I was still at the post office and on a particular day I was sitting at my computer. I now had 43 years of service. The Lord spoke to me saying, *Son I know that you want to retire, but I have specific people whose lives you are to sow into, but I am closing the door.* Over the next few years, I saw a number of those people manifest that I was to sow into; but there was one that stands out over the rest.

She is a young woman whose 15-year-old son had attempted suicide. She attempted the same and her mom had actually committed suicide (This is the result of a generational curse on the family, of which we deal with in the **HTGTTV** course). The boss to her boss had called me and asked if I would counsel her and pray for her. Approximately 4 weeks later, I was in Chicago at a meeting and the Lord told me to call her and pray and counsel her. I did. After my prayer and counseling session, unknown to myself, she then went and prayed for her son, who was on such medication that it kept him in an almost anesthesia state. After her prayer, he was removed from all medications and is living a very successful college life. He is on the dean's list. She herself, has had breakthroughs that are miraculous!

I was also requested to travel to various states and districts in the country within the post office, to do motivational/inspirational talks to enhance the careers of those in various positions in the post office and in management. I was also requested to speak to people outside of the post office. This ended up influencing a wide range of persons and every place I traveled, the people knew the cause of the success was Jesus... I made sure that I let it be known! It's called **LEGACY** and the Lord has a plan for all His people to leave His legacy everywhere our feet travel! Guess what? That is referring to **YOU!!**

How to Keep the Legacy

I am sure that after the prodigal son returned to his father's house and blessings that he stayed in them! As we continue in the thoughts and ways of our Heavenly Father, "If we confess our sins, he is faithful and just to forgive us our sins, and to cleanse us from all unrighteousness" **(1 John 1:9)**.

"He who has an ear, let him hear what the Spirit says to the churches." "And to the angel of the church in Philadelphia write, 'These things says He who is holy, He who is true, "He who has the key of David, He who opens and no one shuts, and shuts and no one opens": "I know your works. See, I have set before you an open door, and no one can shut it; for you have a little strength, have kept My word, and have not denied My name."

~ Revelation 3:6-8 NKJV

In Jeremiah chapter 1 we see that the Lord continued speaking with Jeremiah and Jeremiah kept acknowledging, praying, being in fellowship and hearing; take note of the times the Lord spoke:

"The words of Jeremiah the son of Hilkiah, of the priests who were in Anathoth in the land of Benjamin, to whom the word of the LORD came in the days of Josiah the son of Amon, king of Judah, in the thirteenth year of his reign. It came also in the days of Jehoiakim the son of Josiah, king of Judah, until the end of the eleventh year of Zedekiah the son of Josiah, king of Judah, until the carrying away of Jerusalem captive in the fifth month."

~ Jeremiah 1:1-3 NKJV

Note, in more specific instances, **Jeremiah 1:4, 7, 9, 11, 12-14:**

> (4) "Then the word of the LORD came to me, saying…" (7) "But the LORD said to me…" (9) "Then the LORD put forth His hand and touched my mouth, and the LORD said to me…" (11) "Moreover the word of the LORD came to me, saying…" (12) "Then the LORD said to me…" (13) "And the word of the LORD came to me the second time, saying…" (14) "Then the LORD said to me…" (NKJV).

The Lord continued His message through to verse 19 and spoke further in chapter 2:1, "Moreover the word of the LORD came to me, saying…" **(Jeremiah 2:1 NKJV).**

It is necessary that we continue **hearing, believing** and **obeying** as we release (speak) those things the Lord has revealed to us to get His results, which is His fruit or purposes in the earth ("Thy Kingdom come, thy will be done in earth as it is in heaven"). The Lord's Kingdom coming and will being done has a process that must be followed. Please see the chart entitled, "Seed, Blade, Ear and Fruit," (for chapter 14) on the website, www.guardyourheart.life.

The greatest legacy is sonship thoughts.

God's legacy to us was our receiving the gift of new birth through Jesus' sacrifice of His blood to remove our sins and take death, the separation of Himself from His Father, and then raising us to life; therefore, transferring His life to ourselves. This gave us everlasting life with He and His Father. In this *life* package came the removal of iniquity and receipt of His thoughts, peace with the Father due to Christ being chastised in our stead and healing for ourselves through the stripes He received. He gave us the infilling of the Holy Ghost so that we would become empowered through the 9 **supernatural** gifts of His Spirit so that we can experience and release His kingdom activities into the earth. God has, is and shall perform His word and that which He will say. We therefore have His impossibilities running in our veins to make the impossible happen. "For the mouth of the Lord has spoken it!"

Several years ago, a very dear friend of mine had some brain tumors that were inoperable. He went to the hospital. I think it was the University of Michigan hospital in Ann Arbor, Michigan, and they did various tests and blood work on him. The results were not good. The next morning, he had to fly into Dallas, Texas and go through a procedure whereby the probable results of that procedure were not going to be good and it was based on the blood work results that had manifested the previous day.

The doctors in Dallas, Texas performed a specific brain procedure. They said that if blood work was perfect which it was not, he would not have much of a chance of survival. However, the blood work was very poor from the previous day, so his chances of survival were nil to none. He called me early that morning before I went to work and told me about the situation, and I asked him had the Lord given him a word. He told me that the Lord had spoken to him **Luke 1:37**. I went to **Luke 1:37**, it was referring to Mary the mother of Jesus, soon-to-be pregnancy and the angel that told her that with God nothing is impossible. When I saw that, I saw **IM...POSSIBLE**, not impossible but **IM...POSSIBLE**; so, I told my buddy what the Lord had just shown me, and that's what I prayed over his condition.

I received a call later that evening from him. He was very joyful and laughing. The doctors in Dallas, Texas checked his blood work and in doing so they saw that his blood work was just great. The Dallas doctors called after looking at the information that the doctors sent from Ann Arbor, Michigan on his blood work which was very poor, and they said this is impossible! So, they called the doctors in Ann Arbor and told them what they had found with the blood work. The doctors in Ann Arbor said that's impossible! Here is what we found. At that point the doctors in

Dallas, Texas stated that's impossible there's no way that anyone's blood could change that much in less than 24 hours. Well, the bottom line of all of this was the procedure was not necessary because of the *impossible happy outcome*, all from God speaking regarding the situation, **IM POSSIBLE**.

Now, let's take a glimpse of the Lord's Legacy to His people who have matured to sonship. This means they've become disciples according to **John 8:31-32**. I'm going to take an example of an old manual on finances published almost 40 years ago, and that I used in chapter 9. It referred to some very simple investment principals based on compound interest rates of 5% and 10% on a 1-time investment of $1000.00 over a 70-year period. See below.

% Int.	20 YRS	30 YRS	40 YRS	50 YRS	60 YRS	70 YRS
5%	$2,653	$4,321	$7,039	$11,467	$18,679	$30,426
10%	$6,727	$17,449	$45,259	$117,390	$304,481	$789,747

It does not take a rocket scientist to figure out which interest rate gives the greatest benefit. Now, as it relates to God's legacy toward us let's look at 4 scriptures:

"For My thoughts are not your thoughts, Nor are your ways My ways," says the LORD. "For as the heavens are higher than the earth, So are My ways higher than your ways, And My thoughts than your thoughts."   ~ Isaiah 55:8-9 NKJV

"Will a man rob God? Yet you have robbed Me! But you say, 'In what way have we robbed You?' In tithes and offerings. You are cursed with a curse, For you have robbed Me, Even this whole nation. Bring all the tithes into the storehouse, That there may be food in My house, And try Me now in this," Says the LORD of hosts, "If I will not open for you the windows of heaven And pour out for you such blessing That there will not be room enough to receive it." ~ Malachi 3:8-10 NKJV

"Then He said, "To what shall we liken the kingdom of God? Or with what parable shall we picture it? It is like a mustard seed which, when it is sown on the ground, is smaller than all the seeds on earth; but when it is sown, it grows up and becomes greater than all herbs, and shoots out large branches, so that the birds of the air may nest under its shade." ~ Mark 4:30-32 NKJV

"But these are the ones sown on good ground, those who hear the word, accept it, and bear fruit: some thirtyfold, some sixty, and some a hundred." ~ Mark 4:20 NKJV

Now, comparing the Lord's legacy toward us, as we hear, believe and obey, and **then continue,** we come into the multiple blessing-benefits of the Lord that, as it states in Isaiah, are above our thoughts and ways; inclusive to the compounding of God's interest rates. The Lord does not deal with 5% and 10% as in our example, but instead according to **Mark 4:20,** "…some thirtyfold, some sixty, and some a hundred" (NKJV). For those that obey in the relationship of obedience regarding the tithe, they are spared from the curse and are ushered into the beyond the 100-fold blessing to "open for you the windows of heaven And pour out for you such blessing That there will not be room enough to receive it" (**Malachi 3:10b** NKJV). Finally, the faith as a grain of mustard seed does not relate to the size of the mustard seed but its continual growth to the point of becoming a huge tree. Look at the following pictures.

Mustard seed atop a finger   Corn seed in the hand

Mustard seed tree size   Corn at full maturity (note the boy)

The mustard seed blessing comes down to this, for those in fellowship under anointed services continually according to **Hebrews 10:25**, "…not forsaking the assembling of ourselves together, as is the manner of some, but exhorting one another, and so much the more as you see the Day approaching" (NKJV).

Please note my confession: I have actively sought the Lord for the last 44 years, however, in the writing of this book; I have had to come to a new level. Let me give an example: in December of 2017, I gave my congregation an assignment that the Lord had put on my heart. They had to take nine issues of life and go before the Lord for Him to show them their number one issue that they needed to work on. Next, they were to take 2 scriptures out of the nine that are given or go to the word and get them for themselves and meditate those two scriptures until they receive revelation secrets from God. From that step, they were to proceed on in growth as with the mustard seed, and go from the seed stage, which is receiving a revelation word from God. Then the next stage would be the blade stage, which refers to initiating that which the Lord has spoken in the seed stage, once again from another revelation. Then the next step, according to **Mark 4:28** is the bud stage which comes right before the fruit. The bud stage comes after much tribulation; of course, the enemy trying his best to stop you and even your flesh getting in the way, but you press on to the bud stage. Once again revelation hearing from the Lord and finally of course, the results or the fruit's manifestation.

The Lord showed me via revelation, my chief issue was self-esteem being raised to Christ-esteem, and I really had a problem with that. The Lord went on to show me that he had been on me to get this book written for 3 years and yet it still wasn't written.

The Lord went on to show me that the reason the book was not written was I have compared myself to Bill Winston, Benny Hinn and Jesse Duplantis and the like, such as Joyce Meyers and even those who have *worldwide* ministries and are moving in the fullness of God. I had compared myself to those people and therefore felt that the work that I would put out would not be on the level of them.

The Lord said to me this, *as you seek me, you have the same Lord as do they and I'll give you the same revelations as I do them... write the book!* He said, *this is what I want you to do, start off putting at least one hour in a day in writing, do that and the book will write itself.* I had the hardest time doing that, but finally, in the ensuing months, I began to discipline myself in the **mustard-seed-continuance** and as I did that, I have come into a realm in the Spirit that I have never experienced... all from being diligent. The issue here is this, folks: the Lord has a legacy for us waiting in, and through diligence! Come on in, the water's fine!

The Great Benefits of Spiritual and Natural Legacy

Here's the spiritual legacy, Jesus said:

> "Most assuredly, I say to you, he who believes in Me, the works that I do he will do also; and greater works than these he will do, because I go to My Father." ~ John 14:12 NKJV

> "However, when He, the Spirit of truth, has come, He will guide you into all truth; for He will not speak on His own authority, but whatever He hears He will speak; and He will tell you things to come." ~ John 16:13 NKJV

> "And He said to them, "Go into all the world and preach the gospel to every creature. He who believes and is baptized will be saved; but he who does not believe will be condemned. And these signs will follow those who believe: In My name they will cast out demons; they will speak with new tongues; they will take up serpents; and if they drink anything deadly, it will by no means hurt them; they will lay hands on the sick, and they will recover." ~ Mark 16:15-18 NKJV

These things are happening all over the world and seeing that the Lord is not a respecter of persons, what He does in one that has heard, believed, obeyed and continued... he'll do for all, inclusive of YOU! I am watching the legacy of myself, which is influence in the natural, follow those who followed my example of Hearing, Believing, Obeying and Speaking **(HBOS)** at the work place, come into the success that the Lord gave me. Our children are doing very well financially and will surpass my wife and myself while seeking first His Kingdom and righteousness. They'll accomplish more and do so quicker than did we. That is part of the legacy, that they, and the members of our church have the advantage of starting off in the spirit and in the natural by standing on our shoulders, not bootstraps, and moving onward. Our grandchildren and yours will do the same, and all to the glory of the Lord.

In the spirit, our children are walking in the power of the gifts of the Spirit bringing more people to the Lord at an earlier age than did we. The grandchildren will multiply our loaves and fishes!

"A good man leaves an inheritance to his children's children, But the wealth of the sinner is stored up for the righteous."

~ Proverbs 13:22 NKJV

The Impact of Self-Esteem Transforming to Christ-Esteem, on Legacy

In chapter 3 I introduced how one could have their self-esteem transformed to Christ-esteem. In doing so, I utilized the fact that once a person hears something, an image formed in their mind and *that something that was heard* can be accomplished. This is how faith occurs. I then gave a biological experiment regarding the pike, minnows, aquarium and glass wall. The pike in the aquarium would quickly swim over and eat the minnows that would be introduced to the opposite side of the aquarium. Once the unseen glass wall was inserted into the tank and the minnows introduced on the other side of the unseen glass wall, the pike would ram into the glass causing pain and failure. As this was repeated several times, eventually the introduction of minnows no longer meant food, but pain and failure. The pike's inner image of the minnows became pain and failure, so don't try to eat them. The pike died of starvation, although the glass wall was removed, and the minnows swam in front of him. It would necessitate a series of continued successes in order to re-establish the image that the minnows, once again, meant a food source and not pain, failure and unavailability.

227

So, it is with us. It requires continued successes to establish the image of the transformative Christ-esteem image from the former self-esteem one. As this success continues for a length of time, a *culture* is established. Next, following the established culture comes an inheritance and then a legacy is produced for future generations. The culture from this new inheritance brings about the Kingdom of God on Earth. God's intentions aren't that multiplied continued successes are just for one person coming into victory over the issues of life; but that *new images causing success* is to become contagious. Two persons are to reach pinnacles of success, then eight persons, sixty-four, two-hundred eighty, etc.

The overall purpose of God's Kingdom inheritance, even as it was with Israel in their obedience to God stage, became a way of life. This *way of life* is and will overtake every realm with God's influence... becoming a living legacy for multitudes.

> "Behold, how good and how pleasant it is for brethren to dwell together in unity! It is like the precious ointment upon the head, that ran down upon the beard, even Aaron's beard: that went down to the skirts of his garments; As the dew of Hermon, and as the dew that descended upon the mountains of Zion: for there the Lord commanded the blessing, even life for evermore." ~ Psalm 133:1-3

SPIRITUAL INVENTORY

Give at least 3 scriptures the Lord has given you from which you have received revelation secrets. . . "God's sayings." List your revelation also.

_____

_____

_____

SECTION IX

←——→

ETERNAL REWARDS

The fruit of what you have planted in your life
that is received in the hereafter.

TRANSFORMING CHARACTERISTIC
~ CHARITY ~

Sacrifice for others due to an all caring,
benefiting relationship

KINGDOM BENCHMARK
~ PURPOSE ~

The Kingdom of God's manifestation in
the earth through you.

15

ETERNAL REWARDS:
AN OVERVIEW

Eternal[1] is defined as: without beginning or end; lasting forever; always existing (opposed to <u>temporal</u>): *eternal life.* Secondly: perpetual; ceaseless; endless: *eternal quarreling; eternal chatter.* Thirdly, eternal can be defined as: enduring; immutable: *eternal principles.*

Reward[2] is defined as a sum of money offered for the detection or capture of a criminal, the recovery of lost or stolen property, etc. Secondly: something given or received in return or recompense for service, merit, hardship, etc. Additionally, reward is to recompense or requite (a person or animal) for service, merit, achievement, etc. or to make return for or requite (service, merit, etc.), recompense.

ETERNAL REWARDS: The Kingdom of God Life connector for this final section brought finances together with legacy and then eternal rewards.

Let's put this under the magnifying glass. In reviewing the issue of **FINANCE$**, Psalms 24:1 says that "the earth is the Lord's and the fullness thereof the people and all that is therein." We agree that this earth belongs to the Lord and we understand that the fullness of the earth including the riches and everything in the earth also belong to Him. Going further with this thought is inclusive of the people that dwell in the earth are also subject to Him. Now, it says in **Jeremiah 29:11** that the Lord knows the thoughts that He thinks towards us as thoughts of peace and not of evil to give us His expected end. We're going to share shortly that the Lord is thinking all the time and coordinating all things for us as we follow Him. Let's look at another scripture regarding FINANCE$: as stated in **Deuteronomy 8:18** you should "remember the Lord your God, for it is He who gives you power to get wealth, that He may establish His covenant which He swore to your fathers..." (NKJV). So, the Lord gives us power which is wisdom, understanding and knowledge to cause you to have the savvy to get wealth in order to establish His covenant and therefore His ways in the earth.

Once His covenant is established, it then gives us a legacy. This legacy is the influence on our children and our children's children along with everyone else that we're involved with, now and later. The Lord's thoughts and purposes are not limited to one generation but to all generations, to be influenced regarding His abundant life and living through the example in our lives. Our final issue, Eternal Rewards, is rooted in these things we have spoken of thus far. As we look at **Hebrews 6:1-5** we find that there are nine Foundation Stones available to us and once they are received, applied and experienced effectively, we graduate to learning of and then experiencing the attributes that come from the knowledge of Christ's sacrifice, receiving Him in salvation, being baptized in the Holy Spirit, coming into revelation knowledge and then the powers of the world to come, therefore being restored to the abilities and powers intended by the Lord. In speaking of Eternal rewards, we must understand that anything that's eternally rewarded is in the Heavenly or the Kingdom of God Realm. The Kingdom of God is not natural, but **supernatural.** The miracles that Jesus did, the healings and deliverances never caused Him excitement; why? The **supernatural** is the norm in the Kingdom of God.

Lucifer, who was over the magnificent sounds of worship was an Archangel, a cherub, whose job was to take the worship from the universe up through his viols within his body, to the Heavenly realm of God's Throne. "How art thou fallen from heaven, O Lucifer, son of the morning! how art thou cut down to the ground, which didst weaken the nations! For thou hast said in thine heart, I will ascend into heaven, I will exalt my throne above the stars of God: I will sit also upon the mount of the congregation, in the sides of the north: I will ascend above the heights of the clouds; I will be like the most High. Yet thou shalt be brought down to hell, to the sides of the pit" **(Isaiah 14:12-15)**.

As **Isaiah 14:12-15** points out, Lucifer said in his heart. In the kingdom of God, in the **supernatural** realm, the thought of the heart is the deed. When he thought it, all the angelic beings heard it as well as God. God, who is **supernatural**, and has all of what we call the gifts of the Spirit and the character of Christ, which is His character, heard the thoughts. By His power and ability to discern spirits through the gift of knowledge and word of wisdom, cast Lucifer out with one third of the angels of heaven that had agreed with him. It says in **Hebrews 6:5** that we shall come into the powers of the world to come now! So, part of our Eternal rewards, is moving in the **supernatural** powers and character of Christ now and in eternity with God, Jesus and the Holy Spirit. The gifts, God has planned for us now will be utilized in His Kingdom realm forever. The gifts are the norm.

Further in **Hebrews 11:9-10**, we see how Abraham the father of the faith was content to live in tents waiting for that which was to come, a greater city whose founder and maker is God. There is a greater reward Abraham found, and it is eternal. Finally, we see in **Hebrews 12:1-2**, that seeing that we are surrounded by so great a cloud of witnesses in the heavens let us hold fast to our faith and then we find in verse 2 that Jesus is the author and finisher of all things. That is not just simply referring to the things in our present lives but things that are eternal. So, with that being said let's step into looking at our eternal rewards.

Our eternal rewards come from the things that are sown now in this life that have benefits to be reaped in eternity. Those things that we gain now don't stop here... they begin accumulating, compounding interest rates that will benefit us in the "next quarter."

The 1,000-year reign with Jesus: in **Matthew 25** as the Lord says, for those who have been faithful over the little, He makes to be master over much. The Lord is not only referring to, *here on the earth* but *in the world to come*. Take note of **Hebrews 6:5**, "...And have tasted the good word of God, and the powers of the world to come..." This is referring to those believers who through obedience and diligence have come into a relationship with God whereby they move in God's revelations and <u>supernatural</u> gifts now in their lives and in the world to come. Our natural thinking is so limited and can be compared to **Jeremiah 29:11**, as so many believe that the "expected end" mentioned in the KJV translation refers only to this normal lifespan on earth.

However, Pastor Francis Chan shows a 4 minute 20 second YouTube clip illustrating a *never ending length of rope* that showed two inches of the rope as being the natural lifespan of people here on earth and about one seventh of the two inches as being the person's retirement span.3 He then shows how the 6/7th. length of the rope represents the individual's lifespan up to their retirement years. During that period most individuals work for and save for that very short one seventh period in their retirement years giving little to no effort or *investment* for the remaining everlasting *never-ending length* of the rope which refers to their eternity. The *expected end* in Jeremiah 29:11 is referring to eternity. The Lord is not just referring to long life but eternal life.

Once again, Abraham in **Hebrews 11:10 looked for a city not built with hands.** This city was obviously a city that God had shown him in the heavenlies; his focus was therefore an eternal or heavenly one. God wants our focus to be the same... not on the 10-20 years one might live in *retirement* but that eternal existence in the heavenlies is to be our focus (see **Zechariah 14** regarding Jesus' returning to rule the earth with His saints).

Eternal Rewards are the recompense due to believers for their faith and obedience to God's will and purposes that He gives in judgment for results in our lives. We understand eternal when we think of the aftermath of this life. It simply means to exist through all times, lasting forever or without end. It is unchanging, not affected by the passage of time. By this definition we know that we are not referring to our physical bodies that we live in. We are speaking of the inner part of the believer, the spirit man.

Yes, there is eternity for all. Believers and unbelievers alike have an eternal destiny; an eternal reward that is based on whether you are in the family of God through Christ Jesus, and have continued in obedience, or are not in the family of God. Those in the family, believed and accepted that Jesus took their sins and are judged from their works of obedience through grace and faith. Those who are not in the family are judged without the benefit of the blood and life of Christ because of their unbelief and are still in their sins and condemned to the Lake of Fire.

At this point, let's look at what God expects and rewards to those who have accepted Jesus as their Savior and have followed Him. Below are a few scriptural references denoting the **eternal rewards and eternal judgments:**

"But very truly I tell you, it is for your good that I am going away. Unless I go away, the Advocate will not come to you; but if I go, I will send him to you. *When he comes, he will prove the world to be in the wrong about sin and righteousness and judgment: about sin, because people do not believe in me; about righteousness, because I am going to the Father, where you can see me no longer; and about judgment, because the prince of this world now stands condemned." ~ John 16:7-11 NIV

*<u>Note the Holy Spirit's purpose is to prove to the world that they are wrong regarding sin, righteousness (= hearing and believing what God has said) and judgment.</u> We all receive our <u>eternal rewards and the eternal judgments</u>, based on these 3 factors.

"For we that are in this tabernacle do groan, being burdened: not for that we would be unclothed, but clothed upon, that mortality might be swallowed up of life. Now he that hath wrought us for the selfsame thing is God, who also hath given unto us the earnest of the Spirit. Therefore we are always confident, knowing that, whilst we are at home in the body, we are absent from the Lord: (For we walk by faith, not by sight:) We are confident, I say, and willing rather to be absent from the body, and to be present with the Lord. Wherefore we labour, that, whether present or absent, we may be accepted of him. For we (Believers) must all appear before the judgment seat of Christ; that every one may receive the things done in his body, according to that he hath done, whether it be good or bad." ~ 2 Corinthian 5:4-10

I believe that almost everyone wants and expects a reward of some kind. There will be 9 points listed in the next chapter that will sum-up, I believe, what is clearly referenced in the word of God as His expectations. Of course, the unsaved cannot perform any of these expectations seeing that they are powerless and never got to first base due to their lost condition. They have hell and the lake of fire awaiting them. So, at this juncture, let's dive deeper into what the obedient believer can expect regarding their rewards in the hereafter. *Underlined scriptures denote rewards of the righteous and eternal rewards.

First Stop: Our 1,000 Year Reign on Earth with Jesus

In **Isaiah 14:3-23, Zechariah 14, 1 Corinthians 15:50-57, 1 Thessalonians 4:13-18, Jude 1:14-15** and **Revelations 20,** it is disclosed that toward the end of the age of mankind, Jesus will come with His saints and conquer the rebellious in the earth, along with Satan and his demonic hoards, placing them in captivity for a 1,000 years. During the 1,000 years that Satan and his demonic hoards are bound in hell, Jesus returns with His faithful saints to rule the nations of the earth from Jerusalem until Satan is released for a short 7-year period to again deceive the nations. This will give those on earth an opportunity to choose the Lord or Satan. At that point Jesus will instantly rid the world of Satan, cast him into the Lake of Fire forever and initiate the Great White Throne Judgment.

"On the day the LORD gives you relief from your suffering and turmoil and from the harsh labor forced on you, you will take up this taunt against the king of Babylon: How the oppressor has come to an end! How his fury has ended! The LORD has broken the rod of the wicked, the scepter of the rulers, which in anger struck down peoples with unceasing blows, and in fury subdued nations with relentless aggression. All the lands are at rest and at peace; they break into singing. Even the junipers and the cedars of Lebanon gloat over you and say, "Now that you have been laid low, no one comes to cut us down." The realm of the dead below is all astir to meet you at your coming; it rouses the spirits of the departed to greet you all those who were leaders in the world; it makes them rise from their thrones all those who were kings over the nations. They will all respond, they will say to you, "You also have become weak, as we are; you have become like us." All your pomp has been brought down to the grave, along with the noise of your harps; maggots are spread out beneath you and worms cover you. How you have fallen from heaven, morning star, son of the dawn! You have been cast down to the earth, you who once laid low the nations! You said in your heart, "I will ascend to the heavens; I will raise my throne above the stars of God; I will sit enthroned on the mount of assembly, on the utmost heights of Mount Zaphon. I will ascend above the tops of the clouds; I will make myself like the Most High." But you are brought down to the realm of the dead, to the depths of the pit. Those who see you stare at you, they ponder your fate: "Is this the man who shook the earth and made kingdoms tremble, the man who made the world a wilderness, who overthrew its cities and would not let his captives go home?" All the kings of the nations lie in state, each in his own tomb. But you are cast out of your tomb like a rejected branch; you are covered with the slain, with those pierced by the sword, those who descend to the stones of the pit. Like a corpse trampled underfoot, you will not join them in burial, for you have destroyed your land and killed your people. Let the offspring of the wicked never be mentioned again. Prepare a place to slaughter his children for the sins of their ancestors; they are not to rise to inherit the land and cover the earth with their cities. "I will rise up against them," declares the LORD Almighty. "I will wipe out Babylon's name and survivors, her offspring and descendants," declares the LORD. "I will turn her into a place for owls and into swampland; I will sweep her with the broom of destruction," declares the LORD Almighty." ~ Isaiah 14:3-23 NIV

In **Isaiah 14:3-23**, we see how Lucifer, who was in charge of all the worship for the universe ended up getting expelled from heaven through his pride, as he thought in his heart that he would exalt his throne to the height of God's throne and become like the Most High. (It must be noted that in the spirit realm or Kingdom realm, the thought of the heart is the actual deed, and is heard because in the spirit realm even one's thoughts are heard. Jesus spoke after telling the paralyzed man that his sins were forgiven him. At that instant, Jesus knew the internal thoughts of the Pharisees and teachers of the law that were present. Jesus then spoke in Luke 5:23:

> "Which is easier: to say, 'Your sins are forgiven,' or to say, 'Get up and walk'? But I want you to know that the Son of Man has authority on earth to forgive sins." So he said to the paralyzed man, "I tell you, get up, take your mat and go home." Immediately he stood up in front of them, took what he had been lying on and went home praising God."   ~ Luke 5:23-25 NIV

After the Pharisees and doctors of the law thought regarding the matter, **"who can forgive sins but God alone" (Luke 5:21b** NIV, emphasis added), Jesus being in the spirit realm, heard their thoughts and then responded.

Now back to Lucifer who was to be demoted and become Satan, once he and 1/3 of the Angels joined in his mutiny against God, they were all expelled from heaven, falling to the earth and made the earth void, darkness and disordered. It goes on to say in Isaiah that Satan shall be demoted even further to Hell. We'll see further regarding this matter in Revelations 20. For now, Zechariah 14 says:

> "A day of the LORD is coming, Jerusalem, when your possessions will be plundered and divided up within your very walls. I will gather all the nations to Jerusalem to fight against it; the city will be captured, the houses ransacked, and the women raped. Half of the city will go into exile, but the rest of the people will not be taken from the city. Then the LORD will go out and fight against those nations, as he fights on a day of battle. On that day his feet will stand on the Mount of Olives, east of Jerusalem, and the Mount of

Olives will be split in two from east to west, forming a great valley, with half of the mountain moving north and half moving south. You will flee by my mountain valley, for it will extend to Azel. You will flee as you fled from the earthquake in the days of Uzziah king of Judah. **Then the LORD my God will come, and all the holy ones with him.** On that day there will be neither sunlight nor cold, frosty darkness. It will be a unique day a day known only to the LORD with no distinction between day and night. When evening comes, there will be light. On that day living water will flow out from Jerusalem, half of it east to the Dead Sea and half of it west to the Mediterranean Sea, in summer and in winter. The LORD will be king over the whole earth. On that day there will be one LORD, and his name the only name. The whole land, from Geba to Rimmon, south of Jerusalem, will become like the Arabah. But Jerusalem will be raised up high from the Benjamin Gate to the site of the First Gate, to the Corner Gate, and from the Tower of Hananel to the royal winepresses, and will remain in its place. It will be inhabited; never again will it be destroyed. Jerusalem will be secure. This is the plague with which the LORD will strike all the nations that fought against Jerusalem: Their flesh will rot while they are still standing on their feet, their eyes will rot in their sockets, and their tongues will rot in their mouths. On that day people will be stricken by the LORD with great panic. They will seize each other by the hand and attack one another. Judah too will fight at Jerusalem. **The wealth of all the surrounding nations will be collected great quantities of gold and silver and clothing.** A similar plague will strike the horses and mules, the camels and donkeys, and all the animals in those camps. Then the survivors from all the nations that have attacked Jerusalem will go up year after year to worship the King, the LORD Almighty, and to celebrate the Festival of Tabernacles. If any of the peoples of the earth do not go up to Jerusalem to worship the King, the LORD Almighty, they will have no rain. If the Egyptian people do not go up and take part, they will have no rain. The LORD will bring on them the plague he inflicts on the nations that do not go up to celebrate the Festival of Tabernacles. This will be the punishment of Egypt and the punishment of all the nations that do not go up to celebrate the Festival of Tabernacles. On that day HOLY TO THE LORD will be inscribed on the bells of the horses, and the cooking pots in the LORD's house will be like the sacred bowls in front of the altar. Every pot in Jerusalem and Judah will be holy to the LORD Almighty, and all who come to sacrifice will take some of the pots and cook in them. And on that day there will no longer be a Canaanite in the house of the LORD Almighty."

~ Zechariah 14:1-21 NIV, emphasis added

In Zechariah 14 it was prophesied that toward the end of the age of man, Jesus will return to the earth and interrupt the war against Israel after half of Jerusalem has been plundered. At that point, Jesus will come with His saints and crush the rebellion of the nations of the earth against Israel and establish a 1,000-year rule upon the earth. Those believers who were obedient and faithful will rule with him after He returns (see 1 Thessalonians 4 below)

"**Brothers and sisters, we do not want you to be uninformed about those who sleep in death, so that you do not grieve like the rest of mankind, who have no hope. For we believe that Jesus died and rose again, and so we believe that God will bring with Jesus those who have fallen asleep in him. According to the Lord's word, we tell you that we who are still alive, who are left until the coming of the Lord, will certainly not precede those who have fallen asleep. For the Lord himself will come down from heaven, with a loud command, with the voice of the** archangel and with the trumpet call of God, and the dead in Christ will rise first. After that, we who are still alive and are left will be caught up together with them in the clouds to meet the Lord in the air. And so we will be with the Lord forever. Therefore encourage one another with these words."

~ 1 Thessalonians 4:13-18 NIV, emphasis added

We see in **1 Thessalonians 4**, Jesus returning to the earth after raising-up the dead in Christ and changing the faithful believers in Himself in "the twinkling of an eye, or a flash" of time as spoken of below in 1 **Corinthians 15:50-57:**

"I declare to you, brothers and sisters, that flesh and blood cannot inherit the kingdom of God, nor does the perishable inherit the imperishable. Listen, I tell you a mystery: We will not all sleep, but we will all be changed in a flash, in the twinkling of an eye, at the last trumpet. For the trumpet will sound, the dead will be raised imperishable, and we will be changed. For the perishable must clothe itself with the imperishable, and the mortal with immortality. When the perishable has been clothed with the imperishable, and the mortal with immortality, then the saying that is written will come true: "Death has been swallowed up in victory." "Where, O death, is your victory? Where, O death, is your sting?" The sting of death is sin, and the power of sin is the law. But thanks be to God! He gives us the victory through our Lord Jesus Christ." ~ 1 Corinthians 15:50-57 NIV, emphasis added

In the scripture of Corinthians, we see the long-awaited return of the Lord with the resurrected saints and the transformation of those believers to their kingdom bodies into immortality. Take note of Enoch's and Jude's prophecy:

"Enoch, the seventh from Adam, prophesied about them: **"See, the Lord is coming with thousands upon thousands of his holy ones to judge everyone,** and to convict all of them of all the ungodly acts they have committed in their ungodliness, and of all the defiant words ungodly sinners have spoken against him."

~ Jude 1:14-15 NIV, emphasis added

What makes Enoch's prophecy so interesting is that he prophesied it 3,300 years before Jesus was born. Compared to now, that's 5,370 years ago. He therefore prophesied 5,370 years ago of events that now as of 2020, appear to be near to manifestation. In Revelation 20 below we see that John prophesied what will happen regarding the Israelite nation, Jerusalem and the world and Satan after half of Jerusalem is ransacked for the last time in history, and all the nations defeated and judged. We see that Satan shall be bound for a short period of time and then released briefly before his final judgment and eternal dismissal to the Lake of fire. At this juncture will be the Great White Throne Judgment of those not found in the Book of Life and the eternal reward of the righteous.

"And I saw an angel coming down out of heaven, having the key to the Abyss and holding in his hand a great chain. He seized the dragon, that ancient serpent, who is the devil, or Satan, and bound him for a thousand years. He threw him into the Abyss, and locked and sealed it over him, to keep him from deceiving the nations anymore until the thousand years were ended. After that, he must be set free for a short time. **I saw thrones on which were seated those who had been given authority to judge. And I saw the souls of those who had been beheaded because of their testimony about Jesus and because of the word of God. They had not worshiped the beast or its image and had not received its mark on their foreheads or their hands. They came to life and reigned with Christ a thousand years.** (The rest of the dead did not come to life until the thousand years were ended.) This is the first resurrection. **Blessed and holy are those who share in the first**

<u>resurrection. The second death has no power over them, but they will be priests of God and of Christ and will reign with him for a thousand years.</u> When the thousand years are over, Satan will be released from his prison and will go out to deceive the nations in the four corners of the earth Gog and Magog and to gather them for battle. In number they are like the sand on the seashore. They marched across the breadth of the earth and surrounded the camp of God's people, the city he loves. But fire came down from heaven and devoured them. And the devil, who deceived them, was thrown into the lake of burning sulfur, where the beast and the false prophet had been thrown. They will be tormented day and night for ever and ever. Then I saw a great white throne and him who was seated on it. The earth and the heavens fled from his presence, and there was no place for them. And I saw the dead, great and small, standing before the throne, and books were opened. Another book was opened, which is the book of life. The dead were judged according to what they had done as recorded in the books. The sea gave up the dead that were in it, and death and Hades gave up the dead that were in them, and each person was judged according to what they had done. Then death and Hades were thrown into the lake of fire. The lake of fire is the second death. Anyone whose name was not found written in the book of life was thrown into the lake of fire."

~ Revelation 20:1-15 NIV, emphasis added

<u>DILIGENCE</u>

Be diligent as you come into God's order and attachment to your election.

"And we desire that every one of you do shew the same diligence to the full assurance of hope unto the end..."   ~ Hebrews 6:11

"But without faith it is impossible to please him: for he that cometh to God must believe that he is, and that he is a rewarder of them that diligently seek him."   ~ Hebrews 11:6

Diligent[4]:

1.   Constant in effort to accomplish something; attentive and persistent in doing anything:

2.   Done or pursued with persevering attention, painstaking:

I'm going to revisit diligence in more detail through testimonies that will be given in the next chapter. Years ago, the Lord told my wife to quit her job because ministry needs had grown at such a pace. At this time, we had one four-year-old child and one on the way with both of us working full-time. After quitting her job, one morning the Lord spoke to her, *I am going to show you how I can take care of you.*

My wife went to the meat market that day and while she was standing there trying to decide which meat package to get because there were several meat packages available when buying meat wholesale. The Lord had led us to purchase a large freezer so we could buy our meats wholesale in larger quantities, thereby saving money. As she was standing at the counter trying to decide which package to get; she had taken a flyer out of her purse to the store that had various sales of meat packages. The store owner was looking over at her trying to decide, seeing what she was doing, came over to look at what flyer she had. He was amazed to see that the flyer she had was out of date (The Lord had led her to keep that flyer with the coupons and discounts etc.). Well the manager was just amazed that she still had those old sale papers, so he came over and told her that he was just impressed that she still had that, and he just had to give her something... **he just had to give her something**!

He went back behind the counter and brought out chickens and he begin loading chickens into her cart, while he continued talking about how amazed he was. She had a couple of boxes of meat by the time she had finished, so he pushed the cart out to her car and loaded the meat boxes for her. He then pushed the cart back into the store still talking about how amazing it was that she was so diligent in keeping that old sales flyer with its coupons. As she got in the car and was about to drive off, the Lord spoke to her and said, *see, I told you that I would show you how I would take care of you.*

> "But without faith it is impossible to please Him, for he who comes
> to God must believe that He is, and that He is a rewarder of those
> who diligently seek Him."   ~ Hebrews 11:6

For myself, outside of the Bible class on my route and the teen group at the church, I ran the children's church on Sunday and helped to establish the Central Detroit Full Gospel Businessmen's Fellowship. I was also busy advancing up the ranks in management in the Postal Service. Once when things on the job went through a *dry spell*, opposite the usual success I had become accustomed to. So, I asked Him, *Lord you said for us to seek first your Kingdom and righteousness and all other things would be taken care of?* I left work early one Friday in order to get to the church with my wife to prepare for a weekend speaker. My wife was downstairs while I was upstairs in the balcony preparing to tape the meetings and the Lord spoke this to me, *son, you've taken care of my business, I will take care of yours.* The next week, things turned around greatly on the job and within 3 months I was requested to take over the role as the acting Postmaster of Detroit. Being diligent is rewarded now and in the here-after.

Note what was revealed to the apostle Paul regarding his eternal rewards due to his faithfulness:

> "I have fought the good fight, I have finished the race, I have kept
> the faith. Now there is in store for me the crown of righteousness,
> which the Lord, the righteous Judge, will award to me on that day—
> and not only to me, but also to all who have longed for his
> appearing."   ~ 2 Timothy 4:7-8 NIV

Now, note the Lord's reward for the Philadelphian church:

"Because you have kept My command to persevere, I also will keep you from the hour of trial which shall come upon the whole world, to test those who dwell on the earth." ~ Revelation 3:10 NKJV

The purpose for bringing to your attention how we think of Eternal Rewards, in eternity is for us to compare what we do regarding our deeds and accomplishments in our natural lives to what the ROI (return on investment) they will give us in the hereafter. I retired as the Postmaster of Detroit which was one of the forty executive post offices out of approximately 33,000 in the country. People would sometimes give accolades to the *elevated position* in which I had achieved, and I would quickly tell them, "there are no postmaster positions in heaven." I worked in the U.S. Postal Service for 47 years... but it ended. My *real work* has been and is *Kingdom* work. The other jobs have no heavenly retirement plans. How about your job?

Notice how God worked things in the earth regarding these two scriptures relating to the order of warfare:

"So God led the people around by way of the wilderness of the Red Sea. And the children of Israel went up in orderly ranks out of the land of Egypt." ~ Exodus 13:18 NKJV

"For because you did not do it the first time, the LORD our God broke out against us, because we did not consult Him about the proper order." ~ 1 Chronicles 15:13 NKJV

As the Lord led His people into battle there was always and still is a specific order. Take note that the Lord had them to go out in **orderly ranks** as they left Egypt. Also note as they began moving the ark of the covenant in first Chronicles chapter fifteen, David was very careful to move it according to how the Lord had instructed. In moving the ark, the first time, David failed to follow the exact procedures the Lord had instructed. Uzzah touched the Ark to prevent its falling, the Lord struck him and he died.

Today, in churches there are those who have not attached themselves to their proper position or *church hop*, from church to church, assuring that they never come under authority so that they do not have to submit to anyone. They are free from the authority that God has established to protect them through pastors and other leaders in the church body and are enslaved to the demonic forces that they have stepped into the snare of.

> "And the servant of the Lord must not strive; but be gentle unto all men, apt to teach, patient, In meekness instructing those that oppose themselves; if God peradventure will give them repentance to the acknowledging of the truth; And that they may recover themselves out of the snare of the devil, who are taken captive by him at his will." ~ 2 Timothy 2:24-26

God has an order. God had an order for His temple to be built. Take note:

> "Now all the work of Solomon was well-ordered from the day of the foundation of the house of the LORD until it was finished. So the house of the LORD was completed." ~ 2 Chronicles 8:16 NKJV

God also has an order to bring all of us into peace, health and prosperity as we journey here on the earth.

> "The steps of a good man are ordered by the LORD, And He delights in his way." ~ Psalm 37:23 NKJV

Also take note of God's expectations of our praise and worship that is beyond Sunday or mid-week service at the church. "Whoever offers praise glorifies Me; And to him who orders his conduct aright I will show the salvation of God" **(Psalm 50:23 NKJV)**.

Win Souls to the Lord and Help Their Development

"The fruit of the righteous is a tree of life; and he that winneth souls is wise."   ~ Proverbs 11:30

"I exhort therefore, that, first of all, supplications, prayers, intercessions, and giving of thanks, be made for all men; For kings, and for all that are in authority; that we may lead a quiet and peaceable life in all godliness and honesty. For this is good and acceptable in the sight of God our Saviour; Who will have all men to be saved, and to come unto the knowledge of the truth."

~ 1 Timothy 2:1-4

Win[5]: **1.** to finish first in a race, contest, or the like. **2.** to succeed by striving or effort: **3.** to gain the victory; overcome an adversary:

Lost[6]: **1.** no longer possessed or retained: **2.** no longer to be found: **3.** having gone astray or missed the way; bewildered as to place, direction, etc.:

The purpose for **John 3:16, "For God so loved the world, that he gave his only begotten Son, that whosoever believeth in him shall not perish, but have everlasting life"** (emphasis added), was so that we would believe on Him and receive life. It is therefore God's will that those who have received this life go about His purposes of reaching out to those who are unsaved. Please note, God does not intend that the winning of souls only come through your pastor or the special traveling evangelist, **but through you**.

So, are we to have some special salvation tract that is especially effective in winning souls? Not necessarily. What we are to do is to become established in the faith ourselves having come into the experience of repentance from dead works, faith toward God, being baptized into Christ, in the Holy Spirit, water and fire. After this we begin to follow the Lord through laying on of hands upon those in need of healing or transference of God's several giftings to others coupled with the understanding and acceptance of the doctrines of resurrection from the dead and eternal judgment. This establishes us in the doctrine of Christ.

> "Now therefore ye are no more strangers and foreigners, but fellowcitizens with the saints, and of the household of God; And are built upon the foundation of the apostles and prophets, Jesus Christ himself being the chief corner stone; In whom all the building fitly framed together groweth unto an holy temple in the Lord: In whom ye also are builded together for an habitation of God through the Spirit."   ~ Ephesians 2:19-22

Once we have the foundation of the faith (see also **Hebrews 6:1-6**), we grow into maturity and begin manifesting the **supernatural** gifts of the Spirit which cause people to be drawn to the Lord. (See chapter 7 regarding coming into maturity relating to the 9 Foundation Stones and the 9 Christ Characteristics) In **1 Corinthians 14**, it tells how the gifts of knowledge, wisdom, prophecy, healing, miracles and discerning of spirits impacts the unbeliever and those ignorant of the Lord to acknowledge Him and come to salvation.

> "But if all prophesy, and there come in one that believeth not, or one unlearned, he is convinced of all, he is judged of all: And thus are the secrets of his heart made manifest; and so falling down on his face he will worship God, and report that God is in you of a truth."   ~ 1 Corinthians 14:24-25

I gave examples of persons accepting the Lord through the giftings of God's Spirit manifesting through my witness in chapters 5 and 7. In chapter 5, I shared regarding the lady being raised up from a coma and other serious illnesses, after receiving the last rites from her church; she went on to salvation and baptism. Also, in that same chapter I mentioned the lady working at the Social Security office receiving the Lord and the baptism in the Holy Spirit over a two-day period as I witnessed to her while delivering mail.

During the fall of 2018, my wife ministered to a sister after a business meeting regarding the marriage ministry. The sister had a severe problem in her walking and had surgeries, etc. and had to use a cane in order to walk. My wife told her of the several miracles we are experiencing and ended up having her to sit on a chair as she raised her legs to check their length. One leg was an inch and a half shorter that the other. As my wife prayed the shorter leg began growing in sight of those that were there. In about 1-2 minutes the sister's legs were the same length and she was running, jumping and crying for joy of her ability to walk without pain and the cane. About 2-3 months later she shared her experience with another sister and this sister called and spoke to my wife. We agreed to meet her and her husband for dinner and during that meeting the Lord manifested Himself through words of knowledge and wisdom. The result is both the husband and wife are back in church attendance on a regular basis and are growing in the Lord.

As you mature in the Lord through fellowship, prayer, fasting, the 4 baptisms and obedience, you come into being led of the Spirit of God. This means, as you hear the Lord speaking to you, you follow what He is directing you in. You will find that God will lead you to people who need to accept the Lord and or grow in the Lord. After all, people coming into salvation and then being developed in His doctrines is His purpose and business.

The scriptures below relate to the winning of souls. In **Matthew 25,** although the talents represent money, the principal of the Kingdom law refers to all things that you are faithful in multiplying to greater sums, numbers or events. The same is referred to in John 15 as it speaks to the fruit. Some of the fruit being referred to is souls coming to Christ and being developed.

> "So he who had received five talents came and brought five other talents, saying, 'Lord, you delivered to me five talents; look, I have gained five more talents besides them.' **His lord said to him, 'Well done, good and faithful servant; you were faithful over a few things, I will make you ruler over many things.** Enter into the joy of your lord.'"
>
> ~ Matthew 25:20-21 NKJV, emphasis added

> "This is My commandment, that you love one another as I have loved you. Greater love has no one than this, than to lay down one's life for his friends. You are My friends if you do whatever I command you. No longer do I call you servants, for a servant does not know what his master is doing; but I have called you friends, for all things that I heard from My Father I have made known to you. **You did not choose Me, but I chose you and appointed you that you should go and bear fruit, and that your fruit should remain, that whatever you ask the Father in My name He may give you.** These things I command you, that you love one another."
>
> ~ John 15:12-17 NKJV, emphasis added

I had been invited out to Seattle, Washington to motivate a group of management personnel at a Postal Service development event. It was on a weekend and this day was Sunday. As I had finished the first phase of my presentation I had joined some of the employees for lunch or a break and they stated, "We were so concerned about missing church service at our various churches, but we didn't miss out because you just gave us our message for the week." I quickly responded with, "I didn't note any scriptures in my presentation." They responded back, "No you didn't, but we got God's message today."

I have found that as I have put the Lord first in my life, and winning souls to the Lord which is one of His top priorities, He rewarded me with everything else. That's His business plan and as we take care of His business plan, He rewards us now and here after.

Eternal Reward for the Righteous and Judgment for the Wicked

To get a fuller understanding of **Eternal Reward**, I believe it would benefit all of us to have a good grasp on the following words: **Righteous**: just, lawful, righteous (man). **Righteousness**: as vindicated, justification, salvation of God. It is first mentioned in **Genesis 15:6, "Abram believed the LORD, and he credited it to him as righteousness"** (NIV, emphasis added). From this we see that as we hear the Lord and then believe what He has said, we are counted as righteous before Him. **Vindication**[7]: defense; excuse; justification: **Justification**[8]: a reason, fact, circumstance, or explanation that <u>justifies</u> or defends: **Salvation**[9]: the act of saving or protecting from harm, risk, loss, destruction, etc. **Wicked**[10]: evil or morally bad in principle or practice; sinful; iniquitous: **Iniquity**[11]: gross injustice or wickedness. **Iniquitous**[12]: characterized by injustice or wickedness; wicked; sinful.

In the book of Revelation, one of the last living disciples that walked with Jesus was John. He had been exiled to the island of Patmos because of the persecution he suffered due to his witnessing of Jesus. Christian tradition says that he was banished to Patmos because his testimony of Jesus had caused him to be placed into boiling oil in Rome, yet without any harm coming to him. After which the *entire audience* in the colosseum were converted to Christianity due to the miracle. John was given the *revelation* of Jesus regarding the assessments of the seven churches in Asia-minor, which is an overall synopsis and summary of all church-types throughout history and at the time of Jesus' return to the earth to judge. Check the <u>www.guardyourheart.life</u> website for the synopsis of the seven church types showing the beliefs and behaviors of the churches that would be rewarded and punished. Also given are the Eternal Rewards along with the reasons for the eternal punishments.

After the 1,000-year reign what follows for the righteous are eternal rewards...

"Then I saw "a new heaven and a new earth," for the first heaven and the first earth had passed away, and there was no longer any sea. I saw the Holy City, the new Jerusalem, coming down out of heaven from God, prepared as a bride beautifully dressed for her husband. And I heard a loud voice from the throne saying, **"Look! God's dwelling place is now among the people, and he will dwell with them. They will be his people, and God himself will be with them and be their God. 'He will wipe every tear from their eyes. There will be no more death' or mourning or crying or pain, for the old order of things has passed away."**

~ Revelation 21:1-4 NIV, emphasis added

"It shone with the glory of God, and its brilliance was like that of a very precious jewel, like a jasper, clear as crystal. It had a great, high wall with twelve gates, and with twelve angels at the gates. On the gates were written the names of the twelve tribes of Israel. There were three gates on the east, three on the north, three on the south and three on the west. The wall of the city had twelve foundations, and on them were the names of the twelve apostles of the Lamb. The angel who talked with me had a measuring rod of gold to measure the city, its gates and its walls. The city was laid out like a square, as long as it was wide. He measured the city with the rod and found it to be 12,000 stadia in length, and as wide and high as it is long. The angel measured the wall using human measurement, and it was 144 cubits thick. The wall was made of jasper, and the city of pure gold, as pure as glass. The foundations of the city walls were decorated with every kind of precious stone. The first foundation was jasper, the second sapphire, the third agate, the fourth emerald, the fifth onyx, the sixth ruby, the seventh chrysolite, the eighth beryl, the ninth topaz, the tenth turquoise, the eleventh jacinth, and the twelfth amethyst. The twelve gates were twelve pearls, each gate made of a single pearl. The great street of the city was of gold, as pure as transparent glass. I did not see a temple in the city, because **the Lord God Almighty and the Lamb are its temple. The city does not need the sun or the moon to shine on it, for the glory of God gives it light, and the Lamb is its lamp. The nations will walk by its light, and the kings of the earth will bring their splendor into it.** On no day will its gates ever be shut, for there will be no night there. **The glory and honor of the nations will be brought into it.** Nothing impure will ever enter it, nor will anyone who does what is shameful or deceitful, but **only those whose names are written in the Lamb's book of life.**"

~ Revelation 21:11-27 NIV, emphasis added

The eternal reward package is *out of this world!!!*

"I call heaven and earth as witnesses today against you, that I have set before you life and death, blessing and cursing; therefore choose life, that both you and your descendants may live;"

~ Deuteronomy 30:19 NKJV

"As many as I love, I rebuke and chasten. Therefore be zealous and repent." ~ Revelation 3:19 NKJV

Something for you to consider as we refer to Eternal Rewards. What do you think your Eternal Rewards will look like? Well, it is dependent upon what results you have achieved for the kingdom sake here on the earth. Okay, what does that look like? Let's start off with the character of Christ; what does your character look like compared to Christ? How loving are you? How peaceful, how do you display kindness, gentleness, joy. Etc.? These are some of the fruit of the Spirit of God. On the other side of the coin, is the power of God. What do you display concerning delivering the Kingdom of God into the earth; as in healings getting people delivered from demonic oppression and or possession, receiving words of knowledge and or wisdom from God to manifest the miraculous in your life? Are you discerning spirits and bringing the power of God's Kingdom in the earth? How many people have you personally led to the Lord? I've referred to the scripture in **John 3:16**, "For God so loved the world, that he gave his only begotten Son, that whosoever believeth in him should not perish, but have everlasting life." Further, in **John 15:16** its states:

> "Ye have not chosen me, but I have chosen you, and ordained you, that ye should go and bring forth fruit, and that your fruit should remain: that whatsoever ye shall ask of the Father in my name, he may give it you." ~ John 15:16

A major portion of God's fruit is bringing forth His Kingdom into the earth. So, as I've said before how many people have you personally brought to the Lord and then secondly how has your life caused other people to be developed in Christ. These are the things that will determine your Eternal Rewards. If you need improvement in these areas, ask the Lord for His direction and He will show you the next steps.

SPIRITUAL INVENTORY

Give at least 3 scriptures the Lord has given you from which you have received revelation secrets. . . "God's sayings." List your revelation also.

_____

_____

_____

_____

_____

_____

16

HOW TO GUARD
YOUR HEART

*"Above all else, guard your heart, for everything
you do flows from it." ~ Proverbs 4:23*

ote the process in **Proverbs 4:20-24.** First there are the words, then by paying special focused attention to them one is given revelation *a spoken word from God…His sayings.* Then, focusing on the *sayings,* or *revelation* and following them, will bring one into health (of the body or anything else, such as lack, relationship-building, etc., anything that needs restoration, receives resolution). However, we must *fight, protect and guard* what has been revealed to our mind, **as it is the issue (direction) for our life**. Now to further protect what has been received, you must discard any negativity or complaining and murmurings of our mouth and deceit of your tongue so as not to agree with the world.

GUARD OVERVIEW

Guard means to: **1.** Keep safe from harm or danger; protect; watch over. **2.** Keep under close watch to prevent escape, misconduct, etc. **3.** Keep under control or restraint as a matter of caution or prudence.[1]

The Lord Birthed Us into His Kingdom

Notice the three special births that the Lord has brought forth into the world for the purpose of bringing forth His Kingdom and its purposes.

1. Genesis 18:14:

"Is any thing too hard for the LORD? At the time appointed I will return unto thee, according to the time of life, and Sarah shall have a son." Sarah had never given birth to children and was now 89, beyond the childbearing age and Abram was 99.

2. Isaiah 7:14:

"Therefore the Lord himself shall give you a sign; Behold, a virgin shall conceive, and bear a son, and shall call his name Immanuel."

Luke 1:30-37:

"And the angel said unto her, Fear not, Mary: for thou hast found favour with God. And, behold, thou shalt conceive in thy womb, and bring forth a son, and shalt call his name JESUS. He shall be great, and shall be called the Son of the Highest: and the Lord God shall give unto him the throne of his father David: And he shall reign over the house of Jacob for ever; and of his kingdom there shall be no end. Then said Mary unto the angel, How shall this be, seeing I know not a man? And the angel answered and said unto her, The Holy Ghost shall come upon thee, and the power of the Highest shall overshadow thee: therefore also that holy thing which shall be born of thee shall be called the Son of God. And, behold, thy cousin Elisabeth, she hath also conceived a son in her old age: and this is the sixth month with her, who was called barren. For with God nothing shall be impossible."

Isaiah speaks of a virgin giving birth and in Luke we find the virgin's name is Mary. Before Mary conceived her cousin, Elizabeth, who was well-stricken in age had conceived and was in her sixth month of pregnancy.

3. **1 Peter 1:23:**

"Being born again, not of corruptible seed, but of incorruptible, by the word of God, which liveth and abideth for ever."

2 Corinthians 5:17:

"Therefore if any man be in Christ, he is a new creature: old things are passed away; behold, all things are become new."

Romans 8:29:

"For whom he did foreknow, he also did predestinate to be conformed to the image of his Son, that he might be the firstborn among many brethren."

Christians are the ones who through God's miracle of faith in Christ Jesus, have been born of the seed of God. We therefore have been given His nature (Christ), are being formed into His image. The word IMAGE continues to come forth. As I related about the motivational speaking that I would be requested to do; I would ask someone from the audience to do a thing. They couldn't achieve it because the first 3 times I made the request within myself, where they couldn't hear and therefore had no image until I spoke audibly. As they heard they received the IMAGE and with it could do the task. The pike, minnows, aquarium and glass wall prevented the pike from being able to get the minnows and therefore the IMAGE created in his mind now spoke he was unable to eat the fish even when the glass wall was removed.

Romans 8:29 shows that those born of the seed of Christ (**1 Peter 1:23**) and are new creatures (**2 Corinthians 5:17**) have taken on the IMAGE of Christ (**Romans 8:29**). Jesus states in **John 14:12, "Verily, verily, I say unto you, He that believeth on me, the works that I do shall he do also;**

and greater works than these shall he do; because I go unto my Father"
(emphasis added). Jesus was manifested to destroy the works of the devil
(1 John 3:8). So, we received the same *offensive weapons* as our elder
Brother!

BRINGING UP THE GUARD

Guard that which God has revealed in the soul realm… guard your heart
with all diligence for out of it flows the issues of life **(Prov.4:23
paraphrase)** — guard it, protect it and keep it — keep it in front of you,
keep praying over it and keep praying in the spirit over it. Understand that
you're not at the level of spirit and revelation that God has so you're
guarding what He's going to reveal in the future that's even more. You're
guarding that which "…eye has not seen, nor ear heard, neither have
entered into the heart of man…" **(1 Corinthians 2:9)**… the deep things
of God that you can't see yet, as Joseph with his dreams… that's what you
are guarding. The Lord spoke 3 things about *guarding your heart* as
follows:

1. You must *fight fire with fire*. This equates to the fact that Satan is a
   spirit and therefore has **supernatural** abilities. However, God is a Spirit
   that has all power because He is the Almighty! This is wonderfully
   illustrated in **Exodus 7:1-5**:

   "Then the LORD said to Moses, "See, I have made you like God
   to Pharaoh, and your brother Aaron will be your prophet. You are
   to say everything I command you, and your brother Aaron is to tell
   Pharaoh to let the Israelites go out of his country. But I will harden
   Pharaoh's heart, and though I multiply my signs and wonders in
   Egypt, he will not listen to you. Then I will lay my hand on Egypt
   and with mighty acts of judgment I will bring out my divisions, my
   people the Israelites. And the Egyptians will know that I am the
   LORD when I stretch out my hand against Egypt and bring the
   Israelites out of it" (NIV).

Moses per the instructions of God, had Aaron to throw down his rod before Pharaoh and his rod became a serpent.

"Pharaoh then summoned wise men and sorcerers, and the Egyptian magicians also did the same things by their secret arts: Each one threw down his staff and it became a snake. But Aaron's staff swallowed up their staffs."   ~ Exodus 7:11-12 NIV

After this God had Moses to bring forth 10 plagues against the Egyptians that caused them to free the Israelites and ultimately destroyed the nation of Egypt and Pharaoh and his army in the Red Sea. This guarded the word of the Lord and His people.

2. The weapons that God will give you through His spoken word (sayings), will not be of the human intellect, but instead of the mind and ways of God.

"For though we walk in the flesh, we do not war according to the flesh. For the weapons of our warfare are not carnal but mighty in God for pulling down strongholds, casting down arguments and every high thing that exalts itself against the knowledge of God, bringing every thought into captivity to the obedience of Christ, and being ready to punish all disobedience when your obedience is fulfilled."   ~ 2 Corinthians 10:3-6 NKJV

These verses emphasize that our warfare is not human but spiritual; so, we must use the weapons from and in God's arsenal to win it.

Also note that what God will speak to us will not be natural, or with human limitations, but God's **supernatural** ways!

"For our light affliction, which is but for a moment, worketh for us a far more exceeding and eternal weight of glory; While we look not at the things which are seen, but at the things which are not seen: for the things which are seen are temporal; but the things which are not seen are eternal."   ~ 2 Corinthians 4:17-18

<u>We are not to depend on the things that we can see through our natural</u> <u>human understanding as a *guard against the things of our enemy*,</u> but instead depend on what is unseen of God that He will speak to us that will give us the advantage over the enemy.

3. The Lord has therefore given us a total arsenal of weapons to *guard ourselves from Satan's attacks*. This is shown in ***Ephesians 6:10-18***:

"Finally, be strong in the Lord and in his mighty power. Put on the full armor of God, so that you can take your stand against the devil's schemes. For our struggle is not against flesh and blood, but against the rulers, against the authorities, against the powers of this dark world and against the spiritual forces of evil in the heavenly realms. Therefore put on the full armor of God, so that when the day of evil comes, you may be able to stand your ground, and after you have done everything, to stand. Stand firm then, with the belt of truth buckled around your waist, with the breastplate of righteousness in place, and with your feet fitted with the readiness that comes from the gospel of peace. In addition to all this, take up the shield of faith, with which you can extinguish all the flaming arrows of the evil one. Take the helmet of salvation and the sword of the Spirit, which is the word of God. And pray in the Spirit on all occasions with all kinds of prayers and requests. With this in mind, be alert and always keep on praying for all the Lord's people" (NIV).

We are exhorted to take on the full armor of God, because as mentioned before, we are not warring against mankind but against the **supernatural** spiritual forces of Satan and his host. The Roman empire had the supremacy over other countries because they had developed their soldiers to a higher degree of military expertise. In **Ephesians 6:14-18**, you will note 9 specific strategies and weaponry that they were trained and equipped with that gave them this supremacy. The number 9 represents completeness in biblical numerology which gives the significance of the numbers used by the Lord.

The <u>first</u> weapon or strategy was the soldiers were taught to stand in battle. <u>To stand was more than to be upright upon one's feet but was a state of mind whereby the soldiers were taught to be firm and steadfast,</u> not surrendering their cause or position in battle. The Greek Spartans and Japanese were known for the rigid discipline of their soldiers in their attitude as regards to not giving-up in the fight. We as Christians must have God's mindset to **"...having done all, to stand. Stand therefore..."** (**Eph. 6:13b-14a,** emphasis added).

<u>Secondly,</u> the Roman soldiers were equipped with a belt around their waist that they could hang their sword, knife and other fighting instruments. This gave them the advantage of always having what was needed with them in the battle; they could also attach their shield to the belt as they traveled. <u>We must be equipped with all the things of God, being in His will, which is the flow of His current strategy and purpose or that which He is doing and speaking, so that we are in His strength and not ours.</u>

<u>Thirdly,</u> they had the most vulnerable part of their body, the heart and lung area, covered with a breastplate of movable, pliable metal that gave protection. In **Proverbs 4:23** we are admonished to, "Above all else, guard your heart, for everything you do flows from it" (NIV). The breastplate is that of *righteousness*. This places the absolute importance and necessity of *hearing from God and then coming into believing what has been heard;* <u>this is after-all, what righteousness is.</u> We must be in a *hearing from God mode* as we battle the enemy!

The **fourth** armor piece is having the **feet fitted with the readiness that comes from the gospel of peace.** With the feet protected with the knowledge, understanding and wisdom **(KUW)** of the gospel, you will flourish in the war. <u>Take note, we are cautioned throughout scripture that</u>

God's people are destroyed for a lack of knowledge **(Hosea 4:6)**, not to be ignorant of the devil's devices **(2 Corinthians 2:11)**, our weapons are not carnal but mighty through God, to the pulling down of strongholds **(2 Corinthians 10:3-6)**, and that we are not to be ignorant of our spiritual gifts **(1 Corinthians 12:1, 4-11)**.

The **fifth** piece of armor is the **shield of faith.** The Roman soldier's shield was that which provided a rigidity to repel the sword or spears and other weaponry of the enemy but also it was moist so that the flaming arrows of the enemy would be extinguished. Satan is forever throwing "lying flaming thoughts" at us along with, deceptions **(Genesis 3:1)** and lies **(Genesis 3:4-5)**. He's a murderer **(John 8:44)**, thief, destroyer and killer **(John10:10)**. Satan is always trying to take advantage of us **(2 Corinthians 2:10-11)**. Satan's thoughts are fiery darts **(Ephesians 6:16)**. He uses snares to capture us **(2 Timothy 2:25-26)**, he's a specialist at devouring **(1 Peter 5:8)** and is the accuser of the brethren **(Revelation 12:10)**. Be aware and fend them off!

In **sixth** place, the Roman soldier had a **helmet** to protect his head in the battle… if one *loses their head,* everything else is lost! So is it in the spirit; we have God's thoughts to be the *lifter up of our head* (Psalm 3:3).

The **seventh** piece of armor was an **offensive** one, the soldier's **sword,** that would take down or destroy the enemy effectively. For us, this is the **"sword of the Spirit, which is the word of God" (Ephesians 6:17b,** emphasis added).

The **eighth** piece for us is our praying in the spirit (tongues). As we pray in the spirit, God prays through us His thoughts regarding the big picture of the *unseen things that are causing our circumstances that we can see.* **(Romans 8:26-27, 1 Corinthians 2:9-16, 2 Corinthians 4:17-18)** Prayer in the spirit also opens the door for us to hear the heavenly things of God, so that we can speak those things that be, as though they are and to prophesy **(Romans 4:17, 1 Corinthians 14:1-5, 22-26)**. Prayer in the spirit also breaks down satanic strongholds **(2 Corinthians 10:3-6).** Prayer in the spirit increases the faith of the individual that is praying and therefore builds up the inner man, which is the spirit man.

Lastly, the armor piece in the **ninth** place was the Roman soldiers care for his companions. The Roman soldiers lived together for long stretches of time during their battle campaigns as they traveled to other countries. They became a caring close-nit family that watched out for the needs of one another. If your fellow soldier was weak or in need it impacted the whole unit inclusive of yourself; it was therefore beneficial to care for one another.

In our Christian warfare it is wise and loving to *always keep on praying for all the Lord's people.* **Galatians 5:6** states, "For in Jesus Christ neither circumcision availeth any thing, nor uncircumcision; but faith which worketh by love." Finally, regarding that which keeps our armor together: **"And now these three remain: faith, hope and love. But the greatest of these is love"** (**1 Corinthians 13:13** NIV, emphasis added). Our greatest weapon is our love one for another.

Another way of guarding your heart is given in **Proverbs 4:24: "Put away from you a deceitful mouth, And put perverse lips far from you"** (NKJV, emphasis added). A deceitful mouth is one that twists awry or out of shape, or that makes something crooked or deformed, while giving a false, perverted, or disproportionate meaning to or misrepresenting something or someone. Perverse lips are lips that are willfully determined or disposed to go counter to what is expected or desired; contrary. In short put away and protect from being negative or willingly going against what is needed or expected. But remember what you spend time thinking on is what you'll fill your tank with. **"A good man out of the good treasure of his heart brings forth good; and an evil man out of the evil treasure of his heart brings forth evil. For out of the abundance of the heart his mouth speaks"** (**Luke 6:45 NKJV**, emphasis added).

We must close the doors of Satanic entrance:

> "These six things the LORD hates, Yes, seven are an abomination to Him: A proud look, A lying tongue, Hands that shed innocent blood, A heart that devises wicked plans, Feet that are swift in running to evil, A false witness who speaks lies, And one who sows discord among brethren." ~ Proverbs 6:16-19 NKJV

Add to these immorality, not being holy, disobedience, unforgiveness, bitterness, non-tithing, non-diligence, inconsistent fellowship, witchcraft and rebellion and you have fixed your heart (mind) to cause yourself not to receive the things of God's kingdom. (See the **HTGTTV** website Section 2 The Parable of the Sower)

We Guard Ourselves with Things that Appear Little

Jesus tells us that as we are faithful over the little, He makes us master over much **(Matthew 25:14-30)**. Therefore, as we continue to follow the sayings of God, they are multiplied by His power to overcome any foe or situation. Look at the story of the teenager David as he fought the almost 10-foot soldier, Goliath, and slew him with a rock.

> "David took off the armor and picked up his shepherd's stick. He went out to a stream and picked up five smooth rocks and put them in his leather bag. Then with his sling in his hand, he went straight toward Goliath. Goliath came toward David, walking behind the soldier who was carrying his shield. When Goliath saw that David was just a healthy, good-looking boy, he made fun of him. "Do you think I'm a dog?" Goliath asked. "Is that why you've come after me with a stick?" He cursed David in the name of the Philistine gods and shouted, "Come on! When I'm finished with you, I'll feed you to the birds and wild animals!" David answered: You've come out to fight me with a sword and a spear and a dagger. But I've come out to fight you in the name of the LORD All-Powerful. He is the God of Israel's army, and you have insulted him too! Today the LORD

will help me defeat you. I'll knock you down and cut off your head, and I'll feed the bodies of the other Philistine soldiers to the birds and wild animals. Then the whole world will know that Israel has a real God. Everybody here will see that the LORD doesn't need swords or spears to save his people. The LORD always wins his battles, and he will help us defeat you. When Goliath started forward, David ran toward him. He put a rock in his sling and swung the sling around by its straps. When he let go of one strap, the rock flew out and hit Goliath on the forehead. It cracked his skull, and he fell facedown on the ground. David defeated Goliath with a sling and a rock. He killed him without even using a sword. David ran over and pulled out Goliath's sword. Then he used it to cut off Goliath's head."   ~ 1 Samuel 17:39b-51a CEV

David had a "stick and a stone" that you could see as his weapons. What he had that couldn't be seen was the backing and favor of Almighty God!

Let's look at a few of God's laws that supported David and ourselves also as it relates to our faith in what we have heard from God. Things may look small in the natural eyes, but faith in God grows, is alive and powerful!

1. Job 8:7:

"Though thy beginning was small, yet thy latter end should greatly increase" (emphasis added).

2. Zechariah 4:6-10:

"Then he answered and spake unto me, saying, This is the word of the LORD unto Zerubbabel, saying, Not by might, nor by power, but by my spirit, saith the LORD of hosts. Who art thou, O great mountain? before Zerubbabel thou shalt become a plain: and he shall bring forth the headstone thereof with shoutings, crying, Grace, grace unto it. Moreover the word of the LORD came unto me, saying, The hands of Zerubbabel have laid the foundation of this house; his hands shall also finish it; and thou shalt know that the LORD of hosts hath sent me unto you. For who hath despised the day of small things? for they shall rejoice, and shall see the plummet in the hand of Zerubbabel with those seven; they are the eyes of the LORD, which run to and fro through the whole earth."

3. Matthew 17:20-21:

"And Jesus said unto them, Because of your unbelief: for verily I say unto you, If ye have faith as a grain of mustard seed, ye shall say unto this mountain, Remove hence to yonder place; and it shall remove; and nothing shall be impossible unto you. Howbeit this kind goeth not out but by prayer and fasting."

4. Mark 4:30-32:

"And he said, Whereunto shall we liken the kingdom of God? or with what comparison shall we compare it? It is like a grain of mustard seed, which, when it is sown in the earth, is less than all the seeds that be in the earth: But when it is sown, it groweth up, and becometh greater than all herbs, and shooteth out great branches; so that the fowls of the air may lodge under the shadow of it."

5. Mark 11:22-23:

"And Jesus answering saith unto them, Have faith in God. For verily I say unto you, That whosoever shall say unto this mountain, Be thou removed, and be thou cast into the sea; and shall not doubt in his heart, but shall believe that those things which he saith shall come to pass; he shall have whatsoever he saith."

Elisha's servant had told him once he saw the Syrian army surrounding the city, "Master, what are we going to do for we're surrounded by this great army" (paraphrase 2 Kings 6:15b NKJV)? Elisha told his servant, not to fear for there were more *with* them than those that were *against* them (those he had seen with his natural eyes). He then prayed to the Lord asking that his servant's eyes (inner eyes) would be opened. The Lord then showed Elisha's servant the Assyrian army was surrounded by God's

Angels in chariots of fire (**2 Kings 6:15-17**). So it is with us as we press in to hear God and continue, He will show us His battle plan and provisions are far greater in our favor to guard our hearts and to destroy the forces of the enemy.

The last portion concerning guarding your heart comes down to being in the spirit, otherwise praying, singing and worshiping in the spirit. As you do so it tells you very clearly in **Romans 8:26-27** that we don't know what to pray for, as we ought and it goes further to tell us that as we're praying in the spirit, the Holy Spirit is praying through us the mind of God. Also in **1 Corinthians 2:6-9**, it speaks very clearly that had the secrets of God been known by the princes of darkness, Satanic demons, they would have never crucified the Lord Of Glory; because they would not have allowed Jesus to get in on their territory and take over which He was going to do once He came to hell after dying. He came to hell and took over. It says in **Colossians 2:15**, Jesus made "an open show," in front of the entire universe, in crushing the head of Satan's power and taking away from him the keys of death, praise the Lord!

In **1 Corinthians 2:16** scripture speaks of our having the mind of Christ; so, as you pray in the spirit your faith is built up. Therefore, for faith to be built up God has got to speak to you, so He speaks a word to you as you pray in the spirit and that word gives His thoughts which is His mind.

I opened this book up showing that when the light came in **Genesis 1:2-5**: it was not sunlight that was brought forth, but the same light shown in **Psalms 119:130**... the light from the word of God... otherwise, God-light. When God said, "Let there be light," it was God-light He was calling forth, which destroyed all darkness. Therefore, the atmosphere was and is changed because of the light that comes from the word and from the word comes faith and from faith comes favor. We're told in **Isaiah 55:8-9** that God's thoughts and ways are high above our thoughts and ways as the heavens are galaxies, as minister Carolyn Robinson has spoken to our church, galaxies above the earth. So, that's how much higher His thoughts are than our thoughts! As we pray in the spirit, we leave the limitedness of our thinking and we get up into God's thoughts which is so much further above our own thoughts, and the enemy's or Satan's thoughts.

Now let's look at this: It says in **Isaiah 14** that Satan thought in his heart that he would raise his throne up to God's throne and become like the Most High. I made mention earlier that *when* Satan thought that, God heard it... which means there definitely was a sound produced by the thought.

While praying in the spirit concerning the things of this chapter, the Lord showed me that the sound of Lucifer's thoughts is slow compared to God's speed and He said look up the speed of sound. The speed of sound is 767 miles per hour or 343 meters per second; it is so much slower than the light of God which comes from his word. The speed of light is 670,616,629 miles per hour, which equates to in 1 second, light travels around the earth seven and a half times! The faster something goes the more powerful or the greater power it has; what this means is light is 874,337.2 times faster than sound. It is therefore no comparison between the speed of light and the speed of sound. Of course, this is far less as it comes down to comparing Satan to God; there is no comparison of the power difference. Therefore, as we pray in the spirit God equips us with the mind of Christ and the power of Christ makes us far greater than Satan. **1 John 4:4, "Greater is He that is in you (us), than he that is in the world"** (brackets and emphasis added).

It really brings guarding your heart, to light! Spiritual light travels far faster and is far, far, far more powerful than natural light. It is indeed a treasure in earthen vessels **(2: Corinthians 4:7)** and a down payment from the kingdom realm of God's Spirit of Grace into our heavenly inheritance **(Ephesians 1:13)**. "And it shall come to pass, that before they call, I will answer; and while they are yet speaking, I will hear" **(Isaiah 65:24)**.

In 1995 I became the Acting Postmaster for the city of Detroit. During the early stages of this period, the Lord gave me specific directions (a word from Him which brought light) and as I implemented it, we experienced operational success that was off the chart's success-wise! When I state off the charts that's exactly what I mean. No one in the country was achieving success at the rate that we were. Headquarters sent a group of people to my office to see what I had deployed so they could share it with the rest of the country. Although they took and implemented the "witty inventions" **(Proverbs 8:12**, "I wisdom dwell with prudence, and find out knowledge of witty inventions."), they didn't receive the testimony of where they came from. They, therefore, only had partial success.

Because of the tremendous success we had in implementing the *light* ideas from God into the delivery operations, we were able to improve production, reduce costs, enhance service and improve morale to a degree that was unparalleled in Postal history. As an example, in one specific area of operational efficiency, the impact of the success was so astounding that one of the union presidents filed between 45-60 grievances that went to arbitration and our win rate equated to 100%! This was so dramatic and unheard of in Postal history that the president of that union ended-up apologizing to me in front of his union officers and my staff, asking for forgiveness of particular things he had done against me... and then requested me to pray for him in the meeting! I forgave him and then prayed for him. This was unheard of and I'm sure has never happened before or since. The scriptures highlight this:

> "Arise, shine; for thy light is come, and the glory of the LORD is risen upon thee. For, behold, the darkness shall cover the earth, and gross darkness the people: but the LORD shall arise upon thee, and his glory shall be seen upon thee. And the Gentiles shall come to thy light, and kings to the brightness of thy rising. Lift up thine eyes

round about, and see: all they gather themselves together, they come to thee: thy sons shall come from far, and thy daughters shall be nursed at thy side. Then thou shalt see, and flow together, and thine heart shall fear, and be enlarged; because the abundance of the sea shall be converted unto thee, the forces of the Gentiles shall come unto thee."

~ Isaiah 60:1-5

You are Not on the Defence!

I shared in chapter 4, how the Lord brought me into healing of stroke level blood pressure.

1. He had me to repent and obey His word in forgiving a person and praying and doing well towards them while "blessing them," which is speaking good things toward them (**Matthew 5:44-48**).

2. He had me to meditate **Isaiah 53:4-5**, which speaks of how Jesus has carried our griefs and borne our sorrow while healing our afflictions through the stripes He had received.

3. From this meditation the Lord spoke a *saying*, to me regarding my high blood pressure stating, *you are not on the defensive.* Upon my questioning Him regarding the application of this revelation to bring about the manifestation of health in my body, the Lord further revealed:

4. That most of the church and myself had interpreted **Matthew 16:18**, "And I say also unto thee, That thou art Peter, and upon this rock I will build my church; and the gates of hell shall not prevail against it," in error. We had taken the verse to mean that we were behind the gates and Satan was in front of them, kicking them down. Therefore, we see ourselves in a protection mode... NOT SO! As I stated, the Lord showed me that the gates of hell were anything that was not in God's kingdom. "Thy kingdom come, Thy will be done in earth, as it is in heaven" (**Matthew 6:10**). There is no sickness, fear, lack, poor

relationships, etc. in Heaven! Therefore, "you are not on the defensive," meant that I was on the offense. **I NEEDED TO GUARD THAT TRUTH!**

5. Now, the Lord showed me how to get on the offensive in the matter. He told me to begin speaking aloud to my body functions stating that my blood pressure was better than the normal of 120/80, and instead it became 116/76.

6. He also told me to take off 25 pounds through proper eating, rest, exercise and increased water intake.

7. I obeyed both instructions as I continued in meditation, speaking my new blood pressure numbers… calling those things that be not as though they were **(Romans 4:17B)**. In a very short period, my blood pressure manifested at 116/66! As I continued speaking what the Lord told me to speak, an image developed within me, "as a man thinks in his heart, so is he" **(Proverbs 23:7A)**.

Here is a secret, **in order to guard what God has spoken to you, you must continue meditating it and that which will come after it, while speaking/releasing it into the atmosphere ("And God said, Let there be light: and there was light,"** Genesis 1:3, emphasis added). This simple truth will work for every issue in your life! Please also note that the Lord does most things through the process of diligence. So many think errantly that because they received the first rhema word that they will then see the fruit. In order for fruit to manifest we must first **receive the seed** of the word of God… continue as we plant it in our heart by allowing it to become that which overtakes our thinking in abundance.

> "A good man out of the good treasure of his heart bringeth forth that which is good; and an evil man out of the evil treasure of his heart bringeth forth that which is evil: for of the abundance of the heart his mouth speaketh." ~ Luke 6:45

The seed must grow while becoming the **blade stage,** from the blade stage comes the **bud or ear,** and finally the **fruit results** are produced. After hearing the truth, we must continue in it and become free as Jesus stated in **John 8:31-32.**

Make room for Daddy!

What you hear from God you shall also see...because it becomes your inner IMAGE, that in turn becomes faith. We must have a "priority place" for Our Heavenly Father, so, *"Make Room for Daddy!"* Every image from which a result shall come forth from requires a space, area, room to first be occupied within; therefore, **allow God's sayings that will come forth from your being attentive to His word, to be fully developed.** Once you come into the habit of hearing God and following His directions you will have all you need to guard your heart and come into God's expected end for your life. **Be expecting GREAT THINGS!!**

Of GOD, I am

Lloyd E. Wesley, Jr.

ABOUT THE AUTHOR

 Lloyd took a Bachelor of Science degree in education from Wayne State University and did substitute teaching for a short period. In 1968 he began working as a letter carrier for seven years and then followed the vision that his wife, Pat, received in 1977 and went into management for the USPS. He and Pat dedicated their lives to the Lord and began teaching in-home Bible classes that initiated on his route on every other Thursday for about 15 years. During that time, the classes expanded, and many were won to the Lord, experienced the baptism in the Holy Ghost, healings, and restoration of relationships. Lloyd helped to establish the Central Detroit Full Gospel businessmen's fellowship in 1976. He began working in a supervisory capacity in 1977 and rapidly moved up the ranks to the executive level as Postmaster of Detroit in 1996, achieved exemplary results over a 47-year career, retiring in 2015. He and Pat have pastored Grace Refuge Chapel church since 2000.

The Wesley's recently celebrated their 50th wedding anniversary and have counseled both singles and married couples for over forty years and have seen lives strengthened and marriages restored through Christ in the "**Power of Two Marriage Ministry**."

In 1980 the Lord showed Lloyd the first of four visions. In the first one the Lord showed him leaving the house at night with his family and driving to the downtown area of a large city. At the time of leaving the house it was dark beyond anything he had ever experienced, and the Lord spoke, "this is spiritual darkness." As they drove towards the downtown area, skyscrapers exploded with their rubble falling into the streets. The Lord spoke, "this is the world system coming to naught." Driving away from the chaos, the road kept getting narrower as they drove far from the city. The Lord spoke again, "wide is the way that leads to destruction and many are on that road, narrow is the way that leads to life, and few there be that find it." The road became so narrow only the wheels of the left side of the car fit the road. At that point they left the car as they saw a small church in the wilderness. As they mounted the stairs, two things stood out: the church was made of one stone and was red. Again, the Lord spoke, "those within this structure stand on my word and the blood of Jesus washes them of their sins." Immediately, Lloyd was carried by the Spirit to above the exploding buildings downtown. Being above the buildings, he descended through a glass dome of a large church without breaking the glass or harming himself. Being fifty-sixty feet above the floor, the insides of the church were ornate and magnificent, but he noticed the structure was not stone nor red. As he peered upward through the glass dome, the Lord spoke, "yes, I can see right through it!" It exploded as did the skyscrapers surrounding it. Finally, the Lord translated Lloyd swiftly to the small church in the wilderness and oceans of people were coming into it through the roof. The Lord spoke one last time, "teach them how to go through tribulation!"

Around 1995-97, Lloyd asked the Lord three questions regarding the vision. "Father, the city that was seen could not have been Detroit, as there were too many skyscrapers that were taller than Detroit's and how could all the non-ending oceans of people fit into the church in the wilderness without it bulging at the seams?" The Lord's response was that the city's name was not important as He had said that the exploding skyscrapers represented the "world system." The "world system" was greed, lust, envy, ungodly behavior, etc." Regarding the "oceans of people" never filling-up the wilderness church the Lord stated, "what you saw was the internet." The Lord could not have told him about the internet in 1980, as there was none, and he would not have understood. About eleven years ago the Lord had Lloyd to place the classes of **"How to Go Through Tribulation Victoriously"** on the internet.

The book **"Guard Your Heart, Hearing God to Master the Nine Issues of Life,"** is a supplement of God's instruction at the end of the vision to "Teach them how to go through tribulation." The present times we are living in represent "darkness covering the earth and gross darkness the people" that the Lord spoke of in Isaiah 60:2, and people are going through growing "tribulation" at present that they must learn to go through victoriously.

APPENDIX / WEBSITE AVAILABILITY

***The 3 asterisks represent items, tools, and information that's available free of charge on the **www.guardyourheart.life** website, under tools.

Introduction: For tools, downloads and How to Go Through Tribulation Victoriously course, go to **www.guardyourheart.life.com.**

***Of GOD, I Am* meditation in 2-page double-sided download free of charge, also *Of GOD, I Am* meditation with heart shaped design within the letters in hard plastic protected cover 1-sided 8.5 x 11 inch $2.50, Picture Frame Of GOD, I am meditation with heart shaped design within the letters 1-sided 8.5 x 11 inch **www.guardyourheart.life** website entry, *What is Iniquity?*

Chapter 3: Raising Our Self-Esteem to Christ-Esteem

The Pursuit of Purpose, Dr. Myles Munroe definition and reason of purpose reference.

9 Issues of Life Issues with 9 scriptures for each issue along with scriptures to assist regarding overcoming grief. This is a 12-page document that has a 2-page format that assists you in coming into hearing God's revelation secrets on your issue.

Chapter 4: Relationship with God

Scriptures on Favor

1. **Psalm 5:12,** "For You, O Lord, will bless the righteous; With favor You will surround him as with a shield." Scripture 5 shows because one has heard God, believed and obeyed they come into a relationship called "righteousness" and are benefitted with special treatment that blocks negative environments in life.

2. **Psalm 30:5,** "For His anger is but for a moment, His favor is for life; Weeping may endure for a night, But joy comes in the morning." Scripture 6 displays even in lack of performance of an individual, they receive benefits of God anyway, shortly thereafter.

3. **Proverbs 3:1-4,** "My son, do not forget my law, But let your heart keep my commands; For length of days and long life And peace they will add to you.

Let not mercy and truth forsake you; Bind them around your neck, Write them on the tablet of your heart, And so find favor and high esteem In the sight of God and man." Scripture 7 reveals that the individual who has God's word and keeps them are blessed above others to the point of a good change upward in their self-esteem.

4. *Proverbs 18:22, "He who finds a wife finds a good thing, And obtains favor from the Lord."* Scripture 8 shows that the man that obeys the Lord and marries is benefitted and promoted of the Lord.

5. **Luke 1:28**, "And having come in, the angel said to her, "Rejoice, highly favored one, the Lord is with you; blessed are you among women!"… Luke 1:30, "Then the angel said to her, "Do not be afraid, Mary, for you have found favor with God." Scripture 9 shows how Mary's obedience to the Lord placed her on a good path that led to the creation of a vessel that is positioned under the pouring out of God's blessings from heaven into her life.

6. **Luke 2:52**, "And Jesus increased in wisdom and stature, and in favor with God and men." Scripture 10 shows that at the Passover Feast Jesus and His family had traveled to Jerusalem for its observance and when his family left to go back to Nazareth Jesus remained in the temple asking questions and giving answers to the religious leaders. The leaders were amazed at His knowledge and understanding and after His parents had not found Him in the caravan amongst family and friends they went back to Jerusalem and found Him after 3 days. His parents asked why He had stayed behind and He told them that he had to be about His Father's business. He returned home with His parents, as he submitted Himself to them, although they did not understand His statement regarding His Father's business. What stands out is that although He was only 12 years of age, in His absence from His parents which had to have been 3-7 days, the knowledge, understanding and wisdom that He had kept Him, regarding food, shelter and protection without His parents. It then states that "Jesus increased in wisdom and stature, and in favor with God and men."

7. **Psalm 23:5-6**, "You prepare a table before me in the presence of my enemies; You anoint my head with oil; My cup runs over. Surely goodness and mercy shall follow me All the days of my life; And I will dwell in the *house of the*

LORD Forever." Scripture 11 links with scripture 10 in that Jesus was kept by the relationship of righteousness that grew out of the knowledge, understanding and wisdom provided through God's word coupled with Favor's provision that comes with it.

8. **John 15:14,** "Ye are my friends, if ye do whatsoever I command you. Henceforth I call you not servants; for the servant knoweth not what his lord doeth: but I have called you friends; for all things that I have heard of my Father I have made known unto you. Ye have not chosen me, but I have chosen you, and ordained you, that ye should go and bring forth fruit, and that your fruit should remain: that whatsoever ye shall ask of the Father in my name, he may give it you." The last verses given in scripture 12 does not mention favor but it shows the results of it in one becoming a friend of God through having His word and obedience to it. Because of the "right relationship with God, righteousness, The Lord makes known His secrets while anointing them (empowering with God's ability and favor) to accomplish above and beyond what others achieve for God's purposes in the earth while receiving whatever is desired for them.

Chapter 6: Relationship With Those Who Do Wrong to You

1. Jayla's drawing of, *Into Each Life Some Rain Must Fall.* Available upon request please call 313-592-1717, for size desired and cost.

Chapter 7: MEDITATION: How to Meditate Effectively to Hear God's Direction: www.guardyourheart.life

1. www.guardyourheart.life: 2-page format of the Meditation Exercise Tool to assist in hearing God and getting revelation from His scriptures. (free download) ***

2. www.guardyourheart.life: 2-page format of the ABC's of the Kingdom Document for an initial check on new student to show their scriptural knowledge (free download) ***

3. www.guardyourheart.life: 3-page format of scriptures relating to praying in the spirit or tongues. (free download) ***

4. **www.guardyourheart.life:** 5-page format of meditation of Proverbs 4 to assist in getting revelation (free download) ***

5. **www.guardyourheart.life:** 7-page format of meditation of Isaiah 58 to assist in getting revelation (free download) ***

6. **www.guardyourheart.life:** 6-page format of meditation of Exodus 20 to assist in getting revelation (free download) ***

7. **www.guardyourheart.life:** 5-page format of meditation of 2 Peter 1 to assist in getting revelation (free download) ***

8. **www.guardyourheart.life:** 5-page format of meditation of 1 Corinthians 12 to assist in getting revelation (free download) ***

9. **www.guardyourheart.life:** 5-page format of meditation of Mark 4 to assist in getting revelation (free download) ***

Chapter 13: FINANCE$

*Tracking and Disciplining Your Finance$

Please see the 4 budgets provided on the website. They, with the video presentations will walk you through populating a very thorough budget, then balancing it out to a zero balance by the end of a month in budget number **1**. Budget number **2** shows that budget balanced out to a monthly zero balance. Budget number **3** is a blank budget for our own personal use. Budget number **4** shows one method of paying off the 3 bills given in the "populating data example." Budget number **5** shows a beginning of wealth development after the 3 bills were paid off for years 2-4. Budget number **6** shows years 4-10, the beginning stages of wealth development on a larger scale without debt. Budget number **7** shows how to calculate APR, wealth and other investment strategies.

ENDNOTES

Introduction

1. www.dictionary.com
2. www.dictionary.com
3. Strong's Concordance
4. Strong's Concordance
5. Strong's Concordance
6. Strong's Concordance

Chapter 1

1. www.dictionary.com

Chapter 2

1. www.dictionary.com
2. www.dictionary.com
3. Frederick Sanger - Wikipedia
4. https://en.wikipedia.org/wiki/Frederick_Sanger
5. YouTube video named Transformations-Revival Almolonga, Guatemala

Chapter 3

1. Dr. Myles Munroe, *In Pursuit of Purpose* (Shippenburg: Destiny Image Publishers, 1992), 28.

Chapter 4

1. Jerry Bridges, *The Pursuit of Holiness* (Colorado Springs: Navpress, 1996), 7–8.

Chapter 6

1. Jayla Wesley, 2019

Chapter 7

1. www.dictionary.com
2. www.dictionary.com
3. www.dictionary.com
4. Strong's Bible Concordance

Chapter 9

1. Elder Morris Thomas, Spiritual Aspects Ministries, Teaching on Prayer, January 30, 2011

Chapter 11

1. www.dictionary.com

2. www.dictionary.com

3. www.dictionary.com

4. www.dictionary.com

5. www.dictionary.com

6. www.dictionary.com

7. www.dictionary.com

8. www.dictionary.com

9. History of Harvard's walls, www.wikipedia.org

Chapter 14

1. McMillan dictionary

Chapter 15

1. www.dictionary.com

2. www.dictionary.com

3. YouTube, Pastor Francis Chan, Cornerstone Church, Simi Valley, CA, Rope Illustration from the sermon "Living Eternally, March 8, 2009

4. www.dictionary.com

5. www.dictionary.com

6. www.dictionary.com

7. www.dictionary.com

8. www.dictionary.com

9. www.dictionary.com

10. www.dictionary.com

11. www.dictionary.com

12. www.dictionary.com

Chapter 16

1. www.dictionary.com

<u>NOTES</u>

Chapter 5: Relationship with Others in the Body of Christ

<u>A Few Scriptures to assist in our having the nature of Christ</u>

Romans 12:1-2: "I beseech you therefore, brethren, by the mercies of God, that ye present your bodies a living sacrifice, holy, acceptable unto God, which is your reasonable service. And be not conformed to this world: but be ye transformed by the renewing of your mind, that ye may prove what is that good, and acceptable, and perfect, will of God."

Matthew 5:44-48: "But I say unto you, Love your enemies, bless them that curse you, do good to them that hate you, and pray for them which despitefully use you, and persecute you; That ye may be the children of your Father which is in heaven: for he maketh his sun to rise on the evil and on the good, and sendeth rain on the just and on the unjust. For if ye love them which love you, what reward have ye? do not even the publicans the same? And if ye salute your brethren only, what do ye more than others? do not even the publicans so? Be ye therefore perfect, even as your Father which is in heaven is perfect."

Luke 24:49: "And, behold, I send the promise of my Father upon you: but tarry ye in the city of Jerusalem, until ye be endued with power from on high."

1 Corinthians 13:1-8: "Though I speak with the tongues of men and of angels, and have not charity, I am become as sounding brass, or a tinkling cymbal. And though I have the gift of prophecy, and understand all mysteries, and all knowledge; and though I have all faith, so that I could remove mountains, and have not charity, I am nothing. And though I bestow all my goods to feed the poor, and though I give my body to be burned, and have not charity, it profiteth me nothing. Charity suffereth long, and is kind; charity envieth not; charity vaunteth not itself, is not puffed up, Doth not behave itself unseemly, seeketh not her own, is not easily provoked, thinketh no evil; Rejoiceth not in iniquity, but rejoiceth in the truth; Beareth all things, believeth all things, hopeth all things, endureth all things. Charity never faileth: but whether there be prophecies, they shall fail; whether there be tongues, they shall cease; whether there be knowledge, it shall vanish away."

Galatians 5:6: "For in Jesus Christ neither circumcision availeth any thing, nor uncircumcision; but faith which worketh by love."

Galatians 5:22-24: "But the fruit of the Spirit is love, joy, peace, longsuffering, gentleness, goodness, faith, Meekness, temperance: against such there is no law. And they that are Christ's have crucified the flesh with the affections and lusts."

Galatians 6:1-10: "Brethren, if a man be overtaken in a fault, ye which are spiritual, restore such an one in the spirit of meekness; considering thyself, lest thou also be tempted. Bear ye one another's burdens, and so fulfil the law of Christ. For if a man think himself to be something, when he is nothing, he deceiveth himself. But let every man prove his own work, and then shall he have rejoicing in himself alone, and not in another. For every man shall bear his own burden. Let him that is taught in the word communicate unto him that teacheth in all good things. Be not deceived; God is not mocked: for whatsoever a man soweth, that shall he also reap. For he that soweth to his flesh shall of the flesh reap corruption; but he that soweth to the Spirit shall of the Spirit reap life everlasting. And let us not be weary in well doing: for in due season we shall reap, if we faint not. As we have therefore opportunity, let us do good unto all men, especially unto them who are of the household of faith."

1 Peter 3:7-9: "Likewise, ye husbands, dwell with them according to knowledge, giving honour unto the wife, as unto the weaker vessel, and as being heirs together of the grace of life; that your prayers be not hindered. Finally, be ye all of one mind, having compassion one of another, love as brethren, be pitiful, be courteous: Not rendering evil for evil, or railing for railing: but contrariwise blessing; knowing that ye are thereunto called, that ye should inherit a blessing."

Chapter 15: ETERNAL REWARDS

*Tree of Life References

Proverbs 3:13-19: "Happy is the man that findeth wisdom, and the man that getteth understanding. For the merchandise of it is better than the merchandise of silver, and the gain thereof than fine gold. She is more precious than rubies: and all the things thou canst desire are not to be compared unto her. Length of days is in her right hand; and in her left hand riches and honour. Her ways are ways of pleasantness, and all her paths are peace. She is a tree of life to them that lay hold upon her: and happy is every one that retaineth her. The LORD by wisdom hath founded the earth; by understanding hath he established the heavens."

Proverbs 11:30: "The fruit of the righteous is a tree of life; and he that winneth souls is wise."

Proverbs 13:12: "Delayed hope makes one sick at heart, but a fulfilled longing is a tree of life." (GWT)

Revelation 2:7: "He that hath an ear, let him hear what the Spirit saith unto the churches; To him that overcometh will I give to eat of the tree of life, which is in the midst of the paradise of God."

Revelation 22:14: "Blessed are they that do his commandments, that they may have right to the tree of life, and may enter in through the gates into the city."

GLOSSARY

Chapter 1: The Issues of Life

Nine, according to the book written by E. W. Bullinger, NUMBER in Scripture, "is the completeness, the end and issue of all things as to man-the judgment of man and all his works." Page 235

Chapter 2: Self-Esteem

Breaking Generational Curses by Marilyn Hickey

Purging Your House Pruning Your Family Tree by Perry Stone.

Made in the USA
Monee, IL
09 September 2020

41790629R00187